Lecture Notes in Computer Science 12008

More information about this series at http://www.springer.com/series/7409

Renata Borovica-Gajic · Jianzhong Qi ·
Weiqing Wang (Eds.)

Databases Theory
and Applications

31st Australasian Database Conference, ADC 2020
Melbourne, VIC, Australia, February 3–7, 2020
Proceedings

 Springer

Editors
Renata Borovica-Gajic
University of Melbourne
Parkville, Australia

Weiqing Wang
Monash University
Clayton, Australia

Jianzhong Qi
School of Computing
and Information Systems
University of Melbourne
Parkville, VIC, Australia

ISSN 0302-9743   ISSN 1611-3349 (electronic)
Lecture Notes in Computer Science
ISBN 978-3-030-39468-4   ISBN 978-3-030-39469-1 (eBook)
https://doi.org/10.1007/978-3-030-39469-1

LNCS Sublibrary: SL3 – Information Systems and Applications, incl. Internet/Web, and HCI

This Springer imprint is published by the registered company Springer Nature Switzerland AG
The registered company address is: Gewerbestrasse 11, 6330 Cham, Switzerland

Preface

It is our pleasure to present to you the proceedings of the 31th Australasian Database Conference (ADC 2020), which took place in Melbourne, Australia. ADC is an annual international forum for sharing the latest research advancements and novel applications of database systems, data driven applications, and data analytics between researchers and practitioners from around the globe, particularly Australia and New Zealand. The mission of ADC is to share novel research solutions to problems of today's information society that fulfil the needs of heterogeneous applications and environments and to identify new issues and directions for future research and development work. ADC seeks papers from academia and industry presenting research on all practical and theoretical aspects of advanced database theory and applications, as well as case studies and implementation experiences. All topics related to database are of interest and within the scope of the conference. ADC gives researchers and practitioners a unique opportunity to share their perspectives with others interested in the various aspects of database systems.

As in previous years, the ADC 2020 Program Committee accepted those papers to be considered as being of ADC quality without setting any predefined quota. The conference received 30 submissions and accepted 20 papers, including 14 full research papers and 6 short papers. Each paper was peer reviewed in full by at least three independent reviewers, and in some cases four referees produced independent reviews. A conscious decision was made to select the papers for which all reviews were positive and favorable. The Program Committee that selected the papers consists of 35 members from around the globe, including Australia, China, New Zealand, Japan, the UK, and the USA, who were thorough and dedicated to the reviewing process.

We would like to thank all our colleagues who served on the Program Committee or acted as external reviewers. We would also like to thank all the authors who submitted their papers, and the attendees. This conference is held for you, and we hope that with these proceedings, you can have an overview of this vibrant research community and its activities. We encourage you to make submissions to the next ADC conference and contribute to this community.

December 2019

Renata Borovica-Gajic
Jianzhong Qi
Weiqing Wang

General Chair's Welcome Message

On behalf of the organizers and Steering Committee for ADC 2020, I am honored to welcome you to the proceedings from the conference. The Australasian Database Conference has an extensive history; this is the 31st occurrence of the conference. In the past decade, ADC has been held in Sydney (2019), Gold Coast (2018), Brisbane (2017), Sydney (2016), Melbourne (2015), Brisbane (2014), Adelaide (2013), Melbourne (2012), Perth (2011), Brisbane (2010), Wellington (2009), and Wollongong (2008). This year, ADC was run under the umbrella structure of the Australasian Computer Science Week, organized at Swinburne University in Melbourne.

The technical program was arranged by Dr. Renata Borovica-Gajic (The University of Melbourne) and Dr. Jianzhong Qi (The University of Melbourne), who managed the review process by a panel of distinguished researchers from many countries, and then selected the papers from 30 submissions. The proceedings publication was arranged and supervised by Dr. Weiqing Wang (Monash University). We also sincerely thank the publicity chairs, Dr. Zhifeng Bao (RMIT University) and Zeyi Wen (National University of Singapore), for all their efforts. We are all the beneficiaries of their dedication.

As well as the conference, whose papers are found here, we held a co-located workshop aimed at PhD students and early career researchers, with a range of outstanding speakers, especially a keynote from Dr. Devish Srivastava (AT&T). This all shows the vibrancy of the database research community in Australia and New Zealand, and contributes to its continuation.

Best wishes to all
Chengfei Liu

Organization

General Chair

Chengfei Liu   Swinburne University of Technology, Australia

PC Co-chairs

Renata Borovica-Gajic   The University of Melbourne, Australia
Jianzhong Qi   The University of Melbourne, Australia

Publication Chair

Weiqing Wang   Monash University, Australia

Steering Committee

Rao Kotagiri   The University of Melbourne, Australia
Timos Sellis   RMIT University, Australia
Gill Dobbie   The University of Auckland, New Zealand
Alan Fekete   The University of Sydney, Australia
Xuemin Lin   University of New South Wales, Australia
Yanchun Zhang   Victoria University, Australia
Xiaofang Zhou   The University of Queensland, Australia

Program Committee

Zhifeng Bao   RMIT University, Australia
Renata Borovica-Gajic   The University of Melbourne, Australia
Huiping Cao   New Mexico State University, USA
Xin Cao   University of New South Wales, Australia
Muhammad Aamir Cheema   Monash University, Australia
Lisi Chen   University of Wollongong, Australia
Farhana Murtaza   The University of Melbourne, Australia
   Choudhury
Gianluca Demartini   The University of Queensland, Australia
Janusz Getta   University Of Wollongong, Australia
Yusuke Gotoh   Okayama University, Japan
Michael E. Houle   National Institute of Informatics, Japan
Wen Hua   The University of Queensland, Australia
Guangyan Huang   Deakin University, Australia
Zi Huang   The University of Queensland, Australia
Jianxin Li   The University of Western Australia, Australia

Lei Li	The University of Queensland, Australia
Rong-Hua Li	Beijing Institute of Technology, China
Jixue Liu	University of South Australia, Australia
Jiaheng Lu	University of Helsinki, Finland
Parth Nagarkar	New Mexico State University, USA
Quoc Viet Hung Nguyen	Griffith University, Australia
Jianzhong Qi	The University of Melbourne, Australia
Lu Qin	University of Technology Sydney, Australia
Junhu Wang	Griffith University, Australia
Sheng Wang	RMIT University, Australia
Sibo Wang	The University of Queensland, Australia
Yajun Yang	Tianjin University, China
Hongzhi Yin	The University of Queensland, Australia
Weiren Yu	Aston University, UK
Wenjie Zhang	University of New South Wales, Australia
Ying Zhang	University of Technology Sydney, Australia
James Xi Zheng	Macquarie University, Australia
Rui Zhou	Swinburne University of Technology, Australia
Yi Zhou	University of Technology Sydney, Australia
Yuanyuan Zhu	Wuhan University, China

Contents

Short Papers

Full Research Papers

Semantic Round-Tripping in Conceptual Modelling Using Restricted Natural Language

Bayzid Ashik Hossain[✉] and Rolf Schwitter

Department of Computing, Macquarie University, Sydney, Australia
{bayzid-ashik.hossain,rolf.schwitter}@mq.edu.au

Abstract. Conceptual modelling plays an important role in information system design and is one of its key activities. The modelling process usually involves domain experts and knowledge engineers who work together to bring out the required knowledge for building the information system. The most popular modelling approaches to develop these models include entity relationship modelling, object role modelling, and object-oriented modelling. These conceptual models are usually constructed graphically but are often difficult to understand by domain experts. In this paper we show how a restricted natural language can be used for writing a precise and consistent specification that is automatically translated into a description logic representation from which a conceptual model can be derived. This conceptual model can be rendered graphically and then verbalised again in the same restricted natural language as the specification. This process can be achieved with the help of a bi-directorial grammar that allows for semantic round-tripping between the representations.

Keywords: Conceptual modelling · Restricted natural language · Knowledge representation · Round-tripping

1   Introduction

Information systems can be defined as a collection of relevant components that work together to accumulate, process, store, and disperse information to support decision making, coordination, analysis, and visualization in an organization [1]. A successful information system highly depends on its design. Conceptual modelling is the first step towards designing an information system and is the most important task in the planning and requirement analysis phase of the system development life cycle [2]. The best way to specify an information system in conceptual modelling is to use a language with names for individuals, concepts and relations that are easily understandable by the domain experts in order to maintain accurateness, adaptability, productivity and clarity [3]. This conceptual modelling phase generally includes identifying and understanding the data, process and behavioral insights, and designing the actual database management

R. Borovica-Gajic et al. (Eds.): ADC 2020, LNCS 12008, pp. 3–15, 2020.
https://doi.org/10.1007/978-3-030-39469-1_1

system (DBMS) that is used for the design of the information system [3]. Designing a database means constructing a formal model based on any of the available data models of the desired application domain which is often called as universe of discourse (UOD). The conceptual modelling process depends on different parties (e.g., domain experts and knowledge engineers) to brainstorm together and determine the UOD. The knowledge engineers initiate a conceptual modelling process by acquiring the necessary information from the domain experts and then use well established modelling techniques [4–6] to design the information system based on the acquired information. However, it is necessary to have a clear understanding of the application domain as well as an unambiguous information specification scheme to design the UOD. Conceptual models that are built using existing modelling approaches are usually constructed graphically and are therefore often difficult to understand by domain experts [7].

In order to address this problem, we suggest the use of a Restricted Natural Language (RNL) to specify the system requirements and to translate the resulting specification automatically into a formal conceptual model that can be verbalised again in RNL on demand. As we will see, this results in a form of semantic round-tripping that makes the modelling process transparent to the domain experts. An RNL is a subset of a natural language that is obtained by constraining the grammar and vocabulary in order to remove ambiguity and complexity of the natural language [8,9]. In this paper, we show how an RNL can be used to write a specification for a particular information system and how this specification can be processed to generate and verbalise a conceptual model in a round-tripping fashion. The task of the grammar is to process our RNL and to restrict the form of the input sentences. The language processor then translates the individual RNL sentences into a version of description logic (DL). The resulting DL representation can then be used to verify the specification and to generate a conceptual model.

2   Motivation

The idea of using a RNL in conceptual modelling is not new. However, existing RNL based approaches [10,11] do not use description logic for knowledge representation and they have not considered the idea of semantic round tripping. There is also previous research that looked at representing conceptual models formally for verification [12–14] including consistency and redundancy checking. These approaches allow knowledge engineers to build the conceptual model first to represent the UOD and then use a formal language to formalize the conceptual model [15–17]. Later this formal representation is used for reasoning on the UOD during the design phase and also for extracting necessary information through query answering at run time. Popular conceptual modelling techniques such as entity relationship modelling (ERM) and object oriented modelling (e.g., unified modelling language (UML)) are easy to generate and understand for the knowledge engineers as they are well established. However, these conventional modelling approaches also face some problems; they have no formal semantics and verification support, and are therefore not machine processable, and as a result do not offer automated reasoning and question answering support [13]. To overcome these problems, previous approaches used the DL $ALCQI$ to formally represent the conceptual models. The DL $ALCQI$ is well suited to do reasoning with ERM [14], UML [12], and ORM [18]. $ALCQI$ is an extension of the basic propositionally closed description logic AL and includes constructs for complex concept negation, qualified number restriction, and inverse role. Finite model reasoning with DL $ALCQI$ is decidable and ExpTime-complete[1].

However, using logic in the conceptual modelling process has some problems too. It is difficult to generate these logical representations for domain experts, it is also strenuous for them to understand these representations, and there are no well established methodologies to formally represent the conceptual models. A possible solution to these problems is to use an RNL for the specification [19] as well as the verbalisation of conceptual models. RNLs have been used by several existing ontology editing and authoring tools [20–22] for ontology specification and translation into a DL representation. There are also works on mapping a DL representation into an SQL schema and the other way around [23–26].

3   Proposed Approach

We propose to use an RNL as a language for specifying and verbalising conceptual models (in our case an ERM) in order to overcome the problems discussed in the previous section. There are several benefits of using an RNL for specifying and verbalising conceptual models:

(a) An RNL is a subset of a natural language, so it is easy for domain experts to write a specification with a suitable authoring tool and to understand the verbalisation of a conceptual model.
(b) An RNL gets its semantics via translation into a formal target language.
(c) The resulting formal target language can be used further to generate and verbalise conceptual models.

In our previous works [19], we proposed to write the specification of a conceptual model in RNL and then translate the specification into the DL $ALCQI$. We showed that an existing DL reasoner (e.g., HermiT[2]) can be used to check the consistency of the formal representation of the specification and a conceptual model can be generated afterwards from this representation. Our approach was to derive the conceptual model from the formal representation of the specification whereas in conventional approaches knowledge engineers first draw the model and then use programs to translate the model into a formal representation.

This paper refines our previous work and shows that the grammar of the RNL can also be used to analyze as well as to generate a verbalisation for a conceptual model. We show that conceptual modelling can be seen as a round-tripping process where we start from a specification in RNL, translate the specification into a formal representation from which we generate the conceptual model and vice versa. Figure 1 shows the proposed system architecture for conceptual modelling.

---

[1] http://www.cs.man.ac.uk/~ezolin/dl/.
[2] http://www.hermit-reasoner.com/.

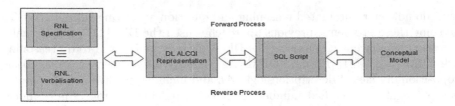

Fig. 1. Conceptual modelling as a round-tripping process.

3.1 Scenario

For demonstration purpose let us consider the example scenario of a learning management system for a university [19]:

> *A Learning Management System (LMS) keeps track of the units the students do during their undergraduate or graduate studies at a particular university. The university offers a number of programs and each program consists of a number of units. Each program has a program name and a program id. Each unit has a unit code and a unit name. A student can take a number of units whereas a unit has a number of students. A student must study at least one unit and at most four units. Every student can enrol into exactly one program. The system stores a student id and a student name for each student.*

First, we reconstruct this scenario in RNL (Table 1) and after that the language processor translates the RNL specification into an internal DL representation using a bi-directional definite clause grammar (DCG) [27]. This internal DL representation can be built up during the parsing process and then translated into another serialization syntax (such as OWL/XML). The DCG follows a similar approach as described in [28]. The advantage of using a DCG is that it implements a logic program that allows us to build a bi-directional grammar where only the pre-terminal rules need to be duplicated.

Our specification in RNL consists of function words and content words. Function words (e.g., determiners, quantifiers and operators) describe the structure of the RNL; the number of these function words is fixed. Content words (e.g., nouns and verbs) are domain specific and can be added to the lexicon during the writing process. It is important to note that the writing of a specification in RNL is supported by a look-ahead text editor [29]. The reconstruction process of the scenario is described in the following:

First, we declare the vocabulary in form of a type system that includes entity types, data types and fact types. This vocabulary is then used to specify the constraints. Entity types declare the entities in the scenario, data types declare the attributes of these entities, and fact types declare the relationships between these entities. All declarations are written without explicit quantifiers. Entity types are declared with the help of a noun in subject position (e.g., *program*), followed by a copula (*is*), and the specific key phrase (*an entity type*) in object position.

To declare a data type, we use a naming convention where the attribute name (e.g., *id*) in subject position is prefixed by an available entity name (e.g., *program*); this data property name (*program id*) is followed by a copula (*is*), and the specific key phrase (e.g., *of integer data type*). To declare a fact type, we use an available entity type name in subject position and an available entity type name in object position with a role name in between (e.g., *Student is enrolled in program*).

Table 1. RNL specification of the example scenario.

Entity types
1. Program is an entity type
2. Student is an entity type
3. Unit is an entity type
Data types
4. Program id is of integer data type
5. Program name is of string data type
6. Student id is of integer data type
7. Student name is of string data type
8. Unit code is of integer data type
9. Unit name is of string data type
Fact types
10. Student is enrolled in program
11. Program is enrolled by student
12. Program is composed of unit
13. Unit belongs to program
14. Student studies unit
15. Unit is studied by student
Constraints
16. Every student is enrolled in exactly 1 program
17. Every program is enrolled by 1 or more students
18. Every program is composed of 1 or more units
19. Every unit belongs to 1 or more programs
20. Every student studies at least 1 and at most 4 units
21. Every unit is studied by 1 or more students
22. Every program has exactly 1 program id and has exactly 1 program name
23. Every student who has exactly 1 student id has exactly 1 student name
24. Every unit has exactly 1 unit code and has exactly 1 unit name

After these types have been declared for the scenario, constrains can be defined using the available vocabulary. To define the constraints, we use all the entity type names and data property names with a quantifying expression: either a quantifier (*every, 1 or more*) or a cardinality constraint (*at least, at most, exactly*).

All the sentences use a universal quantifier in subject position. Sentence (16) uses a cardinality quantifier (*exactly 1*) in object position whereas sentence (20) uses a compound cardinality quantifier (*at least 1 and at most 4*) in the same position. Sentence (17), (18), (19) and (21) use an existential quantifier (*1 or more*) in object position. And finally, sentence (22), (23) and (24) employ a coordinated verb phrase where the noun phrase in object position uses a data property name (*program id, student id, unit code*).

4   RNL Specification to DL *ALCQI* Representation

First we use the bi-directional grammar to translate the RNL specification into an intermediate DL representation (Listing 1.1). The bi-directional grammar has been implemented using a Prolog DCG [27] and is called from a Python programming interface. After that we translate this intermediate DL representation into a DL *ALCQI* representation using the OWL/XML syntax [30]. We discuss the two steps for translating the RNL specification into DL *ALCQI* representation below.

Our RNL specification contains different types of sentences where each type has an identical structure. The bi-directional grammar contains rules to translate every sentence type of the specification. Below, we only show the grammar rules with feature structures for the sentence (20) of the specification. These grammar rules work in both directions from an RNL specification to an intermediate DL representation and the other way around. That means we can feed the output again to the grammar and get a sentence that is semantically equivalent to the input.

Listing 1.1. Grammar Rules for a Constraint

```
% --------------------------------------------------------------------
% Input:   (20) Every student studies at least 1 and at most 4 units.
% Output:  forall(A, student(A)=>exists(B, unit(B) & min(1):study(A, B):max(4)))
% --------------------------------------------------------------------

:- op(900, yfx, '=>').
:- op(800, yfx, '&').
:- op(900, yfx, ':').

s([mode:M, sem:L]) -->
   np([mode:M, num:N, func:subj, arg:X, sco:S, sem:L]),
   vp([mode:M, num:N, arg:X, sem:S]), ['.'].

np([mode:M, num:N, func:subj, arg:X, sco:S, sem:L]) -->
   qnt([mode:M, num:N, arg:X, res:R, sco:S, sem:L]),
   n([mode:M, num:N, arg:X, sem:R]).
```

```
np([mode:M, num:_N, func:obj, arg:X, sco:S, sem:L]) -->
   cst([mode:M, num:N, arg:X, res:R, sco:S, sem:L]),
   n([mode:M, num:N, arg:X, sem:R]).

vp([mode:M, num:N, arg:X, sem:L]) -->
   v([mode:M, num:N, arg:X, arg:Y, sem:S]),
   np([mode:M, num:_N, func:obj, arg:Y, sco:S, sem:L]).

qnt([mode:proc, num:N, arg:X, res:[[]|T]-[R, S], sco:[[]]-T,
     sem:[L1|LR]-[[L2|L1]|LR]]) --> [Wfm|Wfms],
   { lexicon([cat:qnt, wfm:[Wfm|Wfms], num:N, arg:X, res:R, sco:S, sem:L2]) }.

qnt([mode:gen, num:N, arg:X, res:T-[[]], sco:[S, R]-[[]|T],
     sem:[[L2|L1]|LR]-[L1|LR]]) --> { lexicon([cat:qnt, wfm:[Wfm|Wfms],
     num:N, arg:X, res:R, sco:S, sem:L2]) }, [Wfm|Wfms].

cst([mode:proc, num:N, arg:X, res:[[]|T]-[R, S], sco:[[]]-T,
     sem:[L1|LR]-[[L2|L1]|LR]]) --> [Wfm|Wfms],
   { lexicon([cat:cst, wfm:[Wfm|Wfms], num:N, arg:X, res:R, sco:S, sem:L2]) }.

cst([mode:gen, num:N, arg:X, res:T-[[]], sco:[S, R]-[[]|T],
     sem:[[L2|L1]|LR]-[L1|LR]]) --> { lexicon([cat:cst, wfm:[Wfm|Wfms],
     num:N, arg:X, res:R, sco:S, sem:L2]) }, [Wfm|Wfms].

n([mode:proc, num:N, arg:X, sem:[L1|LR]-[[L2|L1]|LR]]) --> [Wfm|Wfms],
   { lexicon([cat:n, wfm:[Wfm|Wfms], num:N, arg:X, sem:L2]) }.

n([mode:gen, num:N, arg:X, sem:[[L2|L1]|LR]-[L1|LR]]) -->
   { lexicon([cat:n, wfm:[Wfm|Wfms], num:N, arg:X, sem:L2]) }, [Wfm|Wfms].

v([mode:proc, num:N, arg:X, arg:Y, sem:[L1|LR]-[[L2|L1]|LR]]) --> [Wfm|Wfms],
   { lexicon([cat:v, wfm:[Wfm|Wfms], num:N, arg:X, arg:Y, sem:L2]) }.

v([mode:gen, num:N, arg:X, arg:Y, sem:[[L2|L1]|LR]-[L1|LR]]) -->
   { lexicon([cat:v, wfm:[Wfm|Wfms], num:N, arg:X, arg:Y, sem:L2]) }, [Wfm|Wfms].

lexicon([cat:qnt, wfm:['Every'], num:sg, arg:X,
         res:R, sco:S, sem:forall(X, R => S)]).

lexicon([cat:cst, wfm:[at, least, L, and, at, most, U], num:pl, arg:X,
         res:R, sco:S, sem:exists(X, R & min(L) : S : max(U))]) :-
   number(L), number(U), L>0, U>0, L<U.

lexicon([cat:n, wfm:[student], num:sg, arg:X, sem:student(X)]).
lexicon([cat:n, wfm:[units], num:pl, arg:X, sem:unit(X)]).
lexicon([cat:v, wfm:[studies], num:sg, arg:X, arg:Y, sem:study(X, Y)]).
```

The first grammar rule states that a declarative sentence (*s*) consists of a
noun phrase (*np*) and a verb phrase (*vp*), followed by a full stop (.). The grammar rule contains additional arguments that implement feature structures in the
form of *attribute:value* pairs whereas the value can be a term or a difference
list (of the form *[Head|Tail]-Tail*). The feature structure *mode:M* specifies the
processing mode. The feature structure *func:F* specifies the syntactic function of
the phrase. The feature structure *sem:L* is used to build up the entire semantic
representation for the constraint, *num:N* deals with number agreement (singular
or plural), and *arg:X* defines the argument of a class. The feature structure *sco:S*

stands for the information derived from the verb phrase. Note that the grammar rules for the quantifier and the cardinality constraint play an important role because they provide the main pattern for the internal representation. For example, the grammar rule for the universal quantifier (*every*) results in a pattern of the form *sem:forall(X, R => S)* that takes a restrictor *R* that contains the information derived from the noun phrase in subject position and the scope *S* of the verb phrase and turns this information into an implication. Finally, *cat:n* defines a noun, *cat:v* defines a verb and *wfm:[Wfm|Wfms]* defines a word form with potentially multiple elements. After generating the intermediate DL representation from the RNL specification, we translate this representation into the corresponding OWL/XML syntax.

An example of the *ALCQI* representation in OWL/XML syntax that is generated by the system for sentence (18) is given in (Listing 1.2). The intermediate representation stated below specifies that the class *program* has an object property *composed_of* with the class *unit* having minimum cardinality of 1 and maximum cardinality of many.

Listing 1.2. ALCQI Representation in OWL/XML Syntax

```
<!-- Input: forall(A, program(A) =>  exists(B, unit(B) &
                min(1):composed_of(A, B):max(*))) -->

<ObjectPropertyDomain>
    <ObjectProperty IRI="#composed_of"/>
    <Class IRI="#program"/>
</ObjectPropertyDomain>
<ObjectPropertyRange>
    <ObjectProperty IRI="#composed_of"/>
    <ObjectSomeValuesFrom>
        <ObjectProperty IRI="#composed_of"/>
        <Class IRI="#unit"/>
    </ObjectSomeValuesFrom>
</ObjectPropertyRange>
```

5   DL *ALCQI* Representation to SQL Script

In the next step, we extract necessary information such as a list of classes, data properties and object properties from the OWL/XML file. This information is extracted by executing XPath[3] queries over the OWL/XML syntax and is then used to build an SQL script. Later, this SQL script is executed to create an SQL schema to generate an ER-diagram. For mapping the DL representation into an ER-diagram, we have used the approach described in [19]. All the classes in the OWL/XML file become entities, object properties are mapped into relations between the entities, and data properties are mapped into attributes for these entities. To generate the SQL script for the database schema, we first create tables for each class from the class list. The data properties for each class

---

[3] https://www.w3schools.com/xml/xml_xpath.asp.

become the attributes in the table. Data properties with the name "id" (e.g., *program_id*) and "code" (e.g., *unit_code*) are considered as primary keys in the table. For each object property we identify the domain, range, and associated cardinality constraints. If the cardinality constraint is "many to one" (i.e., consider the sentence (16) in the RNL specification), then we add a foreign key to the table representing the domain class, and we annotate the object property name to the foreign key name for verbalisation. If the cardinality constraint is "many to many" (i.e., consider the sentence (18) and (19) in the RNL specification) then we create a separate table to represent the object property in the schema. In this case, we annotate the cardinality constraint (i.e., minimum cardinality and maximum cardinality) as well as the object property name with the foreign key name in the connecting table (i.e., *1_4_study__student_id*). We also use a specific naming convention containing the name of both domain and range classes separated by an underscore (_) for the connecting tables. All the tables representing a class have the prefix "et" (i.e, *et_student*) that indicates an entity. All the data properties have the prefix "dp" (i.e., *dp_student_name*) and all the connecting tables representing a "many to many" relationship have the prefix "op" (i.e., *op_student_unit*). Annotated information is separated by a double underscore with the attribute name in the table. Inverse roles (e.g, *enrolled_in* and *enrolled_by*) are also separated by a double underscore during the annotation.

6 Conceptual Model Generation

The SQL script is executed by a MySQL[4] database management system to generate the corresponding database for the specification. After that, we use MySQL workbench to generate the entity relationship diagram (Fig. 2) from the database. We understand conceptual modelling as a round-tripping process. That means a domain expert can write the RNL specification first, then automatically generate the conceptual model from the specification, and then a knowledge engineer might want to modify the conceptual model by following our naming convention. These modifications will then be reflected on the level of the RNL by verbalising the formal representation. During this modification process the DL reasoner can be used to identify inconsistencies found in a given specification and to give appropriate feedback to the knowledge engineer on the graphical level or to the domain expert on the textual level. We generate an SQL script from the modified conceptual model in the MySQL workbench and start the reverse process in conceptual modelling to generate the verbalisation.

---

[4] https://www.mysql.com/.

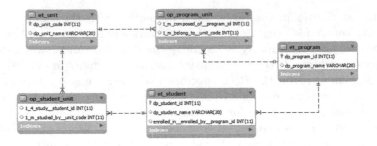

Fig. 2. Entity relationship diagram generated from the DL representation.

7   Database Schema to DL *ALCQI* Representation

The SQL script generated from the conceptual model serves as a starting point for the verbalisation process. If there are any changes in the graphical model then those changes are reflected in the SQL script. After that, we translate the SQL script into a DL *ALCQI* representation. The verbalisation process is done in two steps: 1. we create the database schema from the SQL script and then translate it into OWL/XML syntax; and 2. we generate the intermediate DL representation from the translated OWL/XML syntax.

To generate the OWL/XML syntax from the database schema, we look up the following information by querying the database: 1. list of classes, 2. list of data properties for each class, and 3. list of object properties with domain, range and cardinality information. We get this information by querying the INFOR-MATION_SCHEMA[5] table in the MySQL database management system. At this stage, we take the advantage of the naming convention we followed during the SQL script generation. For identifying the name, minimum cardinality and maximum cardinality for an object property, we use the annotated information. For mapping a SQL schema to the DL representation, we have used an approach that follows the rule based translation of a relational database to OWL ontologies [24]. In this step, we extract the necessary information using XPath[6] queries over the file containing OWL/XML representation to extract a list of classes, data properties and object properties. After that we transform the extracted information into the intermediate DL representation.

8   DL *ALCQI* Representation to RNL verbalisation

Next, we feed the intermediate DL representation to the bi-directional DCG which translates this intermediate representation into an RNL specification. This is the last stage of the reverse process because the DCG verbalises the conceptual model and completes the round-tripping process.

---

[5] https://dev.mysql.com/doc/refman/8.0/en/information-schema-introduction.html.
[6] https://www.w3schools.com/xml/xml_xpath.asp.

9   Evaluation

To evaluate the round-tripping process, we translate the specification $S1$ into the DL representation $R1$ (that is used to generate the conceptual model) and then execute two types of questions that collect the defined content words and used constraints: (1) What are the entity type names/data property names/fact type names? and (2) What are the domain, range and cardinality constraints for the fact type names? and store the answers. Next we take the DL representation $R1$ and generate the verbalisation $S2$ of the specification. We then use the same grammar to translate the verbalisation $S2$ into the DL representation $R2$ and prove that $S1$ and $S2$ are semantically equivalent by showing that $R1$ and $R2$ produce the same answers for the questions (1+2). This mechanism is important because, the sentence (23) *"Every student who has exactly 1 student id has exactly 1 student name"* from the specification and its verbalisation (23') *"Every student has exactly 1 student id and has exactly 1 student name"* are syntactically different but semantically equivalent.

					Specification S1	Verbalisation S2
Entity names	Student, Unit, Program.				√	√
Data property names	Student id, Student name, Unit code, Unit name, Program id, Program name.				√	√
Fact type names with domain, range and cardinality constrains	*Name*	*Domain*	*Range*	*Cardinality Constrains*		
	enrolled in	student	program	exactly 1		
	enrolled by	program	student	1 or more	√	√
	study	student	unit	at least 1 and at most 4	√	√
	studied by	unit	student	1 or more	√	√
	belongs to	unit	program	1 or more	√	√
	composed of	program	unit	1 or more	√	√

Fig. 3. Comparison of specification and verbalisation based on the questions (1+2).

Since the original specification $S1$ and its verbalisation $S2$ produce the same answer (Fig. 3) for the question (1+2), we can conclude that the two textual representations are semantically equivalent.

10   Conclusion

In this paper we showed the outcome of our experiment to justify the proposed approach for conceptual modelling. This experiment shows that it is possible to generate formal representations from RNL specifications and to map these formal representations to a conceptual model. Subsequently, this conceptual model can also be mapped back to a formal representation and can then be verbalised by using the same grammar. The proposed approach for conceptual modelling is novel and addresses two research challenges[7]: (1) Providing the right set of modelling constructs at the right level of abstraction to enable successful communication among the stakeholders (i.e., domain experts and knowledge engineers);

---

[7] http://www.conceptualmodelling.org/Conceptualmodelling.html.

and (2) preserving the ease of communication by using a subset of natural language (RNL) and enabling the generation of a database schema which is a part of the application software. Our approach has several advantages: Firstly, it uses a formal representation to generate conceptual models. Secondly, it makes the conceptual modelling process easy to understand by providing a framework for writing specifications, generating visualizations with the help of a case tool, and verbalisations of these visualizations. Thirdly, it makes the conceptual models machine-processable like other logical approaches and supports verification. Furthermore, the support for verbalisation facilitates better understanding of the modelling process which is only available in limited form in current conceptual modelling frameworks and allows users to manipulate the models in a round-tripping fashion.

References

1. Laudon, K.C., Laudon, J.P.: Management Information Systems: Managing the Digital Firm Plus MyMISLab with Pearson eText - Access Card Package, 14th edn. Prentice Hall Press, Upper Saddle River (2015)
2. Olivé, A.: Conceptual Modeling of Information Systems. Springer, Heidelberg (2007). https://doi.org/10.1007/978-3-540-39390-0
3. Bernus, P., Mertins, K., Schmidt, G.: Handbook on Architectures of Information Systems. Springer, Heidelberg (2013)
4. Halpin, T.: Object-role modeling. In: Liu, L., Özsu, M.T. (eds.) Encyclopedia of Database Systems, pp. 1941–1946. Springer (2009). ISBN 978-0-387-39940-9
5. Frantiska Jr., J.: Entity-relationship diagrams. Visualization Tools for Learning Environment Development. SECT, pp. 21–30. Springer, Cham (2018). https://doi.org/10.1007/978-3-319-67440-7
6. O'Regan, G.: Unified modelling language. In: Concise Guide to Software Engineering, pp. 225–238. Springer (2017). https://doi.org/10.1007/978-3-319-57750-0
7. Jarrar, M., Keet, C.M., Dongilli, P.: Multilingual verbalization of ORM conceptual models and axiomatized ontologies (2006)
8. Schwitter, R.: Controlled natural languages for knowledge representation. In: Proceedings of the 23rd International Conference on Computational Linguistics: Posters, pp. 1113–1121. Association for Computational Linguistics (2010)
9. Kuhn, T.: A survey and classification of controlled natural languages. Comput. Linguist. **40**(1), 121–170 (2014)
10. Ambriola, V., Gervasi, V.: On the systematic analysis of natural language requirements with circe. Autom. Softw. Eng. **13**(1), 107–167 (2006)
11. Harmain, H.M., Gaizauskas, R.: CM-builder: a natural language-based case tool for object-oriented analysis. Autom. Softw. Eng. **10**(2), 157–181 (2003)
12. Berardi, D., Calvanese, D., De Giacomo, G.: Reasoning on UML class diagrams. Artif. Intell. **168**(1), 70–118 (2005)
13. Calvanese, D.: Description Logics for Conceptual Modeling Forms of reasoning on UML Class Diagrams. EPCL Basic Training Camp (2013)
14. Lutz, C.: Reasoning about entity relationship diagrams with complex attribute dependencies. In: Proceedings of the International Workshop in Description Logics 2002 (DL2002), vol. 53, pp. 185-194. CEUR-WS (2002). http://ceur-ws.org
15. Fillottrani, P.R., Franconi, E., Tessaris, S.: The ICOM 3.0 intelligent conceptual modelling tool and methodology. Semant. Web **3**(3), 293–306 (2012)

16. Lembo, D., Pantaleone, D., Santarelli, V., Savo, D.F.: Easy OWL drawing with the graphol visual ontology language. In: Fifteenth International Conference on the Principles of Knowledge Representation and Reasoning (2016)
17. Lembo, D., Pantaleone, D., Santarelli, V., Savo, D.F.: Eddy: a graphical editor for OWL 2 ontologies. In: IJCAI, pp. 4252–4253 (2016)
18. Franconi, E., Mosca, A., Solomakhin, D.: ORM2: formalisation and encoding in OWL2. In: Herrero, P., Panetto, H., Meersman, R., Dillon, T. (eds.) OTM 2012. LNCS, vol. 7567, pp. 368–378. Springer, Heidelberg (2012). https://doi.org/10.1007/978-3-642-33618-8_51
19. Hossain, B.A., Schwitter, R.: Specifying conceptual models using restricted natural language. In: Proceedings of the Australasian Language Technology Association Workshop 2018, Dunedin, New Zealand, pp 44–52, December 2018
20. Davis, B., et al.: RoundTrip ontology authoring. In: Sheth, A., et al. (eds.) ISWC 2008. LNCS, vol. 5318, pp. 50–65. Springer, Heidelberg (2008). https://doi.org/10.1007/978-3-540-88564-1_4
21. Denaux, R., Dimitrova, V., Cohn, A.G., Dolbear, C., Hart, G.: Rabbit to OWL: ontology authoring with a CNL-based tool. In: Fuchs, N.E. (ed.) CNL 2009. LNCS (LNAI), vol. 5972, pp. 246–264. Springer, Heidelberg (2010). https://doi.org/10.1007/978-3-642-14418-9_15
22. Power, R.: OWL simplified English: a finite-state language for ontology editing. In: Kuhn, T., Fuchs, N.E. (eds.) CNL 2012. LNCS (LNAI), vol. 7427, pp. 44–60. Springer, Heidelberg (2012). https://doi.org/10.1007/978-3-642-32612-7_4
23. Brockmans, S., Volz, R., Eberhart, A., Löffler, P.: Visual modeling of OWL DL ontologies using UML. In: McIlraith, S.A., Plexousakis, D., van Harmelen, F. (eds.) ISWC 2004. LNCS, vol. 3298, pp. 198–213. Springer, Heidelberg (2004). https://doi.org/10.1007/978-3-540-30475-3_15
24. Astrova, I., Korda, N., Kalja, A.: Rule-based transformation of SQL relational databases to OWL ontologies. In: Proceedings of the 2nd International Conference on Metadata and Semantics Research. Citeseer (2007)
25. Astrova, I., Korda, N., Kalja, A.: Storing owl ontologies in SQL relational databases. Int. J. Electr. Comput. Syst. Eng. 1(4), 242–247 (2007)
26. Bagui, S.: Mapping OWL to the entity relationship and extended entity relationship models. Int. J. Knowl. Web Intell. 1(1–2), 125–149 (2009)
27. Pereira, F.C.N., Shieber, S.M.: Prolog and Natural-Language Analysis. Center for the Study of Language and Information (CSLI) Publications, Stanford (1987)
28. Schwitter, R.: Specifying and verbalising answer set programs in controlled natural language. Theory Pract. Log. Program. 18(3–4), 691–705 (2018)
29. Guy, S.C., Schwitter, R.: The PENG ASP system: architecture, language and authoring tool. Lang. Resour. Eval. 51(1), 67–92 (2017)
30. Motik, B., Parsia, B., Patel-Schneider, P.F.: OWL 2 web ontology language xml serialization. World Wide Web Consortium (2009)

PAIC: Parallelised Attentive Image Captioning

Ziwei Wang$^{(\boxtimes)}$, Zi Huang , and Yadan Luo

School of Information Techonology and Electrical Engineering,
The University of Queensland, Brisbane, Australia
ziwei.wang@uq.edu.au, huang@itee.uq.edu.au, lyadanluol@gmail.com

Abstract. Most encoder-decoder architectures generate the image description sentence based on the recurrent neural networks (RNN). However, the RNN decoder trained by Back Propagation Through Time (BPTT) is inherently time-consuming, accompanied by the gradient vanishing problem. To overcome these difficulties, we propose a novel Parallelised Attentive Image Captioning Model ($PAIC$) that purely employs the optimised attention mechanism to decode natural sentences without using RNNs. At each decoding phase, our model can precisely localise different areas of image utilising the well-defined spatial attention module, meanwhile capturing the word sequence powered by the well-attested multi-head self-attention model. In contrast to the RNNs, the proposed PAIC can efficiently exploit the parallel computation advantages of GPU hardware for training, and further facilitate the gradient propagation. Extensive experiments on MS-COCO demonstrate that the proposed PAIC significantly reduces the training time, while achieving competitive performance compared to conventional RNN-based models.

Keywords: Image captioning · Self-attention · Parallel training

1 Introduction

Image captioning has inspired research enthusiasm from both academia and industry owing to its power of bridging the modality gap between visual content and natural language. Notably, image captioning is an interesting yet challenging research problem, as it requires high-level visual understanding to interpret the visual information into a natural language caption. Moreover, the explosive growth in the volume of visual content highlights the difficulty in designing efficient and effective image captioning methods.

Despite its challenging nature, many image captioning methods have been intensively studied following the encoder-decoder architecture. Specifically, the convolutional neural network (CNN) encoder encodes the given image into a feature vector, and the recurrent neural network (RNN) decoder generates a sentence. To learn a recurrent neural network, the standard process is utilising back-propagation through time (BPTT) strategy. Consequently, the RNN-based

R. Borovica-Gajic et al. (Eds.): ADC 2020, LNCS 12008, pp. 16–28, 2020.
https://doi.org/10.1007/978-3-030-39469-1_2

PAIC:
A <u>young boy</u> brushing his <u>teeth</u> with a <u>green</u> tooth brush.
LSTM:
A young child brushing his teeth with a toothbrush.
Human:
A young boy is brushing his teeth with a green toothbrush.

PAIC:
A <u>flock of birds</u> flying over a body of water.
LSTM:
A group of people on the beach flying kites.
Human:
A group of birds flying over the water.

PAIC:
An <u>ice cream truck</u> parked in a parking lot.
LSTM:
A white truck with a surfboard on top of it.
Human:
An ice cream truck parked on the side of the street.

PAIC:
A woman standing on a tennis court <u>holding a racquet</u>.
LSTM:
A woman in a defensive stance on a tennis court.
Human :
A woman stands on a tennis court holding a racket.

Fig. 1. Image captions of two different models and human annotated ground-truth for four example images. The LSTM is the baseline Model [27], and the one on the top is generated by the proposed PAIC. It can be observed that PAIC successfully describes major objects and interactions as well as their surrounding environment in details. (Color figure online)

decoder methods often suffer from the issue of the gradient vanishing problem especially in long-term dependencies learning. To this end, a recent surge of interests in finding efficient alternatives for sequence modelling has been widely discussed. Recent attempts on the above problem mainly focusing on extending the original RNN model. For example, the well-known Long-Short-Term-Memory (LSTM [9]) alleviates the gradient vanishing or exploding by introducing the memory cell state. Recent work enhances the object recognition and enrich the interpretation of the critical details by incorporating different learning models, such as object detection [11], semantic attributes [19,30], attention [17,28,29,31], and reinforcement learning [18]. While some encouraging performances are reported, training RNN-based decoder is still time-consuming and incapable of parallel computing due to the limitation of BPTT. Moreover, preserving the long-term dependencies is challenging since memorising all hidden states occupies huge memory overhead, meanwhile the gradient is inevitably vanishing through long path. Consequently, RNN-based decoder becomes a hindrance of the encoder-decoder architecture.

To alleviate the bottleneck of time consuming RNN training, we introduce an efficient Parallelised Attentive Image Captioning Model (PAIC) that leverages the pure attention mechanism as a decoder without RNNs. Inspired by the recent successes of the Transformer model [26] for machine translation task, PAIC employs a stack of multi-head self-attention to capture the word sequence, and utilises another well-designed spatial attention module to localise different areas of image. The Fig. 1 shows some generated captions from the proposed model.

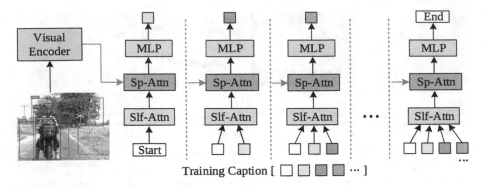

Training Caption [☐ ☐ ■ ■ ⋯]

Fig. 2. Framework overview. The visual regions are firstly extracted from the original image, which is further self-attended via a visual encoder. For language decoding, the self-attention module firstly finds the relevant textual context, and the spatial-attention module shifts the focus on most salient visual regions subsequently. The final word is predicted based on the output from the spatial attention. All the time steps separated by dot lines are able to trained in parallel efficiently.

Figure 2 illustrates an overview of the proposed PAIC. Technically, we develop a new attentive decoder model by introducing a well-defined intra and inter-attention mechanism followed by a simple feed-forward network. Specifically, the self-attention can precisely capture the intra-relevance of the visual regions and history words, and the spatial attention captures the inter-relevance between the textual and visual features. After a stack of attention layers, the outputs are fed to a projection and a softmax layer to predict next word to generate. Compared to LSTM-based decoder model [27], PAIC denotes superior performance with powerful parallel training capability.

The key contributions in this paper are three-fold:

1. This paper proposes a novel framework to explore the pure attention mechanism in image captioning, which allows the model to adaptively highlight salient parts of textual and visual context.
2. The efficient intra and inter-attention mechanisms empower faster parallel training benefits. At the same time, long-term dependencies are easier to be learned during training.
3. Quantitative and qualitative analysis conducted on the challenging MS-COCO dataset illustrate the efficiency and effectiveness of PAIC.

The rest of this paper is organised as follows: Sect. 2 discusses the related work. Section 3 presents the details of the attentive captioning model. Section 4 shows experimental results of our method, followed by the conclusion in Sect. 5.

2   Related Work

2.1   Image Captioning

Image captioning has been widely studied in computer vision community recently. In general, most existing methods can be categorised into two groups: template-based and language-based.

The main idea of template-based methods [6,10,15,20] is to reformulate the captioning task as a ranking and template retrieval problem, and then fills in template slots with outputs from object detection, attribute classification and scene recognition. However, the diversity and complexity of generated captions are limited to achieve satisfied performance due to the confined flexibility on template.

The language-based models [2,5,7,24] intend to learn the mapping function to form a full sentence from visual representations to semantic language embeddings. Benefiting from the prominent representation ability of CNNs, recent literatures focus on extracting effective deep features to guarantee high quality captioning results. Vinyals et al. [27] proposed an end-to-end CNN-LSTM architecture to interpret visual content by generated word sequence.

2.2   Attention Model

Built on the encoder-decoder framework, the attention mechanism has been demonstrated to make encouraging improvements at handling image captioning and machine translation tasks [4,13,21,25]. Xu et al. [29] proposed a visual attention module to align latent correspondence when generating word sequence, and similar visual attention methods [17,22] further improved the learning structure by augmenting focused areas. However, all the existing methods above heavily depend on the hidden states from each time step of recurrent units. Therefore, all these attention mechanisms are hardly trained in parallel, and their long-term dependencies learning abilities are clearly subject to RNNs.

3   Methodology

In this section, we elaborate our Parallelised Attentive Image Captioning Model (PAIC) for efficient image captioning. As shown in Fig. 2, the Faster-RCNN region features [1] are extracted to represent informative visual features. The visual region features are firstly forwarded as the input of a multi-head self-attended visual feature encoder to obtain the visual context vectors. For the decoder, the language model takes the all the previous words as textual inputs to obtain the self-attended textual features. Given the self-attended textual and visual features, the important spatial inter-attention module is constructed to select the focused area and assist its corresponding description at each position. The proposed PAIC trains all time steps in the Fig. 2 in parallel which significantly reduce the number of training iterations.

3.1   Problem Formulation

We denote the RGB-based original images as inputs I. The ultimate objective of the proposed model is to generate a preferable descriptive sentence $\mathbf{S} = \{S_1, ..., S_M\}$ for given I, where M is the sentence length.

3.2   Preliminaries

To enable the parallelised model training, we build the PAIC based on multi-head attention (MHA) following the Transformer model [26]. The attention model maps the queries and a set of contextual key-value pairs to an output. To formalise MHA, we define a set of d_m-dimensional queries as matrices Q, which can be computed simultaneously. Similarly, a set of d_m-dimensional keys and values are denoted as matrices K and V. MHA firstly reduces d_m-dimensional Q, K, V to d_k, d_k and d_v dimensions by learning h linear projections, where h is the number of attention $heads$. Then, each projected "mini" queries, keys and values can be fed to each attention $heads$. The underlying reason is that all the attention $heads$ can capture different implicit alignments in parallel. We define the multi-head attention module and the attention $head$ as follows:

$$MHA(Q, K, V) = Concat(head_1, ..., head_h)W^o \tag{1}$$

$$head_i = Att(QW_i^Q, KW_i^K, VW_i^V) \tag{2}$$

$$Att(Q, K, V) = softmax(\frac{QK^T}{\sqrt{d_k}})V, \tag{3}$$

where $W^o \in \mathbb{R}^{hd_k \times d_m}$ is output weight matrices, $W_i^Q, W_i^K \in \mathbb{R}^{d_m \times d_k}$, $W_i^V \in \mathbb{R}^{d_m \times d_v}$ are projection parameters of Q, K and V respectively. $Concat$ is a concatenation function to join all the outputs from h attention $heads$. $softmax$ is the softmax function to calculate the attention weights.

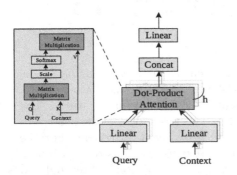

Fig. 3. Multi-head attention module.

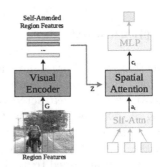

Fig. 4. Spatial attention module.

3.3   The Attentive Encoder-Decoder

This section introduces the attentive encoder-decoder framework in general, and then describes how to incorporate the efficient multi-head attention in the visual feature encoder Sect. 3.4 and language decoder Sect. 3.5.

Existing image captioning models follow the encoder-decoder framework [27]. Given a pair of image I and caption S, the captioning model maximises the probability of the correct image caption. The objective function is defined as:

$$\theta^* = \arg \max_{\theta} \sum_{(S,I)} \log p(S|I;\theta) \tag{4}$$

where θ are the model parameters. The log likelihood over all the time steps S is computed by chain rule:

$$\log p(S|I) = \sum_{t=0}^{M} \log p(S_t|I, S_0, ..., S_{t-1}), \tag{5}$$

where M is the sentence length.

In the encoder-decoder framework, each conditional probability depends on I and all the previous positions in word sequence. The probability at position t is modelled as follows:

$$\log p(S_t|I, S_0, ..., S_{t-1}) = f(c_t^*) \tag{6}$$

$$c_t^* = \sigma(c_t W_1 + b_1)W_2 + b_2 \tag{7}$$

$$c_t = MHA(a_t, Z, Z) + a_t, \tag{8}$$

where f is a non-linear activation function that approximate probability of S_t. c_t^* is output of two linear layers W_1, W_2, σ denotes ReLU function, the dimension of inputs and outputs of Eq. 7 is $d_m = 512$, and the inner-layer has the dimension of $d_{ff} = 2048$. c_t is the contextual visual attention output at position t, and a_t is the self-attended language attention output at position t. Z is the self-attended visual feature encoder output which will be discussed in Sect. 3.4. The details of contextual vectors c_t and a_t will be explained in Sect. 3.5.

3.4   Visual Feature Encoder

The Faster-RCNN features are firstly forwarded to a self-attention mechanism to calculate the relevance between different object regions. We notate the region features as $G = [g_0, g_1, \cdots, g_k]$, k is the number of object regions. Since the feature encoder extracts the intra-relationships between the regions, so the queries, keys and values are from the place:

$$Z = [MHA_{encoder}(G, G, G) + G]_{\times N} \tag{9}$$

$$G = [g_0, g_1, \cdots, g_k], \tag{10}$$

where the subscripts N indicates we forward through a stack of N identical MHA layers.

3.5   Language Decoder

In the decoder, the self-attention reasons the relevance of the previous and current words, then this self-attended textual feature a_t is further utilised to find the related visual regions, computing spatial attention c_t for final word prediction.

Language Self-attention. As mention in Sect. 3.2, a_t is calculated given all the previous and current positions. For self-attention, the queries, keys and values are from same place. The self-attended feature a_t is modelled as:

$$a_t = MHA(q_t, q_t, q_t) + q_t \tag{11}$$

$$q_t = [x_0, ..., x_t], \tag{12}$$

where q_t is the queries sequence at position t, and the key-value pairs are essentially queries themselves q_t, $x_i \in x_0, ..., x_t$ is all the word vectors in previous positions upon up to the current position t, v_g is the d_m-dimensional global visual feature of the image. It is worth to mention in Eq. 11, we add second term q_t to serve as residual connection [8].

Spatial Attention. As formulated in Eq. 8, given a_t, we forward the textual feature to second MHA spatial attention module to calculate the c_t.

The spatial attention model efficiently learns the weights over image regions given current word sequence representation a_t, and guide the language decoder to focus on the most salient regions to predict next word. Spatial attention illustrated in Fig. 4 is an alignment mechanism to give the language decoder evidence to decide *where* are the most relevant regions at position t. The inputs are the current language feature a_t and the self-attended region features Z.

4   Experiments

4.1   Experimental Settings

Dataset. We evaluate PAIC on on the MS-COCO [16] dataset for sentence captioning generation. For comparison, we follow the "Karpathy" split [12], which provides train, val and test splits with 113 287, 5 000, 5 000 images, respectively.

Implementation Details. The proposed model consists of the region feature extractor, intra-attentive visual feature encoder, language decoder, and spatial attention modules. For region feature extractor, the region visual features are extracted using Faster-RCNN with ResNet-101 following [1]. For all the multi-head attentive modules, in the best model, we stack $N = 3$ layers of MHA, and each layer has $h = 8$ attention heads. The batch size is 100 in all the experiments. The word embedding dimension is empirically set to 512. The optimiser is Adam [14] with learning rate $5e - 4$. All the models are trained on a 40-Core Intel(R) Xeon(R) E5-2660 CPU server, with 2 Nvidia GeForce GTX 1080 Ti GPUs.

Table 1. Performance comparison on MSCOCO Karpathy test split [12]. ***Iter@Best** means the number of iterations taken to train a best model, smaller number indicates faster training.

Model	BLEU-3	BLEU-4	METEOR	Rouge-L	CIDEr	Iter@Best*
NIC [27]	41.60	30.34	25.05	53.58	96.29	33k
Adaptive [17]	42.25	30.88	25.40	53.82	98.26	22k
SCST: Att2in [23]	43.31	31.83	25.73	54.50	102.29	32k
SCST: Att2all [23]	44.70	33.25	26.25	55.19	105.60	31k
UpDown [1]	44.58	33.14	26.45	55.37	106.14	33k
PAIC Small	43.47	32.80	26.53	54.46	105.3	**12k**
PAIC large	**45.52**	**34.96**	**27.58**	**55.82**	**111.89**	15k

Evaluation Metrics. We report the performance using automatic language evaluation protocols [3] including BLEU-3, 4, METEOR, Rouge-L, and CIDEr. All four metrics measures the similarity between the candidate and the reference captions. For example, **BLEU-n** measures the n-gram precision scores for the candidate caption given several reference captions. **Iter@Best** stands for the number of training iterations (100 images per iteration) taken to train the model with best performance.

Compared Methods. The compared methods are all conventional recurrent neural networks based models. Neural Image Captioner (NIC) [27] is a basic encoder-decoder framework, in which the encoder is a CNN extracting global visual features, and the decoder is a LSTM-based language model for sequence generation. Adaptive Attention [17], SCST-Att2in, Att2all [23], and UpDown Attention [1] models are carefully-engineered variants of visual attention-based models.

4.2 Quantitative Analysis

For fair comparison, we firstly extract Faster-RCNN region features following the process similar to [1] for all the baseline models, and the language model is a single-layer LSTM with hidden size of 512. Therefore, the reported results are slightly different to the benchmarks from the original papers.

The main results of image captioning on MSCOCO dataset are demonstrated in the Table 1. In general, the proposed PAIC demonstrates superior performance in all the metrics comparing to the state-of-the-art methods showing the effectiveness of attention-based language decoder with parallel training. In particular, comparing to NIC, PAIC-Large significantly improves BLEU-4, METEOR, and CIDEr by relatively 15%, 10%, and 16%, respectively. Moreover, if we compare the proposed PAIC to the state-of-the-art UpDown [1] model, our model still outperforms it by 5% in both BLEU-4 and CIDEr metrics relatively. This result

| PAIC: a woman **blow drying her hair in a bathroom.** LSTM: a woman taking a selfie in a bathroom mirror. GT: A woman blow drying her hair in a room with a window. | PAIC: A slice of **pizza** on a **white plate.** LSTM: A white plate topped with a sandwich and a salad. GT: A piece of pizza sitting on a white plate | PAIC: A **brown and white dog** standing next to a **red fire hydrant.** LSTM: A dog and a dog are running in the grass. GT: a brown and white dog is sitting in some grass and a red and white fire hydrant | PAIC: A **red car** parked next to a **parking meter.** LSTM: A parking meter sitting on the side of a road. GT: A red car is parked by a parking meter. |

Fig. 5. Case studies of PAIC, LSTM and human annotated captions in different scenes.

indicates that the pure attention model efficiently learns long-term dependencies, therefore improving the ability for better natural language generation.

In regards to the training efficiency, the PAIC takes only 12k iterations (100 images per iteration) to train a best model, while maintaining competitive performance. For example, comparing to SCST: Att2all model, PAIC-Small only takes 39% of training iterations while achieving similar performance. Similarly, PAIC-Big only needs around half of the training iterations comparing to most of the baseline models. Although the Adaptive model takes just 22k iterations, the performance is not comparable without further time-consuming CNN fine-tuning step reported in the original paper. More details with regard to training curve will be discussed in Sect. 4.4.

4.3   Qualitative Analysis

To intuitively understand the performance of the proposed PAIC, we present case studies on randomly chosen images in Fig. 5. The presented sentences are generated by conventional LSTM-based model NIC [27] and the proposed PAIC model. We also provide human annotated ground-truth (GT) captions for reference. With comparisons with LSTM, the PAIC model generates the sentence in an accurate and visual-grounded manner. For example, in the third picture, PAIC can precisely identify the "brown and white" colour of the dog, as well as the "red fire hydrant" next to it. In comparison, the LSTM model successfully describes the dog, but it is lack of accurate details. Another example is the first image, the woman is "blow drying" hair instead of "taking a selfie". The proposed PAIC clearly describes visually-grounded actions, but the LSTM model only considers the general motion which leads to incorrect description. In conclusion, the proposed attentive captioning model can identify more precise details, and organise the words in a more human-readable order.

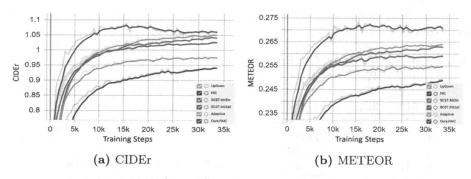

(a) CIDEr   (b) METEOR

Fig. 6. Training steps and performance of CIDEr and METEOR.

4.4 Training Efficiency Analysis

In this section, we study the training efficiency of the PAIC. The detailed performance curves of the validation split are illustrated in Fig. 6. As shown in the training curve, the green line on the top is the proposed PAIC showing faster climbing and higher peak performance in both CIDEr and METEOR. From CIDEr curve in Fig. 6a, we can observe that all the LSTM-based state-of-the-art attention models (e.g. Updown, SCST:Attn2in, SCST:Attn2all) needs around 15k iterations to climb up to CIDEr 1.00, while PAIC only taking around 5k training steps. To achieve the best performance, the LSTM-based baselines grow slowly after 15k steps, and can hardly reach CIDEr 1.05 after 30k iterations for the most competitive model UpDown. In the contract, PAIC demonstrates strong learning ability reaching best performance CIDEr 1.08 within 16k iterations, which is only the half number of steps comparing the baselines. The similar trend also appeared in Fig. 6b for METEOR evaluation, where the PAIC shows even larger relative margin above the baseline methods. However, the only drawback is that CIDEr tends to slightly overfit after reaching the peak due to the complexity of multi-head attention. One of the effective training strategy is to early terminate the model training after seeing the performance drop in several consecutive epochs to eliminate overfitting.

4.5 Model Structure Comparison

In this section, we compare different model structures of PAIC. From Table 2, we can find that the small models A and B ($N = 1$, $d_{model} = 512, 1024$) achieve promising results with fast training time. In practice, these two variants take the smallest memory usage (4 GB among other bigger variants. However, the small versions can hardly achieve better performance due to the limited numbers of learnable neural network layers. Moreover, the learning curve of Model B (navy blue) experience fluctuations after $22k$ iterations. Therefore, it is necessary to train the model with deeper multi-head attention networks. In the further experiments, when we increase the number of attention layers, the models improve their performance as we can see in the model C and D. However,

Table 2. The performance of different model structures in Test Set.

Model	N	d_{model}	Iter@Best	**CIDEr**
A	1	1024	12k	105.30
B	1	512	15k	106.86
C	2	512	20k	109.64
D	**3**	**512**	**15k**	**111.89**
E	4	512	15k	110.03
F	5	512	14k	111.25
G	6	512	15k	110.89

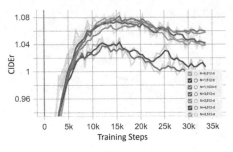

Fig. 7. CIDEr score in validation set for different parameter settings.

further increasing the depth of model does not show significant improvements as shown in Model E, F, and G. On the contrary, over complex models are generally difficult to train and take up huge computation resources. Hence, we choose $N = 3$, $d_{model} = 512$ to build our best PAIC model.

5   Conclusion

In this work, we propose a parallelised attentive model for image captioning. Towards preserving long-term dependences in the sentences, the proposed captioning model attends to visual and textual cues while language decoding. The attentive captioning model is trained in parallel, therefore minimising number of training iterations whilst maintaining superior performance. The experiments demonstrate the effectiveness and efficiency of the proposed PAIC framework.

Acknowledgement. This work is partially supported by ARC DP190102353 and ARC DP170103954.

References

1. Anderson, P., et al.: Bottom-up and top-down attention for image captioning and visual question answering. In: CVPR, pp. 6077–6086 (2018)
2. Bin, Y., Yang, Y., Zhou, J., Huang, Z., Shen, H.T.: Adaptively attending to visual attributes and linguistic knowledge for captioning. In: ACM MM, pp. 1345–1353 (2017)
3. Chen, X., et al.: Microsoft COCO captions: data collection and evaluation server. CoRR abs/1504.00325 (2015)
4. Cheng, J., Dong, L., Lapata, M.: Long short-term memory-networks for machine reading. In: EMNLP, pp. 551–561 (2016)
5. Donahue, J., et al.: Long-term recurrent convolutional networks for visual recognition and description. TPAMI **39**(4), 677–691 (2017)
6. Farhadi, A., et al.: Every picture tells a story: generating sentences from images. In: Daniilidis, K., Maragos, P., Paragios, N. (eds.) ECCV 2010. LNCS, vol. 6314, pp. 15–29. Springer, Heidelberg (2010). https://doi.org/10.1007/978-3-642-15561-1_2

7. Guo, Z., Gao, L., Song, J., Xu, X., Shao, J., Shen, H.T.: Attention-based LSTM with semantic consistency for videos captioning. In: ACM MM, pp. 357–361 (2016)
8. He, K., Zhang, X., Ren, S., Sun, J.: Deep residual learning for image recognition. In: CVPR, pp. 770–778 (2016)
9. Hochreiter, S., Schmidhuber, J.: Long short-term memory. Neural Comput. 9(8), 1735–1780 (1997)
10. Hodosh, M., Young, P., Hockenmaier, J.: Framing image description as a ranking task: data, models and evaluation metrics. In: IJCAI, pp. 4188–4192 (2015)
11. Johnson, J., Karpathy, A., Fei-Fei, L.: Densecap: fully convolutional localization networks for dense captioning. In: CVPR, pp. 4565–4574 (2016)
12. Karpathy, A., Fei-Fei, L.: Deep visual-semantic alignments for generating image descriptions. TPAMI 39(4), 664–676 (2017)
13. Kim, Y., Denton, C., Hoang, L., Rush, A.M.: Structured attention networks. In: ICLR (2017)
14. Kingma, D.P., Ba, J.: Adam: a method for stochastic optimization. In: ICLR (2015)
15. Kuznetsova, P., Ordonez, V., Berg, A.C., Berg, T.L., Choi, Y.: Collective generation of natural image descriptions. In: ACL, pp. 359–368 (2012)
16. Lin, T.-Y., et al.: Microsoft COCO: common objects in context. In: Fleet, D., Pajdla, T., Schiele, B., Tuytelaars, T. (eds.) ECCV 2014. LNCS, vol. 8693, pp. 740–755. Springer, Cham (2014). https://doi.org/10.1007/978-3-319-10602-1_48
17. Lu, J., Xiong, C., Parikh, D., Socher, R.: Knowing when to look: adaptive attention via a visual sentinel for image captioning. In: CVPR, pp. 3242–3250 (2017)
18. Luo, Y., Huang, Z., Zhang, Z., Wang, Z., Li, J., Yang, Y.: Curiosity-driven reinforcement learning for diverse visual paragraph generation. In: ACM MM, pp. 2341–2350 (2019)
19. Luo, Y., Wang, Z., Huang, Z., Yang, Y., Zhao, C.: Coarse-to-fine annotation enrichment for semantic segmentation learning. In: CIKM, pp. 237–246 (2018)
20. Mitchell, M., et al.: Midge: generating image descriptions from computer vision detections. In: EACL, pp. 747–756 (2012)
21. Parikh, A.P., Täckström, O., Das, D., Uszkoreit, J.: A decomposable attention model for natural language inference. In: EMNLP, pp. 2249–2255 (2016)
22. Pedersoli, M., Lucas, T., Schmid, C., Verbeek, J.: Areas of attention for image captioning. In: ICCV, pp. 1251–1259 (2017)
23. Rennie, S.J., Marcheret, E., Mroueh, Y., Ross, J., Goel, V.: Self-critical sequence training for image captioning. In: CVPR, pp. 1179–1195 (2017)
24. Song, J., Gao, L., Guo, Z., Liu, W., Zhang, D., Shen, H.T.: Hierarchical LSTM with adjusted temporal attention for video captioning. In: IJCAI, pp. 2737–2743 (2017)
25. Sukhbaatar, S., Szlam, A., Weston, J., Fergus, R.: End-to-end memory networks. In: NeurIPS, pp. 2440–2448 (2015)
26. Vaswani, A., et al.: Attention is all you need. In: NeurIPS, pp. 6000–6010 (2017)
27. Vinyals, O., Toshev, A., Bengio, S., Erhan, D.: Show and tell: a neural image caption generator. In: CVPR, pp. 3156–3164 (2015)
28. Wang, Z., Luo, Y., Li, Y., Huang, Z., Yin, H.: Look deeper see richer: depth-aware image paragraph captioning. In: ACM MM, pp. 672–680 (2018)
29. Xu, K., et al.: Show, attend and tell: neural image caption generation with visual attention. In: ICML, pp. 2048–2057 (2015)

30. Yao, T., Pan, Y., Li, Y., Qiu, Z., Mei, T.: Boosting image captioning with attributes. In: ICCV, pp. 4904–4912 (2017)
31. Zhang, M., Yang, Y., Zhang, H., Ji, Y., Xie, N., Shen, H.T.: Deep semantic indexing using convolutional localization network with region-based visual attention for image database. In: Huang, Z., Xiao, X., Cao, X. (eds.) ADC 2017. LNCS, vol. 10538, pp. 261–272. Springer, Cham (2017). https://doi.org/10.1007/978-3-319-68155-9_20

Efficient kNN Search with Occupation in Large-Scale On-demand Ride-Hailing

Mengqi Li, Dan He$^{(\boxtimes)}$, and Xiaofang Zhou

The University of Queensland, Brisbane, Australia
mengqi.li2@uqconnect.edu.au, {d.he,uqxzhou}@uq.edu.au

Abstract. The intelligent ride-hailing systems, e.g., DiDi, Uber, have served as essential travel tools for customers, which foster plenty of studies for the location-based queries on road networks. Under the large demand of ride-hailing, the non-occupied vehicles might be insufficient for new-coming user requests. However, the occupied vehicles which are about to arrive their destinations could be the candidates to serve the requests close to their destinations. Consequently, in our work, we study the k Nearest Neighbor search for moving objects with occupation, notated as *Approachable kNN (AkNN) Query*, which to the best of our knowledge is the first study to consider the occupation of moving objects in relevant fields. In particular, we first propose a simple Dijkstra-based algorithm for the AkNN query. Then we improve the solution by developing a grid-based Destination-Oriented index, derived from GLAD [9], for the occupied and non-occupied moving objects. Accordingly, we propose an efficient grid-based expand-and-bound algorithm for the approachable kNN search and conduct extensive experiments on real-world data. The results demonstrate the effectiveness and efficiency of our proposed solutions.

Keywords: Intelligent raid-hailing system · kNN search · Location-based query · Moving object query

1 Introduction

Recent years, there appears a rapid development of on-demand ride-hailing services such as Uber [4] and Didi [3]. With the proliferation of GPS-enabled devices, e.g., smart phone, these ride-hailing services provide significant improvements against traditional taxi service systems in terms of reducing taxi cruising time and passengers' waiting time. Meanwhile, they also foster plenty of studies for location-based queries on road networks. In particular, given a set O of moving objects and a query point q on a road network, the k Nearest Neighbor (kNN) query returns the k nearest objects in O with the shortest road network distance to q. The kNN query on moving objects provides important technical support for the ride-hailing. For instance, in existing ride-hailing services, a traveler may

---

D. He—Equal contribution.

© Springer Nature Switzerland AG 2020
R. Borovica-Gajic et al. (Eds.): ADC 2020, LNCS 12008, pp. 29–41, 2020.
https://doi.org/10.1007/978-3-030-39469-1_3

request a taxi at his/her current location, and ride-hailing services then need to find several taxis in its fleet that are the closest to this location and dispatch one from the kNN results based on a certain strategy.

There exists a plethora of research works [9–13, 17, 20] that address the kNN queries for moving objects on road networks, some of which can achieve very high system throughput. However, most existing solutions query the moving objects, e.g., taxi, under the assumption that all the candidate objects are available, i.e., they can response to the request right after they are assigned. In practice, with the large demand of user requests, there could be insufficient neighboring objects for the new-coming queries, especially during peak hours. To explain, most of the moving objects near the query locations might have been occupied by some previous users. In this case, existing kNN solutions would either return some available results those are very far away from the query locations, or fail to response the requests. Nevertheless, some of occupied objects might arrive their destinations soon. And if the destinations are happen to be close to some query locations, these objects should be considered as the candidate objects to serve the corresponding requests. For example, in Fig. 1, there are 6 moving objects on this road network, while only O_1 (the yellow taxi marked with a red flag) is non-occupied. When there is a query Q, the existing kNN solutions will find O_1 as the nearest object to Q. However, as we can see, O_3 could approach Q much earlier after it gets to its destination D_3.

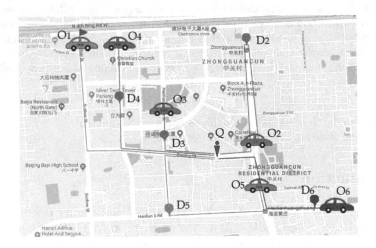

Fig. 1. AkNN example

Consequently, in our work, we study the Approachable kNN (AkNN) query on non-occupied and occupied moving objects, which to the best of our knowledge is the first to consider the occupation of moving objects. Given a set of non-occupied/occupied moving objects and a query point on a road network, we aim to return the k nearest objects those can earliest response the request after they finish the previous journey (arrive the destinations). These objects are regarded as the imminent approachable candidates to serve the requests. Particularly, we measure the distance between the query location and a moving object by combining the distance of the remaining journey and the distance from its destination to the query. In this scenario, directly applying any of the existing kNN solutions would fail to return the correct answers. To explain, after obtaining the k nearest moving objects based on their current locations, we might find some of results with very far destinations. Then the combining distances could be larger than those of some other objects. For instance, in Fig. 1, the objects O_2 and O_5 are the top-2 nearest objects to the query Q based on their current locations, while O_3 and O_6 should be the exact nearest ones considering the combinational distances.

Nevertheless, if the distances between any two nodes could be precomputed in advance, we could slightly modify the existing kNN solutions to address the AkNN query. To be specific, we can get a larger number of nearest candidates and verify the final results by checking the distance from the object to its destination and the distance from its destination to the query location. Obviously, the space consumption for this solution would be huge, which is not desirable. Motivated by this, we employ an efficient hop-labeling algorithm, i.e., the *H2H* [14] for distance calculation, based on which we propose a simple Dijkstra-based algorithm for the approachable kNN query. Then we improve the efficiency by developing a grid-based index for the moving objects with occupation, which is derived from GLAD [9]. In particular, we build a Destination-Oriented index and propose the corresponding algorithm for approachable kNN search. Finally, we conduct extensive experiments on real-world data set and the results show that the grid-based algorithm outperforms the simple solution significantly.

Our work has three primary contributions:

- We introduce a novel and meaningful approachable kNN query on moving objects for the ride-hailing service, which will consider the occupation of objects.
- We first propose a Dijkstra-based algorithm to address the approachable kNN query. Then we improve the efficiency by introducing a grid-based solution, which can achieve a very good performance.
- We develop sufficient experiments with real-world data. And the results demonstrate the superiority of our solution over the competitor.

2   Related Work

In this section, we discuss about the relevant studies of our work, which contains two parts, kNN query and shortest path query.

2.1 kNN Queries

Dijkstra algorithm [7] is the most straightforward solution for the kNN search on the graph, which is the most famous single source shortest path algorithm. Dijkstra's algorithm is simple, requiring only search on the original graph without auxiliary indexing structure. However, due to the large search scope, real-time query cost for Dijkstra is high. ROAD [6] runs a Dijkstra algorithm on the indexing structure of hierarchical subgraphs. By indexing subgraphs, it can reduce the search overhead by skipping the networks that do not contain any object. The defect of ROAD algorithm is that when the objects are evenly distributed, the subgraph structure degrades and the performance would be almost the same as that of Dijkstra. Similarly, G-tree [20] also uses hierarchical subgraph structure. It stores the boundary set of nodes and the corresponding distance matrix for boundary nodes on the subgraph. Then during the exploration, it searches in a top-down manner on the tree structure, and answers kNN query by computing the distance between query node to the objects based on the pre-stored distance matrix. G-tree improves query efficiency through index of tree structure, but at the same time increases space cost. V-tree [17] adds *local nearest active vertex table* on the basis of G-tree, regarding the nodes containing moving objects, to facilitate the query of moving objects. TOAIN [12] uses SCOB index and Contraction Hierarchy (CH) [8] structure. It builds a shortcut on the graph to calculate in advance candidate *downhill* objects for kNN Dijkstra search results. Also, TOAIN has optimized throughputs. GLAD [9] build a grid index to store the moving objects and as for the road network, it applies the state-of-the-art hop-labeling based structure H2H [14] to calculate the road network distance for any two nodes on the graph. GLAD can achieve very little update cost since the update of grid is cheap, thus to improve the system throughput. Meanwhile, it also considers the conflict between queries in the concurrent processing.

2.2   Shortest Path Queries

Querying the shortest path between two nodes on road network has been studied a lot [18–20]. Dijkstra is the most famous method, but it is expensive and not suitable for large-scale road network. Bidirectional-Dijkstra [15] searches from the starting node to the end node by Dijkstra simultaneously, reducing the visited points to reduce the cost. Contraction Hierarchies (CH) [8] first sets the overall order to allow Dijkstra to access the nodes in ascending order. This algorithm calculates distance between pairs of points in advance and reduces the query time for distance by shortcut. TRN [5] adds grid on the road network as an index, then calculates and stores the shortest path of the relatively important points around the grid in advance. Spatially Induced Linkage Cognizance (SILC) [16] stores all the shortest paths in the graph in a summary form to improve efficiency when querying. In addition, there is a lot of research work on shortest path or shortest path query under certain conditions [18,19,21].

3   Preliminary

In this section, we introduce the basic definitions for our work and present our problem statement accordingly.

Definition 1 (Road Network). *We define the road network to be a directed graph, $G = (V, E)$, where V is the set of vertices and E is the set of road segments on this road network. For each edge $(u, v) \in E$, we associate it with a weight $w(u, v)$, which represents the distance from u to v.*

Given two vertices $u, v \in V$, let $P = \langle v_0, v_1, \cdots, v_l \rangle$ be a path from u to v, where $v_0 = u$ and $v_l = v$, then the distance of P is defined as $\sum_{i=0}^{l-1} w(v_i, v_{i+1})$. The shortest distance from u to v is defined as the minimum distance among all the paths from u to v, denoted as $SPD(u, v)$. Consider an object o located on a road segment (u_o, v_o) such that the distance between o and v_o is $w(o, v_o)$. Given a query point q, which is located on a road segment (u_q, v_q), the distance of vertex u_q to q is $w(u_q, q)$. The distance from o to q is then:

$$SPD(q, o) = w(o, v_o) + SPD(v_o, u_q) + w(u_q, q). \tag{1}$$

Following previous works [12, 17, 20], we assume that the query locations and objects are all located on vertices, ignoring the offset of the objects to the vertices (resp. the vertices to query locations) on the road network.

On road networks, it is difficult to monitor the locations of the moving objects in ride-hailing continuously, e.g., taxi. Instead, for the moving objects that include GPSs, the movement of these objects can be tracked periodically with every second, or even with smaller periodicity [1]. In our work, we consider the moving objects that might have been occupied by existing users. Thus we define the moving object as follows.

Definition 2 (Moving Object). *We define a moving object o on the road network to be a tuple, i.e., $o = (v_c, v_d, s)$, where v_c (resp. v_d) indicates the current (resp. destination) location, and s represents the current status (occupied/non-occupied) of the moving object. Note that $v_d = v_c$ if o is non-occupied.*

Next, we define the approachable kNN query on a set of the occupied moving objects on the road network as follows.

Definition 3 (Approachable kNN Query (AkNN)). *Given a query point q, a set M of moving objects on a road network $G(V, E)$, and an integer $k \leq |M|$, the approachable kNN query returns a set $R \subseteq M$ of k moving objects such that for all $o' \in M \setminus R$, the following inequation suffices for any $o \in R$.*

$$SDP(o'.v_c, o'.v_d) + SDP(o'.v_d, q) \geq SDP(o.v_c, o.v_d) + SDP(o.v_d, q)$$

Different from the previous studies on kNN queries for moving objects, we do not consider the distance between the query point to the current location of the moving objects. Since the moving objects could have been occupied, we instead consider the distance between the query location and the destination of the moving objects, combining the distance from the current location to the destination of the moving objects.

4   AkNN Query Algorithms

In this section, we present the algorithms to address the approachable kNN query. We first introduce the simple Dijkstra-based algorithm, followed by the grid-based algorithm which can achieve greater efficiency.

Algorithm 1. Dijkstra AkNN

Input: Road network G, query point q, Distance scheme D
Output: kNN of q
1: Let $D(i)$ be the distance between i and q, and $D(q) = 0$. Let C be the candidate set of kNN queries. Let Q be a priority queue of nodes, and every element in Q has a distance as priority, $Q \leftarrow \{q\}$. Let θ be the upper bound of the distance of the kNN, $\theta \leftarrow \infty$. Let v be the currently accessed node $v.dist \leftarrow 0$, $v.id \leftarrow q$.
2: **while** $(Q \neq \emptyset)$ and $(v.tDist < \theta)$ **do**
3:      $v \leftarrow Q.top$, $dist[v] \leftarrow v.dist$, Remove v from Q
4:      **for** each object o on v node **do**
5:          $D \leftarrow H2H(o_c, o_d) + H2H(o_d, q)$
6:          **if** $C.size < k$ **then**
7:              $C \leftarrow o(D)$
8:          **else**
9:              **if** $D < C[k].dist$ **then**
10:                 $\theta \leftarrow D$, Remove k-th object from C, $C \leftarrow o, D$
11:             **end if**
12:         **end if**
13:     **end for**
14:     **for** each unvisited node u is a neighbor of v **do**
15:         **if** u in Q **then**
16:             **if** $dist[v] + w(v, u) < dist[u])$ **then**
17:                 $dist[u] \leftarrow dist[v] + w(v, u)$
18:             **end if**
19:         **else**
20:             $Q \leftarrow u, (dist[v] + w(v, u))$
21:         **end if**
22:     **end for**
23: **end while**
24: **return** C

4.1   Dijkstra AkNN

In this section, we introduce the simple Dijkstra-base algorithm for the approachable kNN. As we need to consider the distance of the reminding journey of an occupied moving object, applying the basic Dijkstra algorithm straightforwardly will cost huge. This is because, when we observed a moving object by Dijkstra, we can only obtain the distance from the current location to the query, and even might not reveal its destination. And the shortest distance from its current location to its destination is unknown even we observe both locations by Dijkstra from the query node.

Consequently, unlike the traditional Dijkstra algorithm that is totally index-free, in our work, we will need an auxiliary index structure for the AkNN search. Our main observation is that the distance between nodes on the road network does not change and only the objects are dynamically moving. Therefore, we apply the H2H [14] on the road network, which is also used in [9]. We regard the H2H index as a black box of distance scheme that can efficiently retrieve the road network distance between any two nodes. In particular, during the exploration on the graph, whenever we meet a moving object, we calculate the combinational distances to verify if the candidate object could contribute to the final answers. The algorithm terminates when k nearest objects are retrieved in terms of the combinational distances.

The pseudo-code of the kNN query algorithm is as shown in Algorithm 1. We maintain an initially empty candidate set C containing up to k elements for the candidate kNN objects and its combinational distance to q. Initially, the upper bound threshold, θ of the query distance is ∞. If the current access node is further from q than the distance upper bound, or if the queue Q is empty, the algorithm terminates. We perform a basic Dijkstra exploration on the road network. Differently, whenever an object is observed, we will calculate the combinational distance from the current position of object to its destination and then to q with the H2H distance scheme (Line 5). If the current candidate results contain less than k objects, the newly observed object will be added to candidate set C, with the combinational distance as the priority (Line 6–7). Otherwise, we compare the distance of newly observed object with the kth object in C to update the candidate results, as well as the distance upper bound θ (Line 9–10). From line 14–21, the algorithm perform the edge relaxation which is the same the origin Dijkstra algorithm. To this end, we will find the k nearest objects regarding the combinational distance.

4.2 Grid-Based AkNN

In this section, we present a grid-based labeling index structure for moving objects, which is derived from GLAD [9], to support efficient update and query processing. Following the idea of GLAD, we partition the road network into small grids, and then maintain a data structure to record the objects that fall into the grid. However, unlike GLAD, here we consider the remaining trips of the occupied moving objects, which contain two spatial fields. Thus, in this section we introduce the *Destination-Oriented* index, and present the corresponding search algorithm as follows.

We map the moving objects to the grid based on their destinations. In this scenario, the update of the index will be less frequent than the previous type of index, since the moving objects usually change their destination after they finish the service journeys. The space consumption is linear, i.e., $O(|M|)$, as each object contains only one destination in any time. We update the grid index object-by-object, i.e., whenever there is an object changing its destination, we update the corresponding grid cells accordingly. We will show in the experiment study (Sect. 5.3) that the Destination-Oriented index achieves better per-

---

Algorithm 2. Grid-base AkNN

Input: Road network G, query point q, Distance scheme D, Grid index L
Output: kNN of q
1: Let h be the grid containing q, $H \leftarrow \emptyset$, $NH \leftarrow \{h\}$. Let $C(q)$ be the candidate set
   of the kNN queries. Let UB be the upper bound of the distance of the k-th nearest
   neighbor to q and initially set to ∞. Let $LB \leftarrow 0$ and $L(o,q)$ denotes the Euclidean
   distance from q to the destination of object o plus the Euclidean distance from the
   current position of o to the destination of it.
2: **while** $UB > LB$ **do**
3:    Let $L(NH)$ be the set of objects that their destinations fall in any grid in NH
4:    **for** $o \in L(NH)$ with $L(o,q) < UB$ **do**
5:       $dist(o,q) \leftarrow D(o.c, o.d) + D(o.d, q)$
6:       **if** $dist(o,q) < k$-th object in C **then**
7:          $C \leftarrow o$
8:       **end if**
9:    **end for**
10:   $H \leftarrow H \cup NH$
11:   Update UB to the k-th distance in C
12:   Let NH be the set of grids that are neighbors of H but excluding the grids in
      H
13:   Let LB be the Euclidean distance from q to edge of NH
14: **end while**
15: **return** objects in C

---

formance compared with the other two types of indexes (Object-Oriented and Hybrid).

Next, we present the algorithm detail with the Destination-Oriented index as Algorithm 2. Line 1 illustrates the initialization of this algorithm. We maintain a set C to hold candidate kNN objects, and maintain a set H that holds the grid accessed, initially empty. Then we maintain a set NH, to store H's neighbor grids, and add h to NH before the loop starts. We set UB to be the upper bound of the distance of the kth nearest neighbor to q and initially set to ∞. Then let LB be 0. $L(o,q)$ denotes the Euclidean distance from q to the destination of object o plus the Euclidean distance from the current position of o to the destination of it. The algorithm terminates if UB is less than or equal to LB. When searching all objects in the grids of NH, if $L(o,q)$ of o is less than UB for an object, then we calculate the road network distance from the current position of o to its destination and then to q with H2H distance scheme (Line 4–5). We verify the candidates in C if the distance is less than the kth objects (Line 6–7). After checking all the objects in grids of NH, we merge the grids in NH into H (Line 10). Update the upper bound with the combinational distance of the kth object in C (Line 11). Update NH with the surrounding grids of H, and update LB with Euclidean distance from q to the boundary of NH (Line 11–13). Finally, we return the objects in C (Line 15).

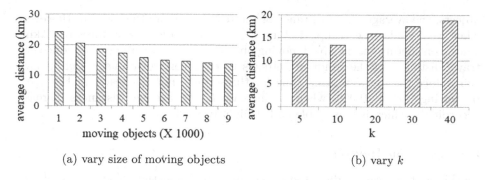

(a) vary size of moving objects   (b) vary k

Fig. 2. Average distance between the query and kNN results

5   Experimental Study

In this section, we experimentally evaluate the proposed solutions for the approachable kNN problem. All methods are implemented in C++ and compiled with full optimizations. All experiments are conducted on an Intel Core M 1.2 GHz CPU with 8 GB RAM running Mac OS Mojave (10.14.6).

5.1   Experiment Setup

We conduct our experiments on the New York (NY) road network, which includes $264K$ nodes and $733K$ edges. We obtain a real dataset from NYC Open Data [2], which has $18K$ taxi trajectories. We map the starting point of each trajectory to the nearest vertex on the road network. Then, the query locations are half generated from random starting points of the trajectories and half generated from random vertices on the road network. The current position of moving objects are generated uniformly from the road network. For the non-occupied objects, the destinations are set to be the same as their current location. For the occupied objects, we generate the destination of half of the objects to be the end points of the trajectories. In terms of the rest, we generate the destinations that are randomly distributed.

5.2   Case Study

In this section, we perform a case study to show the significance of the approachable kNN problem in ride-hailing service. In particular, we generate 10000 moving objects while only 1000 of them are non-occupied. We random generate 5000 query locations, and obtain their kNN moving objects. For each query, we compute the average distance from the query to its kNN results. We first vary the total number of the moving objects and then vary the value of k to conduct the experiment, of which the results are shown in Fig. 2. From Fig. 2(a), the average distances decrease when the number of occupied objects increases. Specifically, when we perform 10NN search on only the non-occupied moving objects, the average travel distance of the results is more than 24 km. However, when we consider the occupied objects, the average distance reduces to 13 km. Thus, considering the occupied moving objects in the ride-hailing can reduce the travel distances of the candidate objects to the query locations, which in fact can reduce the users' waiting time for the service. For the result in Fig. 2(b), by setting $|M| = 10000$, when we increase k, the average distances increase accordingly, which is reasonable and straightforward.

5.3 Different Indexes

In this section, we conduct the experiment to show the effectiveness of the Destination-Oriented index. Alternatively, we implement two other types of indexes, Object-Oriented and Hybrid, as follows.

– **Object-Oriented:** We map the moving objects to the grid based on their current locations. In this case, the index follows the same scheme with the one in GLAD.
– **Hybrid:** In this type of index, we duplicate the moving objects and map each object to the grid twice based on both its current location and destination. For each grid cell, we will maintain two lists for the objects and destinations respectively.

We compare the effectiveness and efficiency of these three types of indexes regarding the query processing time and the update cost. The experimental results are shown in Fig. 3, where OO represents the Object-Oriented index, DO indicates the Destination-Oriented index. Note that in all settings, the size of each grid cell is set to be 100 m × 100 m. As for the query processing time, we perform AkNN search for 5000 queries with three index structures and record the average query time used for each query. We vary the value of k from 5 to 40 as shown in Fig. 3(a). The results show that the Destination-Oriented index always works the best. This is because, when we consider the occupied objects, the distance from their destinations to the query location is the lower-bound of the combinational distance. Thus, indexing the objects only by the

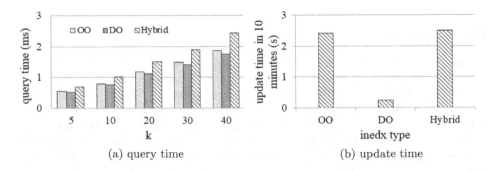

(a) query time   (b) update time

Fig. 3. Effectiveness of different indexes

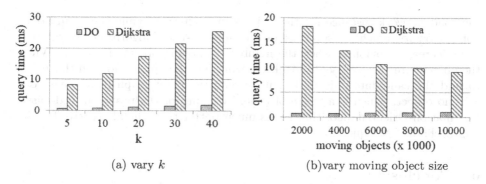

(a) vary k (b)vary moving object size

Fig. 4. Effectiveness of different indexes

destinations can efficiently filter the unnecessary visited objects, i.e., the objects with close current locations but far destinations from the query location. In terms of update, since the destinations of the occupied moving objects will not change frequently, thus the update cost is slight. In the experiment, we assume that the destinations will be updated every 10 min on average, while the current locations update every second. We compute the total update cost needed in every 10 min, where the number of moving objects is 5000, with 1000 non-occupied and 4000 occupied objects. The result in Fig. 3(b) shows that, the Destination-Oriented index needs the least update cost. Besides, the update cost our grid-based index is very negligible.

5.4   AkNN Search Algorithms

In this section, we present the experiment about the efficiency of our proposed grid-based Destination-Oriented AkNN search, compared with the Dijkstra-based algorithm. We vary the parameter of k and the number of moving objects to record the query processing time of each query. For each setting, we run 5000 query and compute the average query cost. Figure 4 shows the results of this set of experiment. Under all the setting, the proposed grid-based algorithm outperforms the Dijkstra-based algorithm. Note that, in Dijkstra-based algorithm, we also map each moving object to the graph according to its destination location with the similar reason as analyzed in Sect. 5.3. In particular, when we increase k, the number of moving objects is set to be 5000. The result in Fig. 4(a) shows that the query time increases for both algorithms, which is straightforward to understand. That is, when k increases, the exploration space has to be enlarged to get more candidates. As we can see, the grid-based algorithm (denote as DO) can always achieve more than 10 times faster than the Dijkstra-based algorithm. Moreover, we vary the size of moving objects to see the performance of both algorithms, where k is set to be 10. Figure 4(b) demonstrates that the query time for the grid-based algorithm increases slightly when the number of moving object increases. This is because, when the moving objects are more dense, there are more objects in each grid. Then the algorithm will need to compute more for the road network distance for the objects in each grid, while the bound does not narrow too much. However, as for the Dijkstra-based algorithm, the running time decreases obviously when the number of moving objects increases. When the objects are very sparse, the Dijkstra will need to explore more on the graph to find the candidate objects, i.e., it encounters many graph nodes that contain no object, which is a waste of time. To sum up, the proposed grid-based Destination-Oriented algorithm works much better than the alternative for the approachable kNN query.

6   Conclusion

In this paper, we study a novel k nearest neighbor search for moving objects with occupation on the road network, namely Approachable kNN Query. It differs from the existing kNN in the measure of distance from objects to query location. Accordingly, we introduce a simple Dijkstra-based algorithm and propose an improved grid-based algorithm to address the approachable kNN search. Our work shows the superiority to the existing related works in the scenario with high-demanded requests in the ride-hailing service systems. As a future work, we tend to study the approachable kNN query on the road network on dynamic road network, i.e., the distance weight on each edge changes overtime.

References

1. https://news.thomasnet.com/fullstory/gps-receiver-provides-20-hz-update-rate-587490
2. https://opendata.cityofnewyork.us/
3. Didichuxing. https://gaia.didichuxing.com/
4. Uber. https://www.uber.com/
5. Bast, H., Funke, S., Matijević, D.: Transit: ultrafast shortest-path queries with linear-time preprocessing. In: 9th DIMACS Implementation Challenge-Shortest Path (2006)
6. Demiryurek, U., Banaei-Kashani, F., Shahabi, C.: Efficient continuous nearest neighbor query in spatial networks using Euclidean restriction. In: Mamoulis, N., Seidl, T., Pedersen, T.B., Torp, K., Assent, I. (eds.) SSTD 2009. LNCS, vol. 5644, pp. 25–43. Springer, Heidelberg (2009). https://doi.org/10.1007/978-3-642-02982-0_5
7. Dijkstra, E.W.: A note on two problems in connexion with graphs. Numerische mathematik 1(1), 269–271 (1959)
8. Geisberger, R., Sanders, P., Schultes, D., Delling, D.: Contraction hierarchies: faster and simpler hierarchical routing in road networks. In: McGeoch, C.C. (ed.) WEA 2008. LNCS, vol. 5038, pp. 319–333. Springer, Heidelberg (2008). https://doi.org/10.1007/978-3-540-68552-4_24
9. He, D., Wang, S., Zhou, X., Cheng, R.: An efficient framework for correctness-aware kNN queries on road networks. In: ICDE, pp. 1298–1309 (2019)
10. He, D., Wang, S., Zhou, X., Cheng, R.: Glad: a grid and labeling framework with scheduling for conflict-aware kNN queries. TKDE (2019)

11. Kolahdouzan, M., Shahabi, C.: Voronoi-based k nearest neighbor search for spatial network databases. In: PVLDB, pp. 840–851 (2004)
12. Luo, S., Kao, B., Li, G., Hu, J., Cheng, R., Zheng, Y.: TOAIN: a throughput optimizing adaptive index for answering dynamic k nn queries on road networks. PVLDB **11**(5), 594–606 (2018)
13. Nutanong, S., Zhang, R., Tanin, E., Kulik, L.: The v*-diagram: a query-dependent approach to moving knn queries. PVLDB **1**(1), 1095–1106 (2008)
14. Ouyang, D., Qin, L., Chang, L., Lin, X., Zhang, Y., Zhu, Q.: When hierarchy meets 2-hop-labeling: efficient shortest distance queries on road networks. In: SIGMOD, pp. 709–724 (2018)
15. Pohl, I.: Bidirectional and heuristic search in path problems. Technical report (1969)
16. Samet, H., Sankaranarayanan, J., Alborzi, H.: Scalable network distance browsing in spatial databases. In: SIGMOD, pp. 43–54 (2008)
17. Shen, B., et al.: V-tree: efficient knn search on moving objects with road-network constraints. In: ICDE, pp. 609–620 (2017)
18. Wang, S., Lin, W., Yang, Y., Xiao, X., Zhou, S.: Efficient route planning on public transportation networks: a labelling approach. In: SIGMOD, pp. 967–982 (2015)
19. Wang, S., Xiao, X., Yang, Y., Lin, W.: Effective indexing for approximate constrained shortest path queries on large road networks. PVLDB **10**(2), 61–72 (2016)
20. Zhong, R., Li, G., Tan, K.-L., Zhou, L., Gong, Z.: G-tree: an efficient and scalable index for spatial search on road networks. TKDE **27**(8), 2175–2189 (2015)
21. Zhu, A.D., Xiao, X., Wang, S., Lin, W.: Efficient single-source shortest path and distance queries on large graphs. In: SIGKDD, pp. 998–1006 (2013)

Trace-Based Approach for Consistent Construction of Activity-Centric Process Models from Data-Centric Process Models

Jyothi Kunchala[1]($^{\boxtimes}$), Jian Yu[1], Sira Yongchareon[1], and Guiling Wang[2]

[1] School of Engineering, Computer and Mathematical Sciences,
Auckland University of Technology, Auckland, New Zealand
{kunchala.jyothi,jian.yu,sira.yongchareon}@aut.ac.nz
[2] Beijing Key Laboratory on Integration and Analysis of Large-Scale Stream Data,
North China University of Technology, Beijing, China
wangguiling@ncut.edu.cn

Abstract. In recent years, artifact-centric paradigm as a data-centric approach to business process modeling has gained momentum. Compared to the traditional activity-centric paradigm that focuses on process control-flow and treats data as simple black boxes that act as input and output to these activities, the artifact-centric paradigm provides equal support to both the control-flow and data. Most of the existing process modeling is activity-centric, although the artifact-centric modeling enables higher process flexibility and reusability. This is mainly due to the existence of numerous notations, tools and technologies that provide increased support to activity-centric process modeling and execution. Therefore, this paper proposes a trace-based approach to transform artifact-centric process models into activity-centric process models and to analyse the consistency of transformed and base models. A case study is utilized to demonstrate the feasibility of the proposed approach.

Keywords: Activity-centric process modeling · Data-centric process modeling · Artifact-centric process modeling · Model transformation

1 Introduction

In the dynamic marketplace, business process modeling (BPM) is a fundamental tool for many organizations to stay competitive and gain operational benefits. The *activity-centric* and *data-centric* approaches are the well-known modeling paradigms in BPM. The activity-centric approach represents the flow of business activities, where the underlying data is annotated as input and output of these activities. There exist a multitude of activity-centric modeling notations including UML, BPMN that provide many intuitive constructs, which can be naturally mapped to executable languages such as BPEL [1]. The activity-centric approach

© Springer Nature Switzerland AG 2020
R. Borovica-Gajic et al. (Eds.): ADC 2020, LNCS 12008, pp. 42–54, 2020.
https://doi.org/10.1007/978-3-030-39469-1_4

is imperative in nature, which requires a process model (or model) to explicitly specify every alternative execution sequence during design-time. Thus, a flow that is not specified in such a model is not allowed [2].

In contrast, the data-centric approach focuses on representing the information about business objects including their attributes and temporal relations. Based on the notion of data-centric modeling, a new approach called artifact-centric approach has been proposed in recent years. Compared to the data-centric approach which is based on a more abstract object-oriented concept that only captures the information aspect of a business object, the artifact-centric approach considers both the information and lifecycle aspects including attributes, states and the interrelations of key business entities called *artifacts* [7], and may also include activities that invoke these artifacts to represent a business process.

The artifact-centric modeling supports a declarative style to describe the process behavior, where the execution sequence of activities can be governed by specifying business constraints [10]. Thus, artifact-centric models are more expressible and offer more freedom compared to the activity-centric models. However, these models are less comprehensible than the activity-centric models, due to their unstructured sets of business rules that often impede their adoption [1,4]. Therefore, this paper proposes an approach to transform artifact-centric models into activity-centric models. Mainly, the proposed approach is comprised of algorithms used to construct an activity-centric model from an artifact-centric model and to check the consistency between the constructed and base models. A case study is also utilized to demonstrate the feasibility of the proposed approach.

This paper is organized into seven sections. Section 2 introduces a motivating example. Section 3 formally defines some key notions. Section 4 presents algorithms for the proposed approach. Section 5 presents a case study. Section 6 discusses the related work. Section 7 concludes this paper.

2   Motivating Example

This section presents an artifact-centric process (ACP) model [10] that describes a customer order processing scenario, which is closely related to the one used in [6] to demonstrate the proposed approach. The ACP model presented in Table 1 consists of *artifacts, services* and *business rules*. Artifacts represent key business entities, which contain a finite set of attributes and states. The *Order, Product* and *Invoice* are the three artifacts of the given process model that have a finite set of states. The attributes, for example, *OrderID* and *CustomerID* are not specified in this model, as we consider them at the implementation level.

Services represent business activities or tasks that take some artifacts as input, and output some artifacts and/or modify their attributes and/or states. The given process model has a set of activities, each of which is labelled with an alphabet to easily referring them throughout the discussion. Business rules are

Table 1. Artifact-centric Process Model (ACP Model)

Artifacts: Order, Product, Invoice **Activities:** InitiateOrder (A), ReceiveOrder (B), AnalyseOrder (C), ConfirmOrder (D), CheckStock (E), PlanProduct (F), ScheduleProduct (G), ManufactureProduct (H), ShipProduct (I), SendInvoice (J), ReceivePayment (K), CloseOrder (L) **Business Rules:** R1, R2, R3, R4, R5, R6, R7, R8, R9, R10, R11	
R1: Initiate order request Pre-condition: λ (Order, wait) Activities: InitiateOrder (Order) Post-condition: λ (Order, init)	Post-condition: λ (Product, planned) ∧ λ (Product, scheduled) **R7: Manufacture the product** Pre-condition: λ (Product, planned) ∧ λ (Product, scheduled) Activities: ManufactureProduct (Product)
R2: Receive order from the customer Pre-condition: λ (Order, init) Activities: ReceiveOrder (Order) Post-condition: λ (Order, received)	Post-condition: λ (Product, made) **R8: Ship product to the customer** Pre-condition: λ (Product, in stock) ∨ λ (Product, made) Activities: ShipProduct (Product, Order)
R3: Analyse the customer order Pre-condition: λ (Order, received) Activities: AnalyseOrder (Order) Post-condition: λ (Order, confirmed) ∨ λ (Order, rejected)	Post-condition: λ (Product, shipped) ∧ λ (Order, shipped) ∧ λ (Invoice, init) **R9: Send invoice to the customer** Pre-condition: λ (Product, shipped) ∧ λ (Order, shipped) ∧ λ (Invoice, init)
R4: Confirm the customer order Pre-condition: λ (Order, confirmed) Activities: ConfirmOrder (Order) Post-condition: λ (Product, init)	Activities: SendInvoice (Order, Invoice) Post-condition: λ (Order, invoiced) ∧ λ (Invoice, sent) **R10: Receive payment from the customer**
R5: Check stock for the product Pre-condition: λ (Product, init) Activities: CheckStock (Product) Post-condition: λ (Product, in stock) ∨ λ (Product, not in stock)	Pre-condition: λ (Order, invoiced) ∧ λ (Invoice, sent) Activities: ReceivePayment (Order, Invoice) Post-condition: λ (Invoice, paid) ∧ λ (Order, paid) **R11: Close the customer order**
R6: Plan and schedule for manufacturing the product Pre-condition: λ (Product, not in stock) Activities: PlanProduct (Product), ScheduleProduct(Product)	Pre-condition: λ (Order, rejected) Activities: CloseOrder (Order) Post-condition: λ (Order, closed)

for associating artifacts with activities, where every rule specifies conditions (pre, post) for one or more activities to invoke the associated artifact(s) by following the Condition-Action [10] style. The complete set of business rules specify the control flow of the ordering process from its initiation to the completion.

It can be observed from Table 1, the process starts with the initiation of an order request by the customer. After receiving the order request for a product, the customer information is analysed to decide whether to confirm the order or to reject it in which case the corresponding order is immediately closed and the process is terminated. When confirmed, the order is analysed to check the availability of the ordered product. The order is shipped to the customer if the requested product is in stock, otherwise, the product is planned, manufactured and then shipped. Then, the order is invoiced and sent to the customer in which case, the process is terminated after receiving the payment from the customer.

Table 2. ACP log

Log traces	Business rules	Activities
1	R1R2R3R4R5R6R7R8R9R10	ABCDEFGHIJK
2	R1R2R3R4R5R8R9R10	ABCDEIJK
3	R1R2R3R11	ABCL

Table 2 presents the process log that contains the execution traces of the ACP model presented in Table 1. These traces can be the recorded traces during the process execution or manually defined traces by analysing the process model. It is assumed that the above process log is compliant with the process model, meaning that it contains every possible execution trace of the given ACP model. This process log is used to check the consistency between the ACP model and the activity-centric process model that will be constructed from this model.

3 Preliminaries

This section formally defines some of the key notions including *ACP Model* (based on [6,10]), *Activity-Centric Process Model*, *Process Log* and *Trace Match*.

Definition 1. *(ACP Model). An ACP model Π is a three tuple (Z, V, B) where,*

- *Z is a finite set of artifacts. Every artifact has a set of attributes, a set of states S, an initial state and a set of final states;*
- *V is a finite set of activities. Every activity contains a label and a finite set of artifacts manipulated by this activity;*
- *B is a finite set of business rules. Every rule consists of a pre (α) and post (β) conditions that comprise a set of in-state (λ) and defined (δ) functions using logical operators ($\wedge$, $\vee$) and activities that manipulate the associated artifacts.*

The logical operators can reveal the relation between artifacts or dependencies between their states that correspond to either a *pre-* or *post-condition* of a business rule. From such a relation/dependency, the control flow relation of activities (executed in *parallel* or *exclusive*) that take these artifacts and states as input or produce them as output can be derived. For example, the states *confirmed* and *rejected* of *Order* artifact have an exclusive relationship between them as they are connected using the $\vee$ operator, therefore, the corresponding activities *ConfirmOrder* and *CloseOrder* must also execute in this exclusive manner. Similarly, the states *planned* and *scheduled* of *Product* artifact connected using the $\wedge$ operator have a parallel relationship, thus the corresponding activities *PlanProduct* and *ScheduleProduct* must also execute in parallel.

The BPMN notation is used to represent the constructed activity-centric process model. Thus, the following definition is based on this notation.

Definition 2. *(Activity-Centric Process (or ACT) Model). An ACT model denoted with Π^P = (E, A, G, F, D, S_p, I, O), where E is a finite set of event nodes, E.Type = {Start, End}; A is a finite set of activity nodes; G is a finite set of gateways, G.Type = {XOR, AND}; F $\subseteq$ (E $\cup$ A $\cup$ G) $\times$ (E $\cup$ A $\cup$ G) is the set of sequence flow relations; D is a finite set of artifacts; S_p is a finite set of states; I and O are the input and output relations among artifacts and activities.*

Definition 3. *(Process Log). A process log P is a finite set of execution traces T_E, where E is the finite set of activities of P. Every trace $t_e = e_1, e_2, ...e_n$ is a finite non-empty sequence of activities, where $e_i \in E$ and $t \in T_E$.*

Definition 4. *(Trace Match). Let $t \in \Pi.T$ and $t_p \in \Pi^P.T_A$, we say t matches t_p that is t $\cong t_p$ if for every $a_i \in t$, $\exists a_j \in t_p$ and $a_i = a_j$. The $\cong$ symbol is used to represent the consistency between two process traces or two process models.*

4   Transformation Approach

This section presents algorithms for each phase of the proposed approach including: *model construction* and *model consistency checking*. In the first phase, an activity-centric process (ACT) model is constructed by obtaining activities and associated artifacts with states from the business rules of the ACP model. In the second phase, the execution traces of the resulting ACT model are extracted and analysed over the ACP traces to check their consistency.

4.1   Model Construction

Algorithm 1 defines the *ConstructACTModel()* function that is recursively invoked for every business rule of the ACP model, from which the activities and the associated input and output artifacts and states are retrieved to construct the ACT model. This function takes as input the ACP model, an ACT model with a *start* node and a data condition (*cond*) based on which a business rule of the ACP model is invoked. Initially, the pre-condition of the first business rule is assigned to the *cond* and is updated with the pre- or post-condition of the corresponding business rule in each invocation of this function and as defined in line 2, a business rule is invoked only if it is not marked as completed, meaning that the activities of this rule were not added in the ACT model.

Algorithm 1 defines three conditions, where every rule needs to satisfy one of these conditions in order to be invoked by the *ConstructACTModel()* function. According to the first condition (line 3) that is when the pre-condition of a rule matches the given data condition (*cond*), the activities of the corresponding rule with their associated artifacts and states are added into the ACT model. In case the pre-condition of a rule is a subset of *cond* (line 24), then for one or more artifacts and states of this *cond*, every next rule is traversed to check if its pre-condition matches with the artifact(s) and state(s) of the given *cond*. Therefore, the recursive function is called for every such rule whose pre-condition is a subset of *cond* (line 28). The third condition is where the *cond* is a subset of the pre-condition of a business rule (line 32). Then the algorithm checks that for every artifact and state of this pre-condition, there an artifact and state associated with an activity node in the ACT model. If these artifacts and states are associated with different activity nodes that belong to different branches of a gateway, then all its open branches are merged using the *MergeBranches()* function (that adds a sequence flow from each branch (activity) node to the close gateway node) before adding the activities of this rule into the ACT model. Then the recursive function is called with this rule and its pre-condition.

The algorithm also defines conditions (line 4 and 14) for adding the activities of each business rule into the ACT model. As in line 4, when a business rule contains a single activity, that it can be added directly to the ACT model with the associated input and output artifacts and states. The algorithm also checks if two states of an output artifact of an activity are in exclusive relation (lines 6–13). In this case, an XOR open gateway node is added in sequence to this activity node in the ACT model. Then, for every artifact and state that is logically connected (using $\lor$ operator), a new branch with that branch condition (artifact [state]) is added to the gateway. To add activities to these branches, every next business rule is traversed until all the activities of rules whose pre-conditions match with the branch conditions are found and added to the corresponding branches of the gateway in the ACT model. The *MergeOpenGatewayBranches()* is for merging those branches that contain no nodes, as their branch conditions do not match the pre-conditions of any rules in the ACP model.

Similarly, a parallel (AND) gateway is used (lines 14–21), when a business rule has more than one activity. In this case, each activity of a business rule is added to a different branch of the AND open gateway node and is annotated with the associated artifacts and states. For each of these branch nodes, the *ConstructACTModel()* function can be called (line 18). This invocation is mainly to add the activities that must be added in sequence to these branch nodes. In this manner, starting at the first rule Algorithm 1 continues until every following rule is invoked and completed, after which an *end* node can be added into the ACT model. Thus the time complexity of this algorithm is analysed as $\mathcal{O}(B \times S)$.

Algorithm 1. Construction of an ACT Model from the ACP Model

Input : ACP Model (Π), ACT Model (Π^P) with start node (n)
Output: Complete ACT Model (Π^P)

1 **Function** ConstructACTModel($rule : \Pi$, $n : \Pi^P$, $cond : rule$):
2   **if** $rule \neq null$ *and is not marked as completed* **then**
3   **if** $rule.\alpha = cond$ **then**
4   **if** $|rule.v| = 1$ **then**
5         $\Pi^P.AddInSequence(v)$
6   **if** $z.s \in v.O$ *and states of z are in exclusive relation* **then**
7           $\Pi^P.AddInSequence(XOR.G^{Open})$
8   **foreach** $z.s \in v.O$ **do**
9             $G^{Open}.AddBranch(branch, z.s)$
10             $ConstructACTModel(GetNext(rule), \Pi^P, z.s)$
11   **end**
12           $MergeOpenGatewayBranches(XOR.G^{Close})$
13   **end**
14   **else if** $|rule.v| > 1$ **then**
15         $\Pi^P.AddInSequence(AND.G^{Open})$
16   **foreach** $v \in rule$ **do**
17           $G^{Open}.AddBranch(branch, v)$
18           $ConstructACTModel(GetNext(rule), \Pi^P, v.O)$
19   **end**
20         $MergeOpenGatewayBranches(AND.G^{Close})$
21   **end**
22       $Mark(rule)$
23       $cond \leftarrow rule.\beta$
24   **else if** $rule.\alpha \subset cond$ **then**
25   **foreach** $z.s \in cond$ **do**
26         $r \leftarrow GetRule(rule, cond)$
27   **while** $r \neq null$ **do**
28   **if** $z.s \in r.\alpha$ **then** $ConstructACTModel(r, \Pi^P, r.\alpha)$
29           $r \leftarrow GetNext(r)$
30   **end**
31   **end**
32   **else if** $cond \subset rule.\alpha$ **then**
33   **foreach** $z.s \in \alpha$ **do**
34   **if** $\exists d.s^p \in \Pi^P$ *and* **then**
35   **if** $d.s^p \in \Pi^P.n_i$ *and* $n_i \in G.branch_i$ **then**
            $MergeBranches(G)$
36             $ConstructACTModel(rule, \Pi^P, rule.\alpha)$
37   **end**
38   **end**
39   **end**
40     $ConstructACTModel(GetNext(rule), \Pi^P, cond)$
41   **end**
42 **End Function**

4.2 Extract Model Traces

Algorithm 2. Extract the Activity-Centric (ACT) Model Traces

Input : ACT Model (Π^P) and its Log (Π_L^P) with empty trace τ^p

Output: Complete Log (Π_L^P) of the ACT Model (Π^P)

1 **Function** BuildTrace($n : \Pi^P$, $\tau^p : \Pi_L^P$):
2 | **if** $n \neq null$ **then**
3 | | **if** $n \in A$ **then**
4 | | | $\tau^p.AddInSeq(n)$
5 | | **else if** $n \in G^{Open}$ *and n is not marked* **then**
6 | | | **if** $n.type = AND$ **then**
7 | | | | **foreach** $bn \in n$ **do**
8 | | | | | **if** *bn is not marked* **then** $BuildTrace(bn, \tau_p)$
9 | | | | **end**
10 | | | **else if** $n.type = XOR$ **then**
11 | | | | **foreach** $bn \in n$ **do**
12 | | | | | **if** *bn is not marked* **then**
13 | | | | | | $BuildTrace(bn, \tau_{new})$
14 | | | | | | $\tau^p.AddInSeq(\tau_{new})$
15 | | | | | | $(\Pi_L^p).Add(\tau^p)$
16 | | | | | **end**
17 | | | | **end**
18 | | | **end**
19 | | **end**
20 | | $Mark(n)$
21 | | $n \leftarrow GetSeqNext(n)$
22 | | $BuildTrace(n, \tau^p)$
23 | **end**
24 **End Function**

Algorithm 2 defines the *BuildTrace()* function that is recursively called to extract each execution trace of the ACT model. This function starts at the *start* node of the ACT model and traverses through every next sequence flow node until it reaches the *end* node and adds the activity nodes (with their input and output artifacts) that it finds on the path to generate a process trace.

As defined in line 3 and 5, the type of each node is checked first, such as *activity* or an open *gateway* node. In the case of activity, the node is added to the process trace. For a gateway type, the algorithm defines two conditions, where, in case of an *AND* gateway (lines 6–9), for every branch of this gateway the *BuildTrace()* function is called with the same process trace that is used to add all the branch nodes of that gateway as all of them are executed.

For every branch of an XOR gateway node (lines 10–18), a new trace is used to traverse through the corresponding branch nodes. After traversing a branch of this gateway, the new trace is appended in sequence to the existing process trace, which is then added to the process log. As defined in line 20, every activity node is marked as visited, once that completes the traversal, while a gateway is marked after all its branches are traced. The time complexity of this algorithm is analysed as $\mathcal{O}(n + e)$, the number of nodes (n) and edges(e) of the ACT model.

4.3   Trace-Based Analysis

Algorithm 3 defines the *ConsistencyCheck()* function for the trace-based analysis of both process logs. This function takes as input the execution traces of the ACP, ACT models and a *count* variable that is initialized to zero and outputs the resulting consistency of the two models. According to the algorithm (lines 2–7), for a trace in the ACP process log if there is a trace that contains the same set of activities in the same execution sequence in the ACT process log, then the value of count is incremented.

Algorithm 3. Analysing the execution traces of ACP and ACT Models

---

Input   : ACP Process Log (Π_L), ACT Process Log (Π_L^P)
Output: Consistency $(\cong)$ of ACP and ACT Models

1 **Function** ConsistencyCheck($\tau : \Pi_L$, $\tau^p : \Pi_L^P$, *count*):
2   **foreach** $\tau \in \Pi_L$ **do**
3   **foreach** $\tau^p \in \Pi_L^P$ **do**
4   **if** $\tau^p \cong \tau$ **then** *count* $\leftarrow$ *count* $+ 1$
5   **end**
6   **end**
7   **if** *count* $= |\Pi_L.\tau|$ **then** $\Pi_L \cong \Pi_L^P$
8 **End Function**

After traversing all the process traces, if the count equals the number of traces in the ACP process log (line 7), then the two models are consistent. The time complexity of this algorithm is analysed as linear $\mathcal{O}(n)$.

5   Case Study

The ACP model and its process log given in Tables 1 and 2 are utilized to demonstrate the feasibility of the proposed approach. To construct an ACT model presented in Fig. 1, Algorithm 1 starts at the rule R1 of the ACP model. As the pre-condition of R1 matches with the *cond* (that contains pre-condition of R1), the *InitiateOrder* activity of this rule is added in sequence to the *start* node of the ACT model with the associated input and output artifacts and states. The algorithm then updates the *cond* with the post-condition of R1. Next, the pre-condition of rule R2 is checked with the *cond*, as there is a match, the *ReceiveOrder* is next added to the ACT model. Similarly, *AnalyseOrder* of R3 is also added, as its pre-condition satisfies the *cond* (post-condition of R2). As the states (*confirmed, rejected*) of R3 are logically connected (using $\vee$ operator), a new XOR open gateway node is added to the ACT model, and for every pair (artifact, state), a new branch with the corresponding branch condition (artifact [state]) is added to the gateway node. Then, the activities of

R4 and R11 that satisfy the branch conditions are added to different branches of the XOR gateway. According to the algorithm, these branches are merged after traversing all the next rules and adding activities of rules that satisfy the branch conditions. For instance, after adding the *ConfirmOrder* activity of R4, the *CheckStock* activity of R5 is added, and again a new XOR open gateway node is added in sequence to this node, as there are logically connected states (*in stock, not in stock*). Similarly, an AND gateway is used for R6 that contains more than one activity including *PlanProduct* and *ScheduleProduct*, which have to be executed in parallel. As shown in the figure, the branches of this gateway are merged before adding the *ManufactureProduct* activity of R7. Similarly, branches of two XOR gateways are merged before adding the activities of R8, R9 and R10.

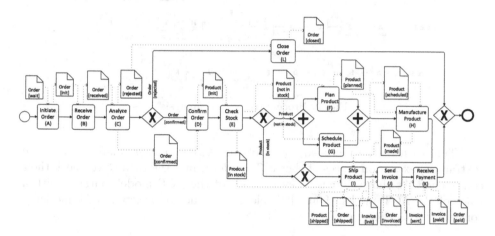

Fig. 1. The constructed Activity-Centric Process (ACT) model

Next, to extract the execution traces of the ACT model, Algorithm 2 starts with an empty trace {} from the *start* node and traverses to the next node *InitiateOrder (A)*, as this node is an activity it is added to the empty trace {A}. Then the next two sequence flow nodes *ReceiveOrder (B)* and *AnalyseOrder (C)* are also added {ABC} in sequence to this trace. Then, for each branch of the first XOR gateway, a new trace is created and used to trace all the branch nodes. For example, in Fig. 1, for the branch that contains a branch condition Order[rejected], a new empty trace is created and the *CloseOrder (L)* node is added {L}. As there is no activity or an open gateway node following this node, the new trace {L} is added to the existing trace {ABCL} and then it is added to the process log. Then a new empty trace is created for the next gateway branch that contains a branch condition Order[confirmed]. The branch nodes *ConfirmOrder (D)* and *CheckStock (E)* are added to the new trace {DE} and is added in sequence to the existing trace {ABCDE}. Then again for the next XOR gateway, similar procedure is followed and the new traces {IJK} and {FGHIJK} are created and they are added in sequence to the existing trace {ABCDE}. The

resulting process traces {ABCDEIJK} and {ABCDEFGHIJK} are then added
to the process log as two different execution traces of the ACT model. For the
AND gateway, the existing trace is used to add all its branch nodes, instead
of adding a new trace for each of its branches. In the resulting trace, a branch
relation is used between the branch nodes of an AND gateway. The extracted
traces can be observed from Fig. 2, where the activities are referenced with their
labels for ease of understanding.

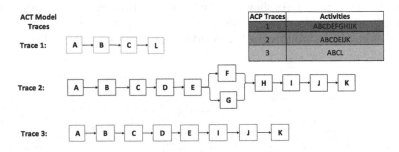

Fig. 2. Process traces and analysis

Then, each of the recorded traces of the ACP model is analysed over the
(extracted) execution traces of the ACT model using Algorithm 3 to check their
consistency. As shown in Fig. 2, every trace of the ACP model matches with a
trace of the ACT model. Thus, it is clear that the constructed ACT model is
consistent with the given ACP model.

6   Related Work and Discussion

There are some approaches to construct activity-centric process models from the
data-centric process models. An approach to transforming declarative models
into Petri Net models is presented in [8]. This approach maps the declarative
constraints of the input model into regular expressions, transforms them into the
Finite State Automaton and then derives a Petri Net. However, this approach
has a drawback that it produces duplicate tasks in the resulting process models
that can increase the complexity with a higher number of execution alternatives.

Algorithms to translate declarative models into the BPMN-D (extension of
BPMN) models have been presented in [2], where a Finite State Automaton of
the input model is first translated into a Finite-state Constraint Automaton,
then into the BPMN-D model. These algorithms do not produce the parallel
states of objects in the BPMN models. Similarly, an approach to automatically
translating artifact-centric models into activity-centric models has been proposed
in [3]. This approach consists of an algorithm that follows a mapping between
the two models to achieve the proposed translation. However, this approach is
also not useful for translating declarative process models.

There exist a few approaches to construct activity-centric models using data-centric counterparts such as the synchronized/unsynchronized object lifecycles. An approach to generate process models from the reference object lifecycles is presented in [5]. The *conformance* and *coverage* notions are used for checking the compliance violations between the generated models and object lifecycles. The approach proposed in [9] is also used to transform the object behaviour models represented in state machines into the YAWL models. The transformation is based on the identification of causal relations in the state machine and encoding those in a heuristics net, from which a Petri Net is generated and further used to derive the YAWL model. The algorithm presented in [6] also uses the synchronized object lifecycles to generate activity-centric models.

As discussed above, there are some approaches for the transformation of data-centric models into activity-centric models. However, these approaches use object lifecycles rather than the declarative models that contain business rules; or they result in models with duplicate tasks and cannot handle parallelism. Therefore, the proposed approach is useful to transform the data-centric models that contain business rules and address the aforementioned limitations. It is worth mentioning that in comparison to the activity-centric models that allow tracing the process flow, the declarative models such as the ACP models can be used to trace both the data and process flows. Due to the nature of the proposed transformation one has to compromise on the limited flexibility and expressibility offered by the resulting activity-centric models [1]. However, the resulting activity-centric models improve the comprehensibility and allow for executing the data-centric models.

7   Conclusion

This paper proposed a trace-based approach to transforming artifact-centric process models into activity-centric process models. The approach is comprised of algorithms to construct an activity-centric process model, extract the execution traces of the constructed model and to analyse these traces over the execution traces of base model in order to check their consistency. A case study is used to demonstrate the feasibility of the proposed approach. In the future, a thorough evaluation of the proposed approach is conducted using real process models.

Acknowledgements. This work is partially supported by the National Key Research and Development Program of China (No. 2018YFB1402500) and National Natural Science Foundation of China under Grant 61832004 and Grant 61672042.

References

1. Caron, F., Vanthienen, J.: Exploring business process modelling paradigms and design-time to run-time transitions. Enterp. Inf. Syst. **10**(7), 790–813 (2016). https://doi.org/10.1080/17517575.2014.986291
2. De Giacomo, G., Dumas, M., Maggi, F.M., Montali, M.: Declarative process modeling in BPMN. In: Zdravkovic, J., Kirikova, M., Johannesson, P. (eds.) CAiSE 2015. LNCS, vol. 9097, pp. 84–100. Springer, Cham (2015). https://doi.org/10.1007/978-3-319-19069-3_6
3. Fan, B., Li, Y., Liu, S., Zhang, Y.: Run JTA in JTang: modeling in artifact-centric model and running in activity-centric environment. In: Bae, J., Suriadi, S., Wen, L. (eds.) AP-BPM 2015. LNBIP, vol. 219, pp. 83–97. Springer, Cham (2015). https://doi.org/10.1007/978-3-319-19509-4_7
4. Haisjackl, C., Zugal, S.: Investigating differences between graphical and textual declarative process models. In: Iliadis, L., Papazoglou, M., Pohl, K. (eds.) CAiSE 2014. LNBIP, vol. 178, pp. 194–206. Springer, Cham (2014). https://doi.org/10.1007/978-3-319-07869-4_17
5. Küster, J.M., Ryndina, K., Gall, H.: Generation of business process models for object life cycle compliance. In: Alonso, G., Dadam, P., Rosemann, M. (eds.) BPM 2007. LNCS, vol. 4714, pp. 165–181. Springer, Heidelberg (2007). https://doi.org/10.1007/978-3-540-75183-0_13
6. Meyer, A., Weske, M.: Activity-centric and artifact-centric process model roundtrip. In: Lohmann, N., Song, M., Wohed, P. (eds.) BPM 2013. LNBIP, vol. 171, pp. 167–181. Springer, Cham (2014). https://doi.org/10.1007/978-3-319-06257-0_14
7. Nigam, A., Caswell, N.S.: Business artifacts: an approach to operational specification. IBM Syst. J. **42**(3), 428–445 (2003). https://doi.org/10.1147/sj.423.0428
8. Prescher, J., Di Ciccio, C., Mendling, J.: From declarative processes to imperative models. In: SIMPDA, vol. 14, pp. 162–173 (2014). http://ceur-ws.org/Vol-1293
9. Redding, G., Dumas, M., Hofstede, A.H.T., Iordachescu, A.: Generating business process models from object behavior models. Inf. Syst. Manag. **25**(4), 319–331 (2008). https://doi.org/10.1080/10580530802384324
10. Yongchareon, S., Liu, C.: A process view framework for artifact-centric business processes. In: Meersman, R., Dillon, T., Herrero, P. (eds.) OTM 2010. LNCS, vol. 6426, pp. 26–43. Springer, Heidelberg (2010). https://doi.org/10.1007/978-3-642-16934-2_6

Approximate Fault Tolerance for Sensor Stream Processing

Daiki Takao[✉], Kento Sugiura, and Yoshiharu Ishikawa

Graduate School of Informatics, Nagoya University, Nagoya, Japan
{takao,sugiura}@db.is.i.nagoya-u.ac.jp, ishikawa@i.nagoya-u.ac.jp

Abstract. Some distributed stream processing systems store their internal states (e.g., partial aggregation results) in non-volatile storage to guarantee fault tolerance, but such checkpointing has a negative effect on system performance. To solve this problem, an existing method proposed to support an approximate guarantee of fault tolerance by omitting some checkpoints based on user-specified thresholds. However, it is difficult for a user to set appropriate thresholds because it is unclear how the thresholds affect the final output. Hence, we propose a method to support approximate fault tolerance for sensor stream processing. In our method, since we use the error bounds and the confidence threshold of recovery as user-specified thresholds, a user can set these thresholds intuitively according to his/her service level agreement (SLA). Our method models the correlation between sensing data by using a multivariate gaussian distribution, and reduces backup data if we can recover such data from the partial backup data and the probabilistic model. In this paper, we focus on average, sum, max, and min queries and propose a greedy-based backup selection algorithm. We evaluate the validity and efficiency of our approach by using synthetic data. Our experimental study shows that our approach achieves both of the reduction of backup data and approximate recovery that satisfies SLA.

Keywords: Stream processing · Fault tolerance · Approximate processing

1 Introduction

Distributed data stream processing systems are used in many applications due to rapidly increasing data size and speed of decision making. Since stream processing assumes that processing data is sent to the system intermittently, stream processing systems require different architecture from batch ones such as Hadoop [2]. Therefore, open-source software of distributed stream processing systems, such as Storm [3], Flink [1], and Samza [5], is being actively developed and attracting a great deal of attention in both industrial and academic fields. Although fault tolerance is one of the important requirements of a distributed stream processing system, it has a negative effect on system performance. In many systems, fault

© Springer Nature Switzerland AG 2020
R. Borovica-Gajic et al. (Eds.): ADC 2020, LNCS 12008, pp. 55–67, 2020.
https://doi.org/10.1007/978-3-030-39469-1_5

tolerance is guaranteed by checkpointing. Checkpointing stores internal states of a system in local or remote storage during processing. Huang et al., however, showed that checkpointing could reduce throughput up to 50% [8]. As such a significant performance decrement is not desirable, it is required to develop a more effective mechanism for fault tolerance.

To solve this problem, Huang et al. proposed an approximate guarantee of fault tolerance [8]. This method requires thresholds of the difference of internal states (input/output queues and intermediate results of processing) and gets a new checkpoint only if the difference between current states and stored ones exceeds thresholds. That is, the existing method improves throughput by reducing the frequency of checkpointing.

However, this method has a problem that it is difficult to set appropriate thresholds to satisfy the user's service level agreement (SLA). Although this method uses thresholds of the difference of internal states, it is unclear how thresholds affect final output. For example, consider the threshold of an input queue. It indicates the number of unprocessed tuples that are allowed to be lost when a failure occurs. If some of the lost tuples have a large effect on processing results, the difference between original output and recovered ones may be unacceptably large. For instance, in the case of `max` aggregation, it is crucial whether lost tuples include the true maximum value.

In this paper, we propose an approximate fault tolerance approach based on a probabilistic model for sensor stream processing. Compared to the existing method [8], we focus on sensing data and simple aggregation queries (i.e., average, sum, max, and min) to use a probabilistic model for recovery. First, we model the correlation between sensors as a multivariate gaussian distribution. Then, we select some sensors that accurately recover aggregation results by using a multivariate gaussian distribution, and store only selected sensors as backup in processing. If a failure occurs, we estimate all sensing data by using stored data and a probabilistic model, and then reprocess aggregation queries to recover internal states. Since we use two user-specified parameters, the error bounds and the confidence threshold of recovery, to select backup sensors, a user can set these parameters intuitively according to his/her SLA. Although our assumption restricts applicable services, existing frameworks, such as Structured Streaming in Spark [6], demonstrate that such simple aggregation queries are sufficiently useful for real applications.

sensor ID	time step					
	1	2	3	4	5	$\cdots$
X_1	21	22	22	23	23	
X_2	21	22	23	23	23	$\cdots$
X_3	19	20	19	19	18	

Fig. 1. A sensor stream

For example, consider a sensor stream shown in Fig. 1. Sensors X_1 and X_2 are correlated in this stream and can be modeled by a multivariate gaussian distribution. That is, we can estimate the value of X_2 (X_1) accurately when we observe that of X_1 (X_2). Thus, we can remove the observations of X_2 (X_1) from backup if this approximate recovery satisfies user's SLA (i.e., the error bounds and the confidence threshold of recovery). In this paper, we also propose how to determine a minimum set of sensors for backup.

The rest of the paper is organized as follows. First, we provide basic concepts to discuss approximate fault tolerance in Sect. 2, and we define our problem in Sect. 3. Next, we explain how partial backup affects the final output for each aggregation query in Sect. 4, and we propose a greedy algorithm to select backup data in Sect. 4.2. Finally, we evaluate validity and efficiency of the proposed method by experiments in Sect. 5, and we conclude the paper in Sect. 6.

2 Preliminaries

In this section, we provide fundamental concepts to discuss approximate fault tolerance. First, we define an input data stream and introduce a sliding window to divide an infinite stream into finite ones. Second, we explain how to estimate sensing data by using a multivariate gaussian distribution. Third, we describe target aggregation queries.

2.1 Data Streams

First, we define a sensor data stream.

Definition 1. *Let n be the number of sensors and let $\boldsymbol{X} = \{X_1, X_2, \ldots, X_n\}$ be the set of all sensors. We assume that all sensors measure simultaneously at a certain interval. A data stream DS is defined as an infinite series of sensing data $\boldsymbol{x}^t = \{x_1^t, x_2^t, \ldots, x_n^t\}$ at each time t:*

$$DS = \langle \boldsymbol{x}^1, \boldsymbol{x}^2, \ldots, \boldsymbol{x}^t, \ldots \rangle. \tag{1}$$

Note that we use the upper case (e.g., X_1) to specify sensor ids or random variables, and the lower case (e.g., x_1) indicates an actual observation of a certain sensor.

To apply aggregation queries, we divide an infinite stream into finite ones by using sliding windows.

Definition 2. *Let w be the width of a time window and let l be the width of slides. A time window $\boldsymbol{x}^{[t,t+w)}$ contains a finite stream in a time span $[t, t + w)$:*

$$\boldsymbol{x}^{[t,t+w)} = \langle \boldsymbol{x}^t, \boldsymbol{x}^{t+1}, \ldots, \boldsymbol{x}^{t+w-1} \rangle. \tag{2}$$

Applying a sliding window, a data stream DS is divided into time windows as follows:

$$W_{DS} = \left\{ \boldsymbol{x}^{[t,t+w)} \mid t = 1 + i \cdot l, i \in \mathcal{N}^0 \right\}. \tag{3}$$

2.2   Estimation Based on a Multivariate Gaussian Distribution

We estimate sensor values by using a multivariate gaussian distribution $\mathcal{N}(x \mid \mu, \Sigma)$ that represents a correlation between sensors X. Suppose that μ and Σ denote a mean vector and a covariance matrix of X, respectively.

We evaluate the validity of estimated values by using the error bounds ϵ and the confidence threshold $1 - \delta$, such as in [7]. Let $Y \in X$ be a target sensor and let v be an estimated value. We can check whether estimation is reliable by using the following equation:

$$P(Y \in [v - \epsilon, v + \epsilon]) = \int_{v-\epsilon}^{v+\epsilon} \mathcal{N}(y \mid \mu_Y, \sigma_Y) dy > 1 - \delta. \tag{4}$$

If this equation is true, we consider that estimation is sufficiently reliable.

Furthermore, estimation quality can be improved by using a posterior probability distribution. Let $O \subseteq X \setminus \{Y\}$ be observed sensors and let o be observed values. We can calculate a posterior distribution $\mathcal{N}(y \mid \mu_{Y|o}, \sigma_{Y|o})$ as follows:

$$\mu_{Y|o} = \mu_Y + \Sigma_{YO} \Sigma_{OO}^{-1} (o - \mu_O) \text{ and} \tag{5}$$

$$\sigma_{Y|o} = \Sigma_{YY} - \Sigma_{YO} \Sigma_{OO}^{-1} \Sigma_{OY}. \tag{6}$$

The subscripts of each symbol indicate corresponding rows/columns in μ and Σ. For instance, Σ_{YO} is a sub matrix of Σ formed by a row Y and columns O (i.e., a covariance vector of Y regarding O). Since a posterior distribution has a smaller variance than a prior one, we can estimate lost data more accurately by using a posterior distribution.

Note that the variance of a posterior distribution is independent of observations o. As shown in Eq. (6), $\sigma_{Y|o}$ is calculated by only sub covariance matrices. It means that we can calculate the variance of a posterior distribution before processing starts. To specify this property, we denote $\sigma_{Y|o}$ as $\sigma_{Y|O}$ in the rest of the paper.

2.3   Aggregation Queries

In this paper, we deal with four aggregation queries: average, sum, max, and min. Aggregation queries are applied to each time window $x^{[t,t+w)} \in W_{DS}$. Let Y_i be a random variable of an aggregation query of $X_i \in X$ at a certain time window. We consider recovery to be sufficiently reliable when a recovered aggregation value v satisfies the following equation:

$$P(Y_i \in [v - \epsilon, v + \epsilon]) > 1 - \delta. \tag{7}$$

3   Problem Definition

In this section, we introduce a problem definition for approximate fault tolerance. First, we define backup cost and a confidence score of approximate recovery. Then, we define a problem of approximate fault tolerance as backup cost minimization.

3.1   Backup Cost

Our approach is based on replay-based recovery and does not use checkpointing. When a failure occurs, all input data is replayed and internal states (i.e., intermittent aggregation results) are recomputed.

However, we do not store all sensing data as backup. As described in Sect. 2.2, we can accurately estimate some observed values by using a multivariate gaussian distribution (i.e., correlation between sensors). That is, we can omit backup of such sensing data to reduce the volume of backup and I/O cost, and replay estimated values if necessary.

Hence, we define backup cost based on the number of stored sensing data.

Definition 3. *Let $o^{[1,t]} \subseteq DS$ be stored backup data at time step t. The cost of backup is the number of stored data:*

$$C(o^{[1,t]}) = \sum_{i=1}^{t} |o^i|. \tag{8}$$

Note that we define an inclusive relation $\subseteq$ between data streams as follows.

Definition 4. *Let $DS = \langle x^1, x^2, \ldots, x^t, \ldots \rangle$ be an infinite stream and let $o^{[1,t]} = \langle o^1, o^2, \ldots, o^t \rangle$ be a finite stream. If all the sensors in $o^{[1,t]}$ is included by DS for every time step in $[1,t]$, there is an inclusive relation between DS and $o^{[1,t]}$:*

$$o^{[1,t]} \subseteq DS \Leftrightarrow \bigwedge_{i=1}^{t} O^i \subseteq X^i. \tag{9}$$

3.2   Confidence Score of Recovery

As described in Sect. 2.3, we have to recover all aggregation results for each time window when a failure occurs. That is, we need to guarantee that all recovered aggregation results satisfy user's SLA (i.e., the error bounds ϵ and the confidence threshold $1 - \delta$). To formalize this requirement, we define a confidence score as the minimum reliability of recovered aggregation results from backup.

First, we define the reliability of recovery for a certain time window.

Definition 5. *Given backup of a certain window $o^{[t',t'+w)}$ and the error bounds ϵ, let Y_i be a random variable of an aggregation query of $X_i \in X$ and let v_i be an estimated aggregation result. The reliability of recovery of this time window is the minimum probability that recovered aggregation results are in the error bounds:*

$$R(o^{[t',t'+w)}) = \min_{X_i \in X} P(Y_i \in [v_i - \epsilon, v_i + \epsilon] \mid o^{[t',t'+w)}). \tag{10}$$

Then, we define overall reliability for all time windows.

Definition 6. *Given backup $o^{[1,t]}$ and the error bounds ϵ, let $W_{o^{[1,t]}}$ be windowed backup, where:*

$$W_{o^{[1,t]}} = \left\{ o^{[t',t'+w)} \mid t' = 1 + i \cdot l, i \in \mathcal{N}^0, t' + w - 1 \leq t \right\}. \tag{11}$$

A confidence score of backup is the minimum reliability of recovery for every window:

$$R(o^{[1,t]}) = \min_{o^{[t',t'+w)} \in W_{o^{[1,t]}}} R(o^{[t',t'+w)}). \tag{12}$$

That is, if a confidence score $R(o^{[1,t]})$ is greater than a confidence threshold $1-\delta$, we consider that recovery is sufficiently reliable.

3.3   Problem Definition

We introduce our problem definition for approximate fault tolerance by using the above cost/confidence functions.

Definition 7. *Given a data stream DS, a window width w, a sliding width l, error bounds ϵ, and a confidence threshold $1 - \delta$, we retain backup $o^{[1,t]}$ at time step t, where:*

$$\begin{aligned} \text{minimize} \quad & C(o^{[1,t]}) \\ \text{subject to} \quad & o^{[1,t]} \subseteq DS \\ & R(o^{[1,t]}) > 1 - \delta. \end{aligned} \tag{13}$$

That is, we try to keep backup data to a minimum as much as possible unless recovered aggregation results become unreliable.

4   Backup Selection for Approximate Fault Tolerance

In this section, we explain how to select sensors for backup. Since we consider the reliability of the final output in this paper, aggregation functions significantly affect backup strategies. For example, consider average/sum aggregation. If we use average aggregation, some estimation errors are obscured because all the aggregated values are flattened in a window. On the other hand, we have to select backup sensors carefully for sum aggregation because estimation errors are stacked up.

Furthermore, we have to select backup sensors before processing starts for efficient backup. Although we can select backup sensors in processing, it is inefficient to check whether sensors are beneficial to recovery at each time step. That is, we have to consider the confidence of recovery based on not observed sensors $O^{[1,t]}$ instead of actual observations $o^{[1,t]}$.

To achieve this requirement, we modify probability distributions of aggregation queries and derive upper bounds of variance for each sensor. As described in Sect. 2.2, the variance of a posterior distribution $\sigma_{Y|O}$ is independent of actual observations. Thus, we derive the required variance of probability distributions for each aggregation query, and then modify it into upper bounds of variance for each sensor.

In the following, we derive upper bounds of variance for each sensor with average/max queries. Then, we propose a greedy-based algorithm for backup sensor selection that satisfies the derived upper bound. Note that we omit the explanations of sum/min queries in this paper because their upper bounds are derived in the same way with average/max queries, respectively.

4.1   Upper Bounds Derivation for Variance of Sensors

Average Queries. Since a gaussian distribution is the family of stable distributions, the sum of gaussian distributions also become a gaussian distribution. Without temporal correlation, an average value Y_i of a sensor $X_i \in X$ and its mean and variance are represented as follows:

$$Y_i = \frac{\sum_{t \in [t', t'+w)} X_i^t}{w}, \tag{14}$$

$$\mu_{Y_i} = \frac{\sum_{t \in [t', t'+w)} \mu_{X_i^t}}{w}, \text{ and} \tag{15}$$

$$\sigma_{Y_i} = \frac{\sum_{t \in [t', t'+w)} \sigma_{X_i^t}}{w^2}. \tag{16}$$

That is, the mean and variance of an average query can be calculated by the linear sum of those of a sensor in a window. Note that the above equations correspond to a prior distribution but those of a posterior distribution can be calculated in the same way.

To consider the confidence of an average query, we regard the mean of a probability distribution (i.e., μ_{Y_i}) as an aggregation result. That is, reliability for Eq. (10) can be calculated as follows:

$$P(Y_i \in [\mu_{Y_i|o^{[t',t'+w)}} - \epsilon, \mu_{Y_i|o^{[t',t'+w)}} + \epsilon] \mid o^{[t',t'+w)})$$
$$= \int_{\mu_{Y_i|o^{[t',t'+w)}} - \epsilon}^{\mu_{Y_i|o^{[t',t'+w)}} + \epsilon} \mathcal{N}(y_i \mid \mu_{Y_i|o^{[t',t'+w)}}, \sigma_{Y_i|o^{[t',t'+w)}}) dy_i. \tag{17}$$

Although this equation depends on actual observations $o^{[t',t'+w)}$, we can remove the dependence by translating a distribution to $\mu_{Y_i} = 0$ [7]:

$$\int_{-\epsilon}^{\epsilon} \mathcal{N}(y_i' \mid 0, \sigma_{Y_i|o^{[t',t'+w)}}) dy_i'. \tag{18}$$

To derive upper bounds of variance of X_i, we consider the maximum variance σ^* of an average query with minimum reliability:

$$\int_{-\epsilon}^{\epsilon} \mathcal{N}(y_i' \mid 0, \sigma^*) dy_i' = 1 - \delta. \tag{19}$$

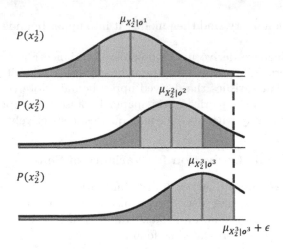

Fig. 2. Confidence calculation for a max query

That is, if the variance of an average query $\sigma_{Y_i|O^{[t',t'+w)}}$ is lower than σ^*, we can recover an average of X_i reliably. We can derive the following relation between the variance of X_i and this reliability requirement by using Eq. (16):

$$\frac{\sum_{t\in[t',t'+w)} \sigma_{X_i^t|O^t}}{w^2} < \sigma^*. \tag{20}$$

When we assume that backup sensors O are unchanged in processing, variance for every time step $\sigma_{X_i^t|O^t}$ has the same value. Hence, we can derive the following upper bound of the variance of X_i:

$$\sigma_{X_i|O} < w\sigma^*. \tag{21}$$

That is, if we can select backup sensors O that satisfies Eq. (21) for every sensor $X_i \in X$, we can recover all averaged values reliably.

Max Queries. Unfortunately, the result of max aggregation does not follow a gaussian distribution. Thus, if we use a straightforward way, we have to calculate the following probability density function:

$$P(Y_i = y_i) = \int_{-\infty}^{\infty} \cdots \int_{-\infty}^{\infty} P(x_i^{[t',t'+w)}) \mathbb{1}[\max(x_i^{[t',t'+w)}) = y_i] dx_i^{[t',t'+w)}, \tag{22}$$

where $\mathbb{1}[\phi]$ is an indicator function. However, as this equation has multiple integral with $\mathbb{1}[\phi]$ function, it is difficult to derive upper bounds of variance for each sensor.

Thus, we derive stricter upper bound for max queries. First, we consider the maximum posterior mean $\mu_{X_i^{t^*}|O^{t^*}}$ as a recovered maximum value and calculate the reliability of a recovered maximum value by using the following equation:

Input: sensors X, variance upper bounds σ^*
Output: backup sensors O

1 $O \leftarrow \emptyset$
2 **while** $Var(O) > \sigma^*$ **do**
3     $X_{new} \leftarrow \underset{X_i \in X \setminus O}{\arg\max}\, Var(X \mid O) - Var(X \mid O \cup \{X_i\})$
4     $O \leftarrow O \cup \{X_{new}\}$

Fig. 3. Greedy-based backup sensor selection

$$P(X_i^{t^*} \in [\mu_{X_i^{t^*}|o^{t^*}} - \epsilon, \mu_{X_i^{t^*}|o^{t^*}} + \epsilon] \mid o^{t^*})$$

$$\prod_{t \in [t', t'+w) \wedge t \neq t^*} P(X_i^t < \mu_{X_i^{t^*}|o^{t^*}} + \epsilon \mid o^t). \tag{23}$$

Figure 2 shows this equation graphically. In Fig. 2, the maximum mean is estimated at time step 3. It corresponds to the first term in Eq. (23) that indicates the estimated maximum value must be in the error bounds (an area filled in red). The other time steps (e.g., X_2^1 and X_2^2) correspond to the second term in Eq. (23) that indicates the other values in a time window must be smaller than the estimated maximum value (an area filled in red and blue). If Eq. (23) is greater than the confidence threshold $1 - \delta$, the reliability requirement (i.e., Eq. (10)) is also satisfied.

However, since Eq. (23) depends on actual observations o^t, we have to remove this dependence. Thus, we narrow down integral interval of the second term in Eq. (23) to the error bounds (an area filled in red in Fig. 2):

$$\prod_{t \in [t', t'+w)} P(X_i^t \in [\mu_{X_i^t|o^t} - \epsilon, \mu_{X_i^t|o^t} + \epsilon] \mid o^t). \tag{24}$$

Although this modification makes upper bound stricter, we can remove the dependence on actual observations by translating gaussian distributions to $\mu = 0$ [7] as follows.

$$\prod_{t \in [t', t'+w)} \int_{-\epsilon}^{\epsilon} N(x_i^t \mid 0, \sigma_{X_i^t|o^t}) dx_i^t \geq 1 - \delta. \tag{25}$$

Since backup sensors O are unchanged in processing, we can derive the following equation:

$$\int_{-\epsilon}^{\epsilon} N(x_i \mid 0, \sigma_{X_i|O}) dx_i \geq (1 - \delta)^{\frac{1}{w}}. \tag{26}$$

That is, we can calculate upper bounds σ^* by solving Eq. (26) with an equal sign.

4.2 Greedy-Based Backup Selection

In the previous subsection, we derive the upper bounds σ^* for each sensor. Although we can recover aggregated values reliably if all sensors satisfy

$\sigma_{X_i|O} < \sigma^*$, the number of candidates of O increases exponentially with the number of sensors n. Thus, we propose greedy-based backup selection.

Figure 3 summarizes our greedy backup selection. In this paper, we use the maximum variance as a greedy objective function:

$$Var(\boldsymbol{X} \mid \boldsymbol{O}) = \max_{X_i \in \boldsymbol{X}} \sigma_{X_i|O}. \tag{27}$$

That is, we select a sensor $X_{new} \in \boldsymbol{X} \backslash \boldsymbol{O}$ that has maximum variance reduction until the variance of all sensors become smaller than upper bounds σ^*:

$$X_{new} = \arg \max_{X_i \in \boldsymbol{X} \backslash \boldsymbol{O}} Var(\boldsymbol{X} \mid \boldsymbol{O}) - Var(\boldsymbol{X} \mid \boldsymbol{O} \cup \{X_i\}). \tag{28}$$

5   Experimental Evaluation

In this section, we demonstrate the efficiency and validity of the proposed method by experiments. We explain experimental settings and then describe the detail experimental results. Note that we omit the results of sum/min queries because they have the same tendency with average/max queries, respectively.

5.1   Experimental Settings

We evaluate the performance of our method by using simple synthetic data. The generated data has $10,000$ tuples for 12 simulated sensors. The sensors are divided into three groups (group A, B, and C) and sensors in each group have a strong correlation as shown in Fig. 4. That is, each sensor's value in the same group can be estimated accurately. To generate such correlated sensing data, we use `rmvnorm` function in R language [4] under the following settings:

- mean: we set mean to 10 for group A, 20 for group B, and 30 for group C, and
- variance and covariancewe set variance of each sensor to 1.0, covariance within the group to 0.8, and covariance between groups to 0.

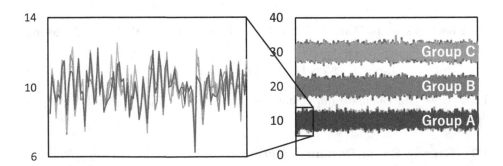

Fig. 4. Simulated sensing data

In the experiments, we evaluate performance by changing the error bounds ϵ and the confidence threshold $1-\delta$ with a static sliding window ($w = 5$ and $l = 5$). That is, each aggregation query is performed to two thousand time windows for each setting, and we check the number of backup sensors and accuracy of recovered aggregation results.

5.2 Experimental Results

We evaluate the performance of the proposed method by efficiency and validity.

Efficiency. We evaluate the efficiency of our approach based on the number of backup sensors. That is, we check how much the volume of backup data decreases.

Figures 5 and 6 show that the number of backup sensors for average/max queries, respectively. These graphs show that the number of backup sensors decreases by increasing the error bounds ϵ and the acceptable error δ. When the reliability requirement is relaxed, we can estimate more sensor values by using a multivariate gaussian distribution. Thus, our approach can reduce the volume of backup data.

Validity. To evaluate the validity of our approach, we calculate the accuracy of recovery. First, we calculate the accuracy for each sensor. We consider the ratio of successful recovery as accuracy in this paper. That is, we count how many times recovered aggregation values are within the error bounds for each sensor. Then, we use the minimum accuracy of all sensors as an overall accuracy score.

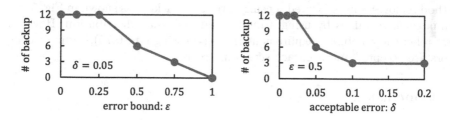

Fig. 5. The number of backup sensors for a max query

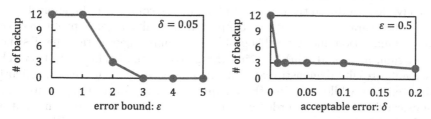

Fig. 6. The number of backup sensors for an average query

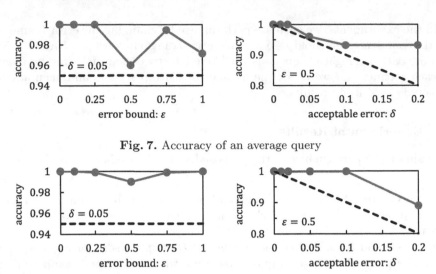

Fig. 7. Accuracy of an average query

Fig. 8. Accuracy of a max query

Figures 7 and 8 show the accuracy of average/max queries, respectively. The dotted lines in the figures show the required accuracy $1 - \delta$. That is, if accuracy scores are above the dotted line, the recovery based on a probabilistic model satisfies the confidence requirement. These graphs show that our approach can recover all the aggregated values reliably from partial backup data.

Note that accuracy scores are variable with the change of parameters. For example, in Fig. 7, the accuracy score decreases with $\epsilon = 0.5$ but increases with $\epsilon = 0.75$. It means that some recovery fails with $\epsilon = 0.5$ because the proposed method removes some observed sensing data from backup, as shown in Fig. 5, and estimates these values by using a multivariate gaussian distribution. However, if we relax the reliability requirement (i.e., increasing ϵ to 0.75), some recovery errors are accepted and accuracy scores improve.

6   Conclusion

In this paper, we proposed approximate fault tolerance based on a probabilistic model for sensor stream processing. To specify the user's reliability requirement intuitively, we introduced the error bounds ϵ and the confidence threshold $1 - \delta$ as user-specified parameters. We defined approximate fault tolerance problem as the backup minimization and solve this problem for simple aggregation queries (i.e., average, sum, max, and min) by using the greedy-based backup selection. The experimental results demonstrated that our approach can achieve a sufficiently reliable recovery while reducing the amount of backup data. Our future work includes consideration of disordered and incomplete data streams, combination with checkpointing-based recovery, and exhaustive experiments with not only synthetic data but also real data.

Acknowledgement. This study was partly supported by KAKENHI (JP16H01722 and JP19K21530) and New Energy and Industrial Technology Development Organization (NEDO).

References

1. Apache Flink: Stateful Computations over Data Streams. https://flink.apache.org/. Accessed 24 Sept 2019
2. Apache Hadoop. https://hadoop.apache.org/. Accessed 24 Sept 2019
3. Apache Storm. https://storm.apache.org/. Accessed 24 Sept 2019
4. Mvnorm function—R Documentation. https://www.rdocumentation.org/packages/mvtnorm/versions/1.0-11/topics/Mvnorm. Accessed 24 Sept 2019
5. Samza. http://samza.apache.org/. Accessed 24 Sept 2019
6. Armbrust, M., et al.: Structured streaming: a declarative API for real-time applications in apache spark. In: Proceedings of SIGMOD, pp. 601–613 (2018)
7. Deshpande, A., Guestrin, C., Madden, S.R., Hellerstein, J.M., Hong, W.: Model-based approximate querying in sensor networks. VLDBJ **14**(4), 417–443 (2005)
8. Huang, Q., Lee, P.P.C.: Toward high-performance distributed stream processing via approximate fault tolerance. PVLDB **10**(3), 73–84 (2016)

Function Interpolation for Learned Index Structures

Naufal Fikri Setiawan[✉], Benjamin I. P. Rubinstein,
and Renata Borovica-Gajic

School of Computing and Information Systems, University of Melbourne,
Melbourne, Australia
{naufal.setiawan,brubinstein,renata.borovica}@unimelb.edu.au

Abstract. Range indexes such as B-trees are widely recognised as effective data structures for enabling fast retrieval of records by the query key. While such classical indexes offer optimal worst-case guarantees, recent research suggests that average-case performance might be improved by alternative machine learning-based models such as deep neural networks. This paper explores an alternative approach by modelling the task as one of function approximation via interpolation between compressed subsets of keys. We explore the Chebyshev and Bernstein polynomial bases, and demonstrate substantial benefits over deep neural networks. In particular, our proposed function interpolation models exhibit memory footprint two orders of magnitude smaller compared to neural network models, and 30–40% accuracy improvement over neural networks trained with the same amount of time, while keeping query time generally on-par with neural network models.

Keywords: Indexing · Databases · Function approximation

1 Introduction

Databases use indexes to organise data for fast data retrieval, with B-trees and variants offering optimal worst-case lookup being the most popular. Viewed through the lens of machine learning, querying a B-tree is analogous to a model prediction, wherein a specific query key—an instance feature vector—is mapped to a record's location—a predicted label. Recent research has introduced the tantalising possibility of replacing classical range indexes with a model learned from data (*e.g.*, a neural network [16]) to perform queries on a pre-sorted set of records, with the aim being to either reduce index space requirements or to improve average-case query time. More broadly, significant efforts have explored the possibility to develop approximate and data-aware structures for specialised purposes [7,17].

For large datasets, maintaining a B-tree can become resource intensive in terms of I/O operations and space requirements. While the space complexity of a B-tree [2] is $\mathcal{O}(N)$ in the number of database records, query time is $\mathcal{O}(\log N)$—space costs are justified given that B-tree's perfect retrieval accuracy minimises

ⓒ Springer Nature Switzerland AG 2020
R. Borovica-Gajic et al. (Eds.): ADC 2020, LNCS 12008, pp. 68–80, 2020.
https://doi.org/10.1007/978-3-030-39469-1_6

subsequent access times. By comparison, deep neural networks [11] have proven capable of generalising in a variety of problem domains: even large network models are compact relative to dataset size, presenting an opportunity to strike desirable trade-offs between the space and time complexity for use in databases, assuming prediction accuracy can be controlled. One cost of such learners is construction time, in that their effective use requires hyperparameter tuning (*i.e.*, grid search over learning rates, network topology, activation functions, and regularisation strategies). While GPUs can be used to accelerate the training of deep neural networks in domains such as computer vision, commodity database servers rarely have access to such hardware [19].

The reduction of index construction and key lookup to supervised learning is via (1) pre-sorting record locators by the key in an auxiliary data structure such as an array or B-tree, and (2) learning to predict a rank from the key. Normalised by the dataset size, this corresponds to fitting a monotonic function with co-domain the unit interval. A core observation in [16] is that such functions are cumulative distribution functions. Based on the association with probability theory, they apply tools from machine learning in supervised regression.

This paper introduces classical polynomial interpolation methods as an alternative approach to supervised regression when learning index models. We note that not only is there no need to generalise from training data to unseen test data in such a case—the typical requirement in statistical learning theory [23]—but that there is no latent population distribution on keys, rather a set (with uniform measure). As such we argue for a function approximation view [5] as opposed to a statistical learning view.

We examine both Chebyshev and Bernstein polynomial bases for function approximation. We find that these methods can outperform single neural network models in terms of query time. Polynomial models also generally occupy less space than neural networks. Fitting of a polynomial model, in most observed cases, also requires fewer resources and less time than do training of neural networks. A key computational requirement of neural networks, that can go unreported, is hyperparameter tuning which also contributes to learned index construction cost. On the contrary, the only hyperparameter needed to create a polynomial model is just the specified degree m.

In the following we discuss related work pertaining to learned and classical indexes. Section 3 summaries necessary background in data structures and polynomial interpolation methods. We describe our main contribution, an approach to index structures based on polynomial approximation, in Sect. 4. Experimental results are presented in Sect. 5, and Sect. 6 offers our conclusions.

2   Related Work

Indexes have for decades attracted the interest of database researchers and practitioners due to substantial query processing speed-ups on offer. We here discuss recent efforts pertaining to reducing the size of indexes through data-, workload- and hardware-aware optimisations or recently introduced learned models.

Space-Aware Indexes. Since traditional B+trees consume a substantial amount of memory space, many alternative approaches have explored techniques to reduce their size, including prefix or suffix truncation, or key normalisation [10,12]. The past decade has also witnessed an increasing number of techniques where the index structure is adjusted to fit the properties of modern hardware, such as CSB+ trees, FAST trees, and Adaptive Radix Trees [15,18,21]. Partial and adaptive indexes similarly aim to reduce the memory footprint of indexes by building an index over a subset of data only, driven by user queries [14,24]. Such techniques are orthogonal to (and could be extended with) our approach that uses function interpolation to approximate the positions of the keys within the leaves of the index.

Learning Indexes. When it comes to reducing the size of indexes the closest to our work is the line of research on approximating indexes with statistical machine learning models, such as learning indexes [16], fitting trees [7], or hybrid models such as sandwiched bloom filters or interpolation friendly B-trees [13, 20]. While the former two use learned models to actually replace the index structure to some extent (they still may use small indexes at the lowest levels to improve approximation accuracy), the latter two focus on improving the index performance by extending indexes with learned models as "helper functions".

3 Background

We now briefly overview the framing of range indexes as approximating a cumulative distribution function, and summarise key results from approximation theory.

3.1 Range Indexes as Cumulative Distribution Functions

The B-tree, and range indexes in general, can be seen as a model that maps a key to a position on disk with perfect accuracy. As records stored in a B-tree require ordering on a column, the positions of records are proportional to a cumulative distribution function (CDF): a monotonic increasing function mapping key space into $[0, 1]$. Suppose we have N records in the database and we are querying a specific key k, then we may conclude that the requested records position as:

$$pos = N \times \Pr(x \leq k). \tag{1}$$

Any model that can approximate the function $f(k) = \Pr(x \leq k)$ can replace the role of a B-tree, provided that an error correction step follows predictions in order to retrieve the data when the model guesses an inaccurate position. This observation was made in [16], where deep neural networks (DNNs) were proposed as a means to approximate cumulative distribution functions.

The modelling choice of (regularised) supervised learning as in a typical DNN [16] presumes that the task of fitting $f(k)$ is one of *inductive learning* wherein the ultimate goal is to minimise risk as measured by expected loss of predictions on random draws of labelled examples from a latent population distribution.

We argue further in Sect. 4 that on fixed datasets[1] the problem of indexing does not require the model to extrapolate outside of existing data. That is, making good predictions on future unseen data is irrelevant to approximating $f(k)$ on existing and known keys.

3.2 Polynomial Interpolation

Interpolation uses a family of functions with uniform domain $\mathcal{B} = \{f_1, f_2, \cdots\}$ (a *basis*) such that any function to be approximated ψ that shares the same domain as the f_i satisfies $\psi(x) \approx \lim_{n \to \infty} \sum_{n=0}^{\infty} \alpha_n f_n(x)$ for some α_i coefficients. Compare this situation with supervised regression. Function approximation seeks accurate reconstruction over the entire domain of target ϕ, while supervised regression trains to fit on a small finite sample of training instances and aims to generalise to any likely inputs in the future.

Since function approximation approaches adopt specific but fixed function bases, only the vector of the coefficients $\langle \alpha_0, \alpha_1, \cdots, \alpha_N \rangle$ need be stored per target ϕ. This allows an interpolation polynomial to act as a lossy compression of a B-tree. The number of coefficients that need to be stored depends on the rate of convergence of the interpolation function and the accuracy that is desired. Most polynomial approaches require that target ϕ be continuous and piecewise smooth in order to provide theoretical guarantees on accuracy, but not in order to yield some approximation. To implement interpolation as a compressed learned index, we simply interpolate over the function ψ that maps a numeric key to a position in an auxiliary array (as the database may be sorted based on different keys rather than the one we are using for the index).

We next summarise the two major polynomial interpolation methods used in the remainder of this paper.

Chebyshev Interpolation Method. The Chebyshev polynomials of the first kind are used in numerical methods in which good approximations and error bounds are needed [4], for example in the solution of least-squared problems. Chebyshev interpolation is regarded as accurate, due to its ability to minimise Runge's phenomenon as with other polynomials that sample from the Chebyshev nodes (the oscillation behaviour that can occur between sample points of the function being interpolated) [3].

Definition 1 (Chebyshev Polynomial). *The Chebyshev polynomials of the first kind are defined by the recurrence relation*

$$T_n(x) = \begin{cases} 1, & \text{if } n = 0, \\ x, & \text{if } n = 1, \\ 2xT_{n-1}(x) - T_{n-2}(x), & \text{o.w.} \end{cases} \quad (2)$$

---

[1] It is sufficient but not necessary to prohibit insertions/deletions as done in [16].

Proposition 1. *An equivalent expression for the Chebyshev polynomials is $T_n(x) = \cos(n \arccos x)$ for $x \in [-1,1]$.*

To express other functions in terms of the Chebyshev polynomials we project into the basis by performing the discrete Chebyshev transformation on the function ψ that we want to interpolate [9].

Definition 2 (Discrete Chebyshev Transform). *The coefficients of the Chebyshev polynomial of the first kind (of degree N) that interpolates ψ are given by:*

$$\alpha_i = \frac{p_i}{N} \sum_{k=0}^{N-1} \psi\left(-\cos\left(\frac{\pi}{N}\left(k + \frac{1}{2}\right)\right)\right) \cos\left(\frac{m\pi}{N}\left(N + k + \frac{1}{2}\right)\right), \quad (3)$$

where $p_0 = 1$ and $p_i = 2$ when $i > 0$.

The Chebyshev interpolation method is used to estimate the **erf** function that is evaluated as part of the cumulative distribution functions of the normal and log-normal distributions [22]. This fact will prove convenient later as the keys in datasets may be distributed in one of these ways.

Bernstein Interpolation Method. The Bernstein polynomials form another important basis. They were originally used in a constructive proof of the Stone-Weierstrass approximation theorem which states that any continuous function can be uniformly approximated by a polynomial. They are also used as the basis for Bézier curves and privacy-preserving function release [1].

Definition 3 (Bernstein Polynomials). *The v-th Bernstein polynomial of order n is defined by the expression*

$$B_v^n(x) = \binom{n}{v} x^v (1 - x)^{n-v}, \quad (4)$$

which corresponds to the Binomial probability mass function representing the probability of observing v heads out of n i.i.d coin flips each with heads probability x.

Definition 4 (Bernstein Interpolation). *Let ψ be an arbitrary continuous function with domain $[0, 1]$. The order n Bernstein interpolation of ψ is defined by*

$$B_n[\psi](x) = \sum_{i=1}^{n} \binom{n}{i} \psi\left(\frac{i}{n}\right) x^n (1 - x)^{n-i}, \quad (5)$$

which corresponds to the expectation $\mathbb{E}_{V \sim \text{Binom}(n,x)}[\psi(V)]$.

4   Indexes by Function Approximation

We next detail the construction and application of indexes based on polynomial interpolation.

As observed in Sect. 3, the existing literature on learned indexes leverages inductive learning: fitting models on existing (training) data to minimise loss on future (test/population) data.

To see why inductive learning is an inappropriate formulation of the range index problem, consider the B-tree and its classical structure variants. The B-tree is prevalent in database systems despite it being an (efficient) lookup table. It does not generalise to new, unseen keys, in that an existing B-tree cannot be used to 'guess' the locations of keys of records not yet stored or encountered.

The astute machine learning reader may then wonder whether our goal should be one of *transductive* learning [8] in which one seeks to minimise loss on specific, given, test cases. While this appears closer to our task, the only test keys we seek to accurately query are in the training set. Further, there is no randomness in the locations of stored records, as would warrant supervised learning. Therefore we advocate for learning without accounting for population sampling or label randomness—pure function approximation.

4.1   Interpolant Construction

To obtain from a database D, a cumulative distribution function for structure construction, we must first extract the (sorted) set of keys. Suppose we choose a column K to be summarised with a range index, then an intermediary array is needed that allows us to map the key that we choose with the actual stored position of the record. Start by generating an array A of pairs $\langle key, pos \rangle$ that is sorted on key. Refer to Fig. 1(a). The position of the entry $\langle key, pos \rangle$ in A will then define an unnormalised cumulative distribution function.

Formally, cumulative distribution functions are right continuous, monotonic and have range space minimum 0 and maximum 1, as depicted in Fig. 1(b). Both polynomial interpolation methods considered require the target function ψ to be continuous and piecewise smooth (*i.e.*, accuracy of the approximation $\psi(x) \approx \lim_{i \to \infty} \sum_{n=0}^{\infty} f_i(x)$ will not typically be guaranteed when ψ is not piecewise smooth and continuous). For this reason, we transform the step-function cumulative distribution function seen in Fig. 1(b) to a piecewise linear, continuous function as in Fig. 1(c). In this step, we also rescale the key from the domain of $[K_{\mathrm{MIN}}, K_{\mathrm{MAX}}]$ to the preferred domain of the interpolation function $[I_{\mathrm{MIN}}, I_{\mathrm{MAX}}]$. In this paper, this is taken as the unit $[0, 1]$ for the Bernstein interpolation method, and $[-1, 1]$ for the Chebyshev interpolation method.

Lastly we choose a degree n and interpolation method (either Chebyshev or Bernstein) for application to the smoothed cumulative distribution function to obtain the parameters α_i for the chosen polynomial basis coefficients. The dashed line $\psi(x)$ in Fig. 1(d) is the original piecewise linear function that passes through all the data points, the (orange) interpolated polynomial example here is $B_5[\psi]$.

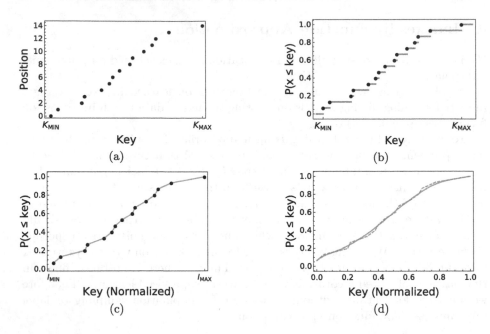

Fig. 1. Transforming (a) key positions to (b) normalised but step-function CDF, (c) piece-wise linear continuous smoothed CDF, (d) polynomial-interpolated CDF. (Color figure online)

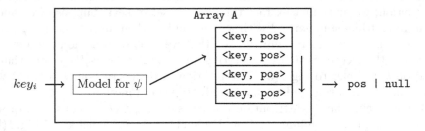

Fig. 2. The polynomial model creates a prediction $p\hat{o}s_A$, then the linear seek error correction algorithm starts looking for the entry with key starting at $p\hat{o}s_A$.

4.2   Query Processing

The lookup process of any record in the database then consists of three steps depicted in Fig. 2 and described as follows:

1. Prediction. First we predict the position of a query key as a location inside the auxiliary index array A. We call this prediction $p\hat{o}s_A$.

2. Error Correction. As predictions are only approximate, some correction/ follow-up search might be necessary. Any incorrect prediction is corrected by linearly seeking through the auxiliary array until the requested key is found or it can be concluded that the key does not exist.

3. Retrieval. After the $\langle key, pos \rangle$ mapping is found in the auxiliary array we can retrieve the record from its actual position on disk.

5   Experimental Results

To investigate how polynomial interpolation performs compared to conventional indexes such as the B-tree, and neural network learned indexes, we performed several experiments reported here. We first explore the model creation time, memory footprint, and query accuracy and time, and then present a sensitivity analysis of interpolation methods with respect to their interpolation degree.

The neural network is set to have 2 hidden layers and 32 neurons. We opted not to use a GPU to reflect the setup of most common database servers—all training and computation was performed by CPU. Neural networks were implemented using the `torch` package [6] and the B-Tree data structure was implemented using the `OIBTree` Python module.

Datasets. We use three different datasets each containing two million entries and build a neural network index on top of it as well as a regular B-tree. These three datasets are created randomly to follow the **uniform**, **normal** and **log-normal** distributions.

Hardware. All experiments are performed on a commodity laptop with 4× Intel i7 CPU cores and 16 GB of RAM. For our implementation we use Linux 5.2.14 and `CPython 3.7.4` running on `gcc 9`.

5.1   Model Creation Time

In our first experiment, we benchmark the time needed to create each polynomial model from degree 1 to degree 50. We use the notation B_n and C_n for Bernstein and Chebyshev polynomials of degree n respectively. We have repeated the experiment on each dataset ten times in succession and report the average time across all, since the overall observed discrepancy was less than 100 ms. Neural networks are not included in this experiment since they are able to be trained

Table 1. Model creation time (in seconds) results for B-tree, and polynomial indexes.

Number of entries	B-tree	B_5	B_{10}	B_{15}	B_{20}	B_{25}	C_5	C_{10}	C_{15}	C_{20}	C_{25}
500,000	7.102	0.786	0.773	0.762	0.765	0.783	0.527	0.581	0.634	0.727	0.820
1,000,000	14.953	1.570	1.551	1.583	1.557	1.547	1.093	1.205	1.362	1.551	1.760
1,500,000	23.611	2.357	2.357	2.350	2.366	2.357	1.661	1.850	2.081	2.395	2.691
2,000,000	34.575	3.279	3.286	3.371	3.277	3.366	2.324	2.631	2.942	3.245	3.809

further for better accuracy while interpolation models have their accuracy and parameters 'set in stone' after creation.

The results in Table 1 show that on existing data, the polynomial models are able to be created significantly faster than B-trees (**by a factor of 10**) for a specified number of entries. This is due to operations performed when assembling the B-tree, since rebalancing a B-tree can be expensive. The time complexity of creating a fresh, full B-tree index is $\mathcal{O}(n \log n)$, where n is the number database records. On the contrary, for m degree of the polynomial approximation, creation of the Bernstein polynomial is fixed $\mathcal{O}(n)$, improvable to $O(m \log n)$, while creation of the Chebyshev polynomial is $\mathcal{O}(m^2 \log n)$.

5.2 Memory Footprint

We next evaluate the size of the polynomial models in comparison to the B-tree and neural network structures, across multiple datasets. We obtain consistent results for all three datasets and hence report only the average results. While conducting this experiment, it is important to note that B-trees do not need to store the $\langle key, pos \rangle$ pairs inside an auxiliary array as these pairs are already stored in the leaves of the B-trees themselves. In this experiment, we refer to the storage of the pair as the 'data segment'. In the case of a B-tree, the term 'data segment' refers to the leaf slots where the $\langle key, pos \rangle$ is stored. In the case of the polynomial models, 'data segment' refers to the auxiliary array.

Table 2. Memory footprint results for B-tree, and Neural Network (in megabytes MB and kilobytes KB).

Dataset entries	B-tree (MB)	Neural network (KB)
500 K	33.034	210.73
1 M	66.126	210.73
1.5 M	99.123	210.73
2 M	132.163	210.73

Table 3. Memory footprint results for the polynomial index models (in bytes B).

Dataset entries	B_5	B_{10}	B_{15}	B_{20}	B_{25}	C_5	C_{10}	C_{15}	C_{20}	C_{25}
500 K	1016	1240	1632	1832	1400	1632	1882	1352	1392	1442
1 M	1016	1240	1632	1832	1400	1632	1882	1352	1392	1442
1.5 M	1016	1240	1632	1832	1400	1632	1882	1352	1392	1442
2 M	1016	1240	1632	1832	1400	1632	1882	1352	1392	1442

Tables 2 and 3 show the memory footprint of the alternatives with the data segment stripped off. This metric shows how much memory overhead is added for the index structure. The overhead introduced by B-tree scales with the size of the data as pointer overheads are needed. The polynomial models require the storage of coefficients only. Similarly, neural networks have a fixed number of parameters, causing them to be independent of the size of database.

According to Table 3, the size of polynomials does not increase with the size of the dataset. This property is also exhibited by the neural networks, although the memory footprint of the polynomial indexes is still **2 orders of magnitude lower**. The higher memory footprint in the case of neural networks is attributed to the larger number of parameters that a neural network has.

5.3 Query Accuracy and Time

We next examine the retrieval accuracy using the polynomial models, and compare them against the classical B-Tree and Neural Network. We present the model prediction time, root mean squared error (RMSE) of the prediction, and the total query time (involving all three steps discussed in Sect. 4.2).

Table 4. Prediction time (in ns), prediction root-mean-squared-error (RMSE) and total query time (in ns) for Normal (No), Uniform (Un) and Log-normal (Ln) datasets.

Dataset	Prediction time (ns)			RMSE			Query time (ns)		
Model type	No	Un	Ln	No	Un	Ln	No	Un	Ln
B_5	133	46.6	148	25805.22	109.55	80214.85	23500	133	92200
B_{10}	158	71.9	189	18014.59	84.90	70304.07	16500	111	65300
B_{15}	196	103	238	14155.66	70.70	57078.78	12400	133	58500
B_{20}	237	133	288	11687.71	68.70	47333.16	9780	151	48100
B_{25}	277	166	336	9973.57	62.58	39566.59	8080	192	40200
C_5	17.9	9.87	27.2	1430.38	57.92	12779.95	10.6	56.3	11800
C_{10}	20.1	11.0	28.4	166.03	52.71	2137.22	11.4	51.6	1860
C_{15}	22.8	12.8	29.2	65.02	45.031	1224.74	68.8	92.2	1020
C_{20}	22.9	14.6	30.4	60.39	28.53	951.37	62.0	48.1	751
C_{25}	25.9	16.4	31.7	57.14	26.39	474.905	62.1	40.2	415
B-tree	24.4	41.5	40.1	N/A			31.5	56.3	46.0
Neural network	433	148	806	105.84	22.67	711.12	402	516	1100

The time taken to predict a key is generally very low in the scenarios examined, being less than 500 ns for all models. However, the total query times for all of the models are always far higher than the time taken simply to predict a key, since most of the cost of retrieving a key is in the error correction. Referring to Table 4, we see that the Bernstein polynomials are far less accurate compared to the Chebyshev polynomials, causing them to take a greater amount of time. A majority of the Bernstein polynomials take longer than our baseline models (*i.e.*, the B-tree and neural network models).

Some of the higher-order Chebyshev models are however significantly faster than the neural networks. Starting at C_{10} onwards the Chebyshev polynomials are able to outperform the neural networks in terms of speed. While the error is generally larger, the Chebyshev polynomial models do not have the operation overhead that neural networks have (attributed to activation functions and matrix multiplication) and are able to outperform the neural network as a result.

5.4   Rate of Convergence of Polynomial Models

The results presented in Fig. 3 show the sensitivity of the polynomial models with respect to the degree increase.

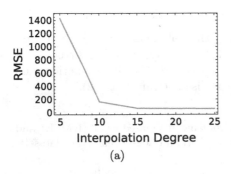
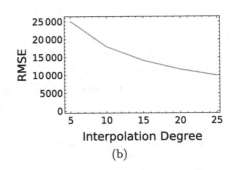

(a)

(b)

Fig. 3. Rates of convergence of the (a) Chebyshev and (b) Bernstein interpolations for the normally distributed dataset.

For the normal dataset, the Bernstein polynomial converges more slowly than the Chebyshev polynomial model, and the Chebyshev polynomial of lower degrees performs far better than the Bernstein polynomial in lower degrees in terms of accuracy. This, consequently leads to them being faster as there is less work required during error correction.

In the log-normal dataset (not presented here due to lack of space), both polynomial models have high errors relative to their performance in the other datasets (see Table 4). The Chebyshev model still performs better than the Bernstein model and still converges faster. To illustrate, C_{10} is 83% faster than C_5 while B_{10} is only 12% faster than B_5.

The uniform distribution is a special case where the Chebyshev model does not converge as fast as it does with the other data sets. However, errors are already minimal even with low-degree models and again, the Chebyshev model still performs better than the Bernstein model.

As seen from Fig. 3(a), the fast rate of convergence of the Chebyshev polynomials allows us to accurately model the cumulative distribution function using a much smaller memory footprint. The Chebyshev interpolation method converges to an interpolant function at an exponential rate [3].

6 Conclusion

We advocate for a function approximation approach to range indexes as an alternative to learned indexes typified by deep neural networks. We argue that supervised learning approaches unnecessarily avoid overfitting in favour of generalisation, and unnecessarily model uncertainty in ground-truth labels. In the range index problem of databases, such considerations are inappropriate.

The two methods introduced in this paper—polynomial bases with corresponding interpolation/fitting operators—have lightweight overhead in construction time and memory footprint compared to neural networks. Moreover polynomial approximation techniques are far simpler to implement. As such, our methods represent feasible options as replacement models for learned indexes, and a tantalising direction for further investigation.

References

1. Aldà, F., Rubinstein, B.I.P.: The Bernstein mechanism: function release under differential privacy. In: AAAI, pp. 1705–1711 (2017)
2. Bayer, R., McCreight, E.: Organization and maintenance of large ordered indices. In: SIGFIDET, pp. 107–141 (1970)
3. Boyd, J.P., Ong, J.R.: Exponentially-convergent strategies for defeating the Runge phenomenon for the approximation of non-periodic functions, part I: single-interval schemes. Commun. Comput. Phys. 5(2–4), 484–497 (2009)
4. Brisebarre, N., Joldeş, M.: Chebyshev interpolation polynomial-based tools for rigorous computing. In: Proceedings of the 2010 International Symposium on Symbolic and Algebraic Computation, pp. 147–154. ACM (2010)
5. Cheney, E.W.: Introduction to Approximation Theory. McGraw-Hill, New York (1966)
6. Collobert, R., Kavukcuoglu, K., Farabet, C.: Torch7: a Matlab-like environment for machine learning. In: BigLearn NIPS Workshop (2011)
7. Galakatos, A., Markovitch, M., Binnig, C., Fonseca, R., Kraska, T.: Fiting-tree: a data-aware index structure. In: SIGMOD, pp. 1189–1206 (2019)
8. Gammerman, A., Vovk, V., Vapnik, V.: Learning by transduction. In: UAI, pp. 148–155 (1998)
9. Gil, A., Segura, J., Temme, N.M.: Numerical Methods for Special Functions. Society for Industrial and Applied Mathematics (2007)
10. Goldstein, J., Ramakrishnan, R., Shaft, U.: Compressing relations and indexes. In: ICDE (1998)
11. Goodfellow, I., Bengio, Y., Courville, A.: Deep Learning. MIT Press, Cambridge (2016)
12. Graefe, G., Larson, P.A.: B-tree indexes and CPU caches. In: ICDE, pp. 349–358 (2001)
13. Hadian, A., Heinis, T.: Interpolation-friendly B-trees: bridging the gap between algorithmic and learned indexes. In: EDBT, pp. 710–713 (2019)
14. Idreos, S., Kersten, M.L., Manegold, S.: Database cracking. In: CIDR, pp. 68–78 (2007)
15. Kim, C., et al.: Fast: fast architecture sensitive tree search on modern CPUs and GPUs. In: SIGMOD, pp. 339–350 (2010)

16. Kraska, T., Beutel, A., Chi, E.H., Dean, J., Polyzotis, N.: The case for learned index structures. In: SIGMOD (2018)
17. Kubica, J.M., Moore, A., Connolly, A.J., Jedicke, R.: Spatial data structures for efficient trajectory-based queries. Technical report, CMU-RI-TR-04-61, Carnegie Mellon University (2004)
18. Leis, V., Kemper, A., Neumann, T.: The adaptive radix tree: artful indexing for main-memory databases. In: ICDE, pp. 38–49 (2013)
19. Microsoft: Hardware and software requirements for installing SQL server
20. Mitzenmacher, M.: A model for learned bloom filters, and optimizing by sandwiching. In: NIPS, pp. 462–471 (2018)
21. Rao, J., Ross, K.A.: Making b+-trees cache conscious in main memory. In: SIGMOD, pp. 475–486 (2000)
22. Schonfelder, J.: Chebyshev expansions for the error and related functions. Math. Comput. **32**(144), 1232–1240 (1978)
23. Shalev-Shwartz, S., Ben-David, S.: Understanding Machine Learning: From Theory to Algorithms. Cambridge University Press, Cambridge (2014)
24. Stonebraker, M.: The case for partial indexes. SIGMOD Rec. **18**(4), 4–11 (1989)

DEFINE: Friendship Detection Based on Node Enhancement

Hanxiao Pan[1], Teng Guo[1], Hayat Dino Bedru[1], Qing Qing[1], Dongyu Zhang[1], and Feng Xia[2(✉)]

[1] School of Software, Dalian University of Technology, Dalian, China
[2] School of Science, Engineering and IT, Federation University Australia, Ballarat, Australia
f.xia@ieee.org

Abstract. Network representation learning (NRL) is a matter of importance to a variety of tasks such as link prediction. Learning low-dimensional vector representations for node enhancement based on nodes attributes and network structures can improve link prediction performance. Node attributes are important factors in forming networks, like psychological factors and appearance features affecting friendship networks. However, little to no work has detected friendship using the NRL technique, which combines students' psychological features and perceived traits based on facial appearance. In this paper, we propose a framework named DEFINE (Node Enhancement based Friendship Detection) to detect students' friend relationships, which combines with students' psychological factors and facial perception information. To detect friend relationships accurately, DEFINE uses the NRL technique, which considers network structure and the additional attributes information for nodes. DEFINE transforms them into low-dimensional vector spaces while preserving the inherent properties of the friendship network. Experimental results on real-world friendship network datasets illustrate that DEFINE outperforms other state-of-art methods.

Keywords: Node enhancement · Friendship detection · Social network

1 Introduction

Information networks are general data structures to explore complex relationships in the real-world. Social networks and academic networks have been widely investigated [8, 21, 23]. Mining friendship in networks also has drawn continuous attention in academia. The data collected by mobile phones can form the dynamic evolution of personal relationships and identify friend relationships accurately [5]. Most friendship detection researches are based on the information obtained from online social networks; little friendship prediction studies focus on social network structure and node attributes. However, exploring the hidden friendship among students is challenging. At present, the existing research literature predicts friendship by depicting characters according to the behavior

© Springer Nature Switzerland AG 2020
R. Borovica-Gajic et al. (Eds.): ADC 2020, LNCS 12008, pp. 81–92, 2020.
https://doi.org/10.1007/978-3-030-39469-1_7

data of students. Attractive appearances and similar psychological characteristics are important factors in the development of friendship [15, 20]. As a kind of social relationship, the formation of friendships is affected by complex social relationships and the students' characteristics. However, little work has been done to detect friendship combining social network structure and node attribute proximity.

To tackle the above challenges, we present a new framework, named **Node Enhancement** based **Friendship Detection** (DEFINE) for predicting friend relationships. Our framework forms an intelligent solution for detecting friend relationship based on hidden attributes in student social network. As shown in Fig. 1, our framework considers both network structure and node attributes which contain students' psychological features and facial perception information. DEFINE transforms the friendship network into low-dimensional vector spaces while preserving the inherent properties of the friendship network to detect friendship accurately.

In summary, our main contributions are concluded as follows:

(1) We propose a framework named DEFINE based on the NRL technique, to discover students' friend relationships by combining the network structure and node attribute proximity.
(2) DEFINE considers both students' psychological factors and facial perception information as node attributes. Experimental results demonstrate the outstanding capabilities of DEFINE on the friendship detection task.
(3) DEFINE not only considers the structural attributes of the social network but also combines node attribute information, which performs better than other NRL models.

We organize the remainder of this paper as follows. Section 2 summarizes related work which contains the theoretical dimensions of the research. In Sect. 3, we focus on the details of problem formulation. Section 4 introduces the details of the proposed framework. We present experiments and results in Sect. 5. In Sect. 6, we present the conclusion of the research.

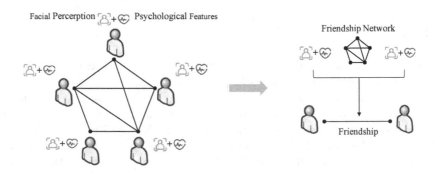

Fig. 1. The overview of friendship detection in our framework.

2   Related Work

2.1   Network Representation Learning

NRL aims to represent the nodes in the network as low-dimensional vectors that are easy to be the input of machine learning classifier and applied in social network tasks. The common network embedding methods are based on network structure information. Perozzi *et al.* [14] proposed the Deepwalk algorithm in 2014, which is the first to consider the introduction of deep learning techniques to express nodes in vector form in the network. Deepwalk uses the random walk that is a repeatable access depth-first search method, to sample the nodes in the network and learns vector representation of nodes using co-occurrence relation between nodes. Since sampling only depends on local information, Deepwalk is suitable for distributed and online systems.

According to the concept of Deepwalk, lots of scholars proposed improved algorithms. Large-scale Information Network Embedding (LINE) [17] considered neighborhood information of nodes in a network and is designed based on the breadth-first search. It redefines the similarity between nodes that contains first-order proximity and second-order proximity and constructs its unique representation. Grover and Leskovec [6] extended Deepwalk and proposed Node2vec by changing the generation of random walk sequence. Node2vec considers the characteristic of depth-first search and breadth-first search while choosing the next node by adding two parameters p and q to control the jumping direction. It also uses the network structure information to learn suitable node representation in a semi-supervised learning approach.

In addition to network structure information, current researches explore the impact of extra information in the network node, such as texts. Some researches combine both the attributes and the network structure to represent the nodes in the network. Yang *et al.* [24] proposed a text-related Deepwalk model named TADW (text-associated DeepWalk), integrating text information of nodes into NRL. This work proves the Deepwalk algorithm is equivalent to matrix decomposition. Graph2Gauss [2] embedded each node as a Gaussian distribution to capture uncertainty about the representation.

2.2   Friendship Prediction

Analyzing and predicting the social relationship between people by using individual information in the social network is the practical application of network link prediction [22]. Parimi *et al.* [13] applied the Latent Dirichlet Allocation (LDA) topic model to quantify users' interest in social media and predict friendship links based on the similarity of users' interest. Zhang *et al.* [26] quantified the distance between user's frequent movement areas and proved the geographic distance is an effective metric for distinguishing friends and strangers. They experimented with Twitter data and applied machine learning classifiers to predict friendship. Valverde-Rebaza *et al.* [18] reviewed research studies about friendship prediction

Table 1. The description of notations

Notation	Description
n	The number of nodes in the friendship network
$\mathbf{s}$	The score of student's psychological and facial perception for each node
$\mathcal{V}$	The set of n nodes
ε	The set of edges
α	Balance module of Skip-gram and the loss of autoencoder
β	The l_2 norm regularizer coefficient
K	The number of encoding layers
T	The weighted average neighbor of each node
$\mathbf{v_i}$	The representations of "context" node
d	The dimension of node representation
$\mathbf{X} \in \mathbb{R}^{n \times m}$	The node attribute information matrix
$\mathbf{Y} \in \mathbb{R}^{|\mathcal{V}| \times d}$	The final representation of the friendship network

in location-based social networks, including their approaches, advantages, and disadvantages, emphasizing the role of location in prediction.

Link prediction has become an interesting focus of friendship prediction, useful models can find the potentially important information in real-world networks. Highly scalable node embedding (HSEM) [1] embedded nodes into a vector with a lower and fix dimension by learning the co-occurrence features of node pairs to solve the link prediction problem in very large-scale networks. Li *et al.* [9] proposed two novel node-coupling clustering approaches and their extensions for link prediction. The models consider the different roles of nodes for prediction and combine the coupling degrees of the common neighbor nodes with the clustering information of a network. DLPA is [4] a novel link prediction approach for dynamic networks using the levels of the related nodes and their attraction force to calculate the connection probability for each potential link.

However, most social network research is based on online social networks; little friendship prediction studies focus on social networks in real life. Zhang *et al.* [25] analyzed the social networks of college students. They collected social networks and appearance data of students and studied the effect of facial perception on social networks. Appearance attributes are considered as features to understand the social status of the student.

3   Problem Formulation

We denote a friendship network $\mathcal{G} = (\mathcal{V}, \varepsilon, \mathbf{X})$, where $\mathcal{V}$ denotes the set of n nodes, and ε is the set of edges. $\mathbf{X} \in \mathbb{R}^{n \times m}$ is a matrix that encodes score s_i for i. $\mathbf{Y} \in \mathbb{R}^{|\mathcal{V}| \times d}$ is the representation of $\mathcal{G}$ in d dimension. The mapping function of $v_i \mapsto y_i \in \mathbb{R}^d$ preserves both network structure and attribute information, where $d \ll |\mathcal{V}|$. z_i is the label in the prediction model. The notations mainly used in this paper are listed in Table 1.

Since we focus on friendship in the student social network, we collect friendship information to construct the friendship network $\mathcal{G} = (\mathcal{V}, \varepsilon, \mathbf{X})$. We assumed that there is a photo of student i and evaluated by attractiveness, trustworthiness, amiableness, and dominance. In the psychological aspect, each student i has extroversion, agreeableness, conscientiousness, and dominance score. Above all, each student i gets score $\mathbf{s}_i$ on psychological features and facial perception dimensions. Our purpose is to detect whether two students will become friends using their psychological features and facial perception information.

Input: Students who are associated with $\mathbf{s}$ and $\mathcal{G}$.
Output: Whether students will become friends?

4   Design of DEFINE

To solve the problem that detects friend relationships in the social network combining psychological features and facial perception, we propose a framework named DEFINE. In this framework, we embed psychological features and facial perception into the network representation, to incorporate both network structure and node attribute information effectively. Then we reconstruct the network via link prediction for the friendship network with node attribute information. DEFINE intelligently combines node attribute information and network construction to detect whether students will become friends. The DEFINE framework is depicted in Fig. 2.

Entropy-Based Pre-processing. As mentioned before, each photo is evaluated by a certain number of participants. To eliminate the impact of noise from participants evaluating photos, we use the method mentioned in [25], which borrowed the concept of entropy in information theory to remove these meaningless data.

$$E = -\sum p(x) \log p(x) \tag{1}$$

where $p(x)$ represents the probability of occurrence of sample x.

Features Processing. Each student has psychological features scores and facial perception scores. We need to convert this information into a matrix which only contains 0 and 1. In the field of network research, the Cora dataset is widely used [10, 16]. The Cora dataset includes 2708 scientific publications. Each publication in the dataset is described by a 0 or 1 valued word vector indicating the absence or presence of the corresponding word from the dictionary. Inspired by the composition of the Cora data set, we map node attributes information into matrix dimensions as follows. First, we made a dictionary according to the psychological features and facial perception scores, each score corresponds to a position in the dictionary. Then, we convert these attributes information score $\mathbf{s}_i$ to a 0 or 1 valued word vector. Finally, we got $\mathbf{x}_i$ for each node to represent node attributes.

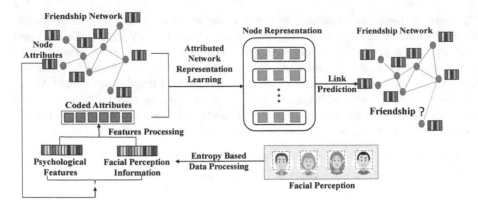

Fig. 2. The framework of DEFINE, which contains four critical components: (1) entropy-based data processing part, (2) feature processing part, (3) attributed network representation part, and (4) link prediction part.

Attributed Network Representation Learning. Attributed network representation learning via deep neural networks (ANRL) can uninterruptedly integrate node attributes affinity and network structural proximity into low-dimensional representation spaces [27]. Therefore, we input each node v_i in friendship network $\mathcal{V}$ and node attributes $\mathbf{X}$ into the ANRL model to get the node representations $\mathbf{Y} \epsilon \mathbb{R}^{|\mathcal{V}| \times d}$.

The goal of the ANRL model is to minimize the objective function:

$$\mathcal{L} = \mathcal{L}_{sg} + \alpha \mathcal{L}_{ae} + \frac{\beta}{2} \sum_{k=1}^{K} (\left\| \mathbf{W}^k \right\|_F^2 + \left\| \mathbf{W}^{\hat{(k)}} \right\|_F^2) \tag{2}$$

where $\mathcal{L}_{sg}$ and $\mathcal{L}_{ae}$ are defined in Eqs. (3) and (6), respectively. For the rest of the formula, α is the hyper parameter which can balance Skip-gram module $\mathcal{L}_{sg}$ and the loss of autoencoder module $\mathcal{L}_{ae}$, and β is the l_2 norm regularizer coefficient. $\mathbf{x}_i$ represents node v_i's feature vector, which includes student psychological features and facial perception information. $\mathbf{y}^{(K)}$ is the representation for node v_i after encoding with K layers. $\mathbf{W}^{(k)}$ is weight matrix in the k-th layer for encoder, and $\mathbf{W}^{\hat{(k)}}$ is same for decoder. u_v corresponds to the v-th column in the weight matrix $\mathbf{U}$ for graph context prediction.

$$\mathcal{L}_{sg} = - \sum_{i=1}^{n} \sum_{c \epsilon C} \sum_{-b \leq j \leq b, j \neq 0} \log p(v_{i+j} | \mathbf{x}_i) \tag{3}$$

where n is the total number of nodes, C is the set of node sequences generated by random walks, and b is the window size. $p(v_{i+j} | \mathbf{x}_i)$ is the likelihood of the target context given the node attributes, and is defined as:

$$p(v_{i+j} | \mathbf{x}_i) = \frac{\exp(\mathbf{v'}_{i+j}^T f(\mathbf{x}_i))}{\sum_{v=1}^{n} \exp(\mathbf{v'}_v^T f(\mathbf{x}_i))} \tag{4}$$

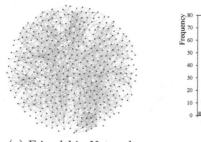

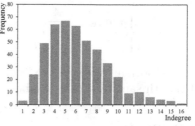

(a) Friendship Network   (b) Histogram of Indegree

Fig. 3. (a) A sketch of friendship network. (b) histogram of indegree for friendship network.

where $\mathbf{v}'_i$ is the representations when node v_i is regarded as "context" node.

When directly optimizing Eq. 4, the summation over the entire set of nodes is computationally expensive. Therefore, sampling multiple negative samples according to some noisy distributions [11] is convenient. In detail, for a specific node-context pair (v_u, v_{i+j}), the objective is as follows:

$$\log \sigma(\mathbf{v}'^T_{i+j} f(\mathbf{x}_i)) + \sum_{s=1}^{|neg|} \mathbb{E}_{v_n \sim P_n(v)}[\log \sigma(-\mathbf{v}'^T_n f(\mathbf{x}_i))] \qquad (5)$$

where $|neg|$ is the number of negative samples and $\sigma(x) = 1/(1 + \exp(x))$ is the sigmoid function. $Pn(v) \propto d_v^{3/4}$ is set as suggested in [11], where d_v is the degree of node v.

$$\mathcal{L}_{ae} = \sum_{i=1}^{n} \|\hat{x} - T(v_i)\|_2^2 \qquad (6)$$

where $\hat{x}$ is the reconstruction output decoder. $T(v_i)$ is adopted by a weighted average neighbor and incorporates prior knowledge into the model to return the target neighbors of v_i. That is to say, $T(v_i) = \frac{1}{|\mathcal{N}(i)|} \sum_{j \in \mathcal{N}(i)} \omega_{ij} \mathbf{x}_j$, where $\mathcal{N}(i)$ is the neighbors of node v_i in the friendship network, $w_{ij} = 1$ for unweighted friendship network, and x_j is the attributes associated with node v_j.

Link Prediction. We generate the labeled dataset of edges [6, 19, 27], which holds out existing links as positive instances randomly. We also sample an equal number of non-existing links randomly to get negative instances. Then, we use the network to train the ANRL model. After having obtained the representations for each node, we use these representations $\mathbf{Y} \in \mathbb{R}^{|\mathcal{V}| \times d}$ to perform link prediction task in the labeled edge dataset. We choose linear SVC as the link prediction model to deal with this task [3, 12, 25], that is,

$$\begin{cases} max_{\mathbf{w},b} & \dfrac{2}{\|\mathbf{w}\|} \\ \quad s.t. & \mathbf{y}_i(\mathbf{w}^T z_i) \geq 1, \quad i = 1, 2, 3 \cdots, \end{cases} \tag{7}$$

where $\mathbf{w}$ is the normal vector of the hyperplane, node representations $\mathbf{y}_i$ is the feature of the ith sample, and z_i is label in the train set.

5   Experiments

In this section, we describe all the data we used in our research and evaluate our framework by comparing it with some classical methods.

5.1   Datasets

We use 454 students' online survey results, which include the Big Five Personality questionnaire results, the dominance scale scores [7], facial images, and questionnaire results about listing their friends. We also collect facial perception scores by recruiting volunteers to rate the facial images. Figure 3(a) shows the sketch of the friendship network. The node represents student i, and the color depth of the nodes in the friendship indicates the indegree of nodes. The darker the color, the higher the indegree. Figure 3(b) is the distribution of indegree for each node in the friendship network which looks like left-skewed bell-shaped curves. Tables 2, 3, and 4 are Pearson's correlation coefficient for psychological features and facial perception information. To distinguish these two features, we marked namesake in Table 3 using P to represent psychological features.

5.2   Prediction

Comparison with DEFINE Variants. The first competitor considers node attributes information only, which is used to verify the validity of NRL in the link prediction task. Then we use competitors to learn low-dimensional vector representations for nodes based on network structure and node attributes. We compare DEFINE with the node attributes that only include psychological features or facial perception. The DEFINE variants are used to verify the performance of our proposed framework.

Table 2. Pearson's correlation coefficient for psychological features

	Dominance	Extroversion	Agreeableness	Conscientiousness
Dominance	-	-	-	-
Extroversion	−0.209**	-	-	-
Agreeableness	−0.488**	0.446**	-	-
Conscientiousness	−0.315**	0.551**	0.580**	-

$*p < 0.05; **p < 0.01$

Table 3. Pearson's correlation coefficient for facial perception

	Attractiveness	Trustworthiness	Agreeableness	Dominance
Attractiveness	-	-	-	-
Trustworthiness	0.664**	-	-	-
Agreeableness	0.425**	0.583**	-	-
Dominance	0.569*	0.470**	−0.012	-

$*p < 0.05; **p < 0.01$

Comparison with Baseline Methods. To prove the advantages of our framework combining network structure and node attributes, we compare DEFINE framework with several classical NRL methods as follows:

- **Structure-only:** This group competitors ignore the node attributes and leverage network structure information only. Node2vec [6] and Deepwalk [19] generate node sequences by using truncated random walks and obtain the latent node representations by feeding them into the Skip-gram model.
- **Attribute + Structure:** The competitor of this group is competitive because it tries to preserve node attributes information and network structure proximity. We consider TADW [24] as our competitor, the detailed descriptions can be found in Sect. 2. It is also used to verify the effectiveness of the Skip-gram model because the main idea of TADW is matrix decomposition.

Prediction Results. In this part, we evaluate the ability of our framework by comparing it with other baseline methods and DEFINE variants. Our goal is to reconstruct the friendship network structure via link prediction. First of all, we learn the representation based on different representation learning algorithms and DEFINE variants. Secondly, we generate the labeled dataset of edges by holding out existing links as positive instances and randomly sample an equal number of non-existing links for negative instances. Then, we use linear SVC to make link prediction. Finally, we divide the labeled nodes into the training set and testing set. The portion ratio of training nodes varies from 50% to 90%. To evaluate the framework quality and the results, we employ the Accuracy, Recall, and F1 score, and higher value indicates a better performance.

Table 4. Pearson's correlation coefficient for psychological features and facial perception

	Dominance (P)	Extroversion	Agreeableness (P)	Conscientiousness
Attractiveness	−0.079	0.129**	0.132**	0.063
Trustworthiness	−0.118**	0.078	0.122**	0.049
Agreeableness	−0.145**	0.088	0.102*	0.039
Dominance	−0.029	0.068	0.062	0.074

$*p < 0.05; **p < 0.01$

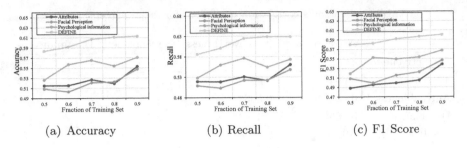

(a) Accuracy   (b) Recall   (c) F1 Score

Fig. 4. The results of the DEFINE variants link prediction experiment with the fraction of the training set.

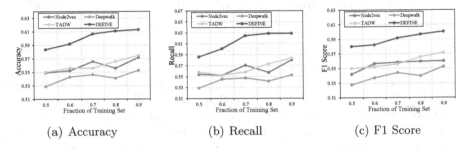

(a) Accuracy   (b) Recall   (c) F1 Score

Fig. 5. Link prediction performance comparison of different baseline methods with the fraction of the training set.

- We can observe that DEFINE performs well than DEFINE variants. Figure 4 presents the result. Even though node attributes can detect friendship, this competitor performs not very well because of lacking NRL.
- Link prediction using each part of node attributes also performs worse, even though converting these attributes and network structure into low-dimensional vectors by the NRL model.
- We can observe that the performance of DEFINE is better than other baseline methods, as seen in Fig. 5.
- Node2vec and Deepwalk both use Skip-gram to represent nodes in the friendship network. Their performance is not good enough because they only consider network structure.
- TADW combines both network structure and node attributes. However, this model is not as good as DEFINE because it is based on matrix decomposition instead of Skip-gram, which does not consider network structure very well.

6   Conclusion

In this paper, we focus on the problem of student friendship detection by developing an effective framework called DEFINE based on Node Enhancement. To our best knowledge, we are the first to combine students' psychological features and facial perceptions with friendship in this problem. Our experiment indicates DEFINE performs well in the prediction of student friendship while compared with the NRL models which use the structure information as the only consideration, such as Deepwalk and Node2vec. Even when both node attributes and network structure are taken into account, our framework still performs better than the NRL model without the leverage of Skip-gram. Compared to the DEFINE variant, experimental results on the real-world friendship network show the outstanding performance of our proposed framework. With its effective and accurate detection in our student friendship network, we consider deploying the framework on larger friendship networks. We also intend to extend DEFINE to the networks with other social relationships such as academic collaboration and trustworthy networks.

References

1. Aakas, Z., Liang, X., Chen, Y.: HSEM: highly scalable node embedding for link prediction in very large-scale social networks. World Wide Web **22**, 1–26 (2018)
2. Bojchevski, A., Günnemann, S.: Deep gaussian embedding of graphs: unsupervised inductive learning via ranking. In: International Conference on Learning Representations, pp. 1–13 (2018)
3. Bottou, L., Curtis, F.E., Nocedal, J.: Optimization methods for large-scale machine learning. SIAM Rev. **60**(2), 223–311 (2018)
4. Chi, K., Yin, G., Dong, Y., Dong, H.: Link prediction in dynamic networks based on the attraction force between nodes. Knowl.-Based Syst. **181**, 104792 (2019)
5. Eagle, N., Pentland, A.S., Lazer, D.: Inferring friendship network structure by using mobile phone data. Proc. Natl. Acad. Sci. **106**(36), 15274–15278 (2009)
6. Grover, A., Leskovec, J.: Node2vec: scalable feature learning for networks. In: Proceedings of the 22nd ACM SIGKDD International Conference on Knowledge Discovery and Data Mining, pp. 855–864. ACM (2016)
7. Hamby, S.L.: The dominance scale: preliminary psychometric properties. Violence Vict. **11**(3), 199 (1996)
8. Kong, X., Shi, Y., Yu, S., Liu, J., Xia, F.: Academic social networks: modeling, analysis, mining and applications. J. Netw. Comput. Appl. **132**, 86–103 (2019)
9. Li, F., He, J., Huang, G., Zhang, Y., Shi, Y., Zhou, R.: Node-coupling clustering approaches for link prediction. Knowl.-Based Syst. **89**, 669–680 (2015)
10. Lu, Q., Getoor, L.: Link-based classification. In: Proceedings of the 20th International Conference on Machine Learning (ICML-2003), pp. 496–503 (2003)
11. Mikolov, T., Chen, K., Corrado, G., Dean, J.: Efficient estimation of word representations in vector space. arXiv preprint arXiv:1301.3781 (2013)
12. Morente-Molinera, J.A., Mezei, J., Carlsson, C., Herrera-Viedma, E.: Improving supervised learning classification methods using multigranular linguistic modeling and fuzzy entropy. IEEE Trans. Fuzzy Syst. **25**(5), 1078–1089 (2016)
13. Parimi, R., Caragea, D.: Predicting friendship links in social networks using a topic modeling approach. In: Huang, J.Z., Cao, L., Srivastava, J. (eds.) PAKDD 2011. LNCS (LNAI), vol. 6635, pp. 75–86. Springer, Heidelberg (2011). https://doi.org/10.1007/978-3-642-20847-8_7
14. Perozzi, B., Al-Rfou, R., Skiena, S.: Deepwalk: online learning of social representations. In: Proceedings of the 20th ACM SIGKDD International Conference on Knowledge Discovery and Data Mining, pp. 701–710. ACM (2014)

15. Pittman, L.D., Richmond, A.: University belonging, friendship quality, and psychological adjustment during the transition to college. J. Exp. Educ. **76**(4), 343–362 (2008)
16. Sen, P., Namata, G., Bilgic, M., Getoor, L., Galligher, B., Eliassi-Rad, T.: Collective classification in network data. AI Mag. **29**(3), 93–93 (2008)
17. Tang, J., Qu, M., Wang, M., Zhang, M., Yan, J., Mei, Q.: Line: large-scale information network embedding. In: Proceedings of the 24th International Conference on World Wide Web, pp. 1067–1077 (2015)
18. Valverde-Rebaza, J.C., Roche, M., Poncelet, P., de Andrade Lopes, A.: The role of location and social strength for friendship prediction in location-based social networks. Inf. Process. Manag. **54**(4), 475–489 (2018)
19. Wang, D., Cui, P., Zhu, W.: Structural deep network embedding. In: Proceedings of the 22nd ACM SIGKDD International Conference on Knowledge Discovery and Data Mining, pp. 1225–1234. ACM (2016)
20. Wang, S.S., Moon, S.I., Kwon, K.H., Evans, C.A., Stefanone, M.A.: Face off: Implications of visual cues on initiating friendship on Facebook. Comput. Hum. Behav. **26**(2), 226–234 (2010)
21. Xia, F., Ahmed, A.M., Yang, L.T., Luo, Z.: Community-based event dissemination with optimal load balancing. IEEE Trans. Comput. **64**(7), 1857–1869 (2015)
22. Xia, F., Ahmed, A.M., Yang, L.T., Ma, J., Rodrigues, J.: Exploiting social relationship to enable efficient replica allocation in ad-hoc social networks. IEEE Trans. Parallel Distrib. Syst. **25**(12), 3167–3176 (2014)
23. Xia, F., Liu, L., Jedari, B., Das, S.K.: PIS: a multi-dimensional routing protocol for socially-aware networking. IEEE Trans. Mob. Comput. **15**(11), 2825–2836 (2016)
24. Yang, C., Liu, Z., Zhao, D., Sun, M., Chang, E.: Network representation learning with rich text information. In: Twenty-Fourth International Joint Conference on Artificial Intelligence (2015)
25. Zhang, D., et al.: Judging a book by its cover: the effect of facial perception on centrality in social networks. In: The World Wide Web Conference, pp. 2290–2300. ACM (2019)
26. Zhang, Y., Pang, J.: Distance and friendship: a distance-based model for link prediction in social networks. In: Cheng, R., Cui, B., Zhang, Z., Cai, R., Xu, J. (eds.) APWeb 2015. LNCS, vol. 9313, pp. 55–66. Springer, Cham (2015). https://doi.org/10.1007/978-3-319-25255-1_5
27. Zhang, Z., et al.: ANRL: attributed network representation learning via deep neural networks. IJCAI **18**, 3155–3161 (2018)

Semi-supervised Cross-Modal Hashing with Graph Convolutional Networks

Jiasheng Duan$^{(\boxtimes)}$, Yadan Luo, Ziwei Wang, and Zi Huang

School of Information Technology and Electrical Engineering,
The University of Queensland, Brisbane, Australia
`j.duan@uqconnect.edu.au`, {`y.luo,ziwei.wang`}`@uq.edu.au`,
`huang@itee.uq.edu.au`

Abstract. Cross-modal hashing for large-scale approximate neighbor search has attracted great attention recently because of its significant computational and storage efficiency. However, it is still challenging to generate high-quality binary codes to preserve inter-modal and intra-modal semantics, especially in a semi-supervised manner. In this paper, we propose a semi-supervised cross-modal discrete code learning framework. This is *the very first work* of applying asymmetric graph convolutional networks (GCNs) for scalable cross-modal retrieval. Specifically, the architecture contains multiple GCN branches, each of which is for one data modality to extract modality-specific features and then to generate unified binary hash codes across different modalities, so that the underlying correlations and similarities across modalities are simultaneously preserved into the hash values. Moreover, the branches are built with asymmetric graph convolutional layers, which employ randomly sampled anchors to tackle the scalability and out-of-sample issue in graph learning, and reduce the complexity of cross-modal similarity calculation. Extensive experiments conducted on benchmark datasets demonstrate that our method can achieve superior retrieval performance in comparison with the state-of-the-art methods.

Keywords: Cross-modal hashing · GCN · Semi-supervised learning

1 Introduction

Multimedia data on the Internet always exist in heterogeneous modalities, such as image, text, video and etc, which gives rise to an increasing requirement of effective multimedia retrieval technology on large-scale multimedia data. In recent years, the analysis of correlations among heterogeneous modalities has been extensively explored. A cross-modal retrieval system generally takes queries from one modality (*e.g.*, text) to search data from the other modalities (*e.g.*, images) with similarity metrics. The key is how to model the similarity relationships across modalities under the heterogeneity of multi-modal data, *i.e.*, data residing in different feature spaces. A common practice is binary representation learning, known as hashing, which aims to project high-dimensional data

© Springer Nature Switzerland AG 2020
R. Borovica-Gajic et al. (Eds.): ADC 2020, LNCS 12008, pp. 93–104, 2020.
https://doi.org/10.1007/978-3-030-39469-1_8

in various modalities into a shared low-dimensional discrete Hamming space, meanwhile the underlying inter- and intra-modal correlations are preserved. The cross-modal hashing work can be roughly categorized into unsupervised hashing and supervised hashing. Unsupervised hashing [3,9,12,15,17,18,20,25,27] learns similarity relationships based on the data distribution with none but numeric features available, while supervised hashing [1,5,7,10,13,21–24,26] adopts guidance information, *e.g.*, class labels, to define the similarity among heterogeneous data. It is worth mentioning that most deep supervised hashing methods are proposed in an end-to-end fashion to build modality-specific pathways for encoding data features into binary hash codes, respectively, such as DCMH [7], MCSCH [23] and etc. However, the similarity computation for each pair of data across modalities results in excessive memory and time cost. To be specific, for m text entities and n images, the computational complexity of directly calculating the similarity of all image-text pair is $\mathbf{O}(mn)$. Compared to supervised learning, unsupervised methods are obviously easier to cater large amount of unlabeled data since the acquisition of labeled data consumes expensive human labors, while supervised methods usually achieve better training results due to the guidance from discriminative semantic information. Hence, semi-supervised hashing provides a feasible solution to benefit from both supervised information and cheap unsupervised data to produce considerable learning performance.

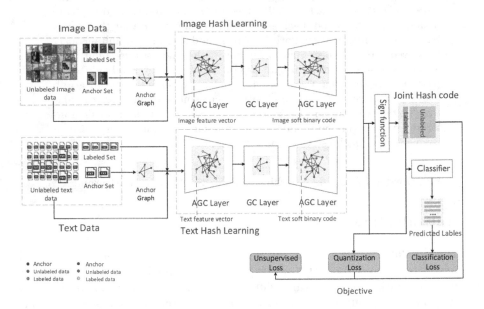

Fig. 1. The Architecture of Asymmetric Graph Convolutional Network for semi-supervised Cross-modal Hashing.

To overcome these limitations, we propose a novel semi-supervised cross-modal graph convolutional network hashing (CMGCNH) method, which *for the first time* exploits asymmetric GCN architecture in scalable cross-modal retrieval tasks. Without loss of generality, in this paper, we concentrate on bi-modal (images and text) hashing, and our framework can be easily extended to multiple branches to handle more modalities. As shown in Fig. 1, we first select a small number of paired anchors from different modalities, then image and text data points are organized into two undirected graphs, in which the nodes represent data entities and edges are defined as their relationships with the anchors. Then, a dual-branch asymmetric GCN framework is designed to learn specific-modality hash functions by implementing the convolution operations on the two graphs. The outputs of these two branches are integrated and sent into the well designed loss functions, so that we can implement cross-modal cooperative learning strategy. Since the graph structure is fixed during the forward propagation through multiple layers in the learning process, the semantic relationships within a modality are well preserved, meanwhile, the information of semantic labels directly propagates from the labeled data to the unlabeled data through the anchors. Besides, within one modality, the computational complexity is reduced from $O(n^2)$ to $O(np)$ ($p \ll n$), where n and p are the number of data points and the pairs of anchors, respectively, because for one data entity, the similarity calculation is only needed between itself and the anchors of the same modality rather than with all data points of the other modality. With the asymmetric architecture, anchors receive information from some data and pass it to other data, so that the convolution operations are only implemented on these small number of anchors, which allows to split large-scale dataset into small batches in the learning process instead of passing all data into the network at a time.

The key contributions of this paper are summarized as follows. Firstly, we propose a novel Asymmetric Graph Convolutional Network (CMGCNH) method for semi-supervised cross-modal hashing. To the best of our knowledge, this is the first attempt to employ asymmetric GCNs for scalable cross-modal hashing. Secondly, CMGCNH carries out cooperative learning strategy to preserve the inter-modality similarity relationships and the graph-based architecture within each branch to achieve the preservation of intra-modality correlation structure. Thirdly, different from other multi-pathway architecture, which directly calculate the similarity score of each image-text pair, CMGCNH only computes the similarity with p anchors within a branch, where $(p \ll m) \vee (p \ll n)$. The complexity is reduced to $O(m+n)$. Finally, extensive experiments on two cross-modal benchmark datasets demonstrate that CMGCNH can achieve superior performance in comparison with other cross-modal hashing methods.

2   Related Work

A rich line of existing cross-modal hashing work have been proposed, which are roughly categorized into unsupervised and supervised hashing. Unsupervised hashing [3,9,12,15,17,18,20,25,27] learns similarity relationships based on data distribution or structure property with only numeric features available, such as Canonical correlation analysis (CCA) [4], predictable dual-view hashing (PDH) [15], collective matrix factorization hashing (CMFH) [3], cross-view hashing (CVH) [9] and Composite Correlation Quantization hashing (CCQ) [12]. The most significant advantage of unsupervised hashing is the large amount of cheap data which can be easily collected, but it is performance is limited due to no additional guidance information. Supervised hashing [1,5,7,10,13,21–24,26] typically works with guidance information, such as common class labels and pair-wise information of modalities, to define the similarity relationships among heterogeneous data, such as semantic correlation maximization (SCM) [24], semantics-preserving hashing (SePH) [10] and Metric Learning by Similarity-Sensitive Hashing (CMSSH) [1]. It generally achieves better performance due to the guidance information but is limited by data collection, since the acquisition of labeled data is quite expensive. Hence, we propose a semi-supervised hashing method in this paper to benefit from both of the learning strategies.

3   Proposed Method

In this section, we describe the dual-branch Asymmetric Graph Convolutional Network for semi-supervised Cross-modal Hashing (CMGCNH) network. We first introduce the Graph Convolutional Networks (GCNs) as the base algorithm, and then discuss the proposed architecture and the objective functions in details.

3.1   Preliminaries

Graph Convolutional Network (GCN) is the base algorithm of CMGCNH. A typical GCN applies spectral graph theory with parameterized filters to integrate information from the neighbors of a node into the features of itself. It consists of one or multiple convolutional layers that conduct spectral convolution operations on a given graph. Kipf et al. [8] simplified this operation by approximating the Chebyshev polynomials and defined the graph convolution as:

$$\mathbf{H}^{(l+1)} = \sigma\big(\hat{\mathbf{A}}\mathbf{H}^{(l)}\mathbf{W}^{(l)}\big) \tag{1}$$

where $\mathbf{H}^{(l)}$ and $\mathbf{H}^{(l+1)}$ denote the input and output features of layer l, respectively; $\hat{\mathbf{A}} = \tilde{\mathbf{D}}^{-\frac{1}{2}}\tilde{\mathbf{A}}\tilde{\mathbf{D}}^{-\frac{1}{2}}$ is the normalized adjacency matrix of all the graph nodes with self-connected edges, in which $\tilde{\mathbf{A}} = \mathbf{A} + \mathbf{I}$ ($\mathbf{A}$ represents the node relationships, $i.e.$, edges; $\mathbf{I}$ is the graph node identity matrix), and $\tilde{\mathbf{D}}$ is the diagonal node degree matrix of $\tilde{\mathbf{A}}$; $\mathbf{W}^{(l)}$ represents the weight matrix of layer l that is what is aimed to learn; σ is an activation function selected in line with the specific tasks.

3.2   Problem Formulation

In CMGCNH, given a set of n multi-modal objects, we denote it as $\mathbf{O} = [\mathbf{O}_l, \mathbf{O}_u]$, since it consists of two data subsets, $i.e.$, supervised data $\mathbf{O}_l$ and unsupervised data $\mathbf{O}_u$. In the supervised set, images and texts are in pairs with class labels, so we define $\mathbf{O}_l = [\mathbf{V}_l, \mathbf{T}_l]$ indicating the labeled image set and labeled text set. In the unsupervised set, there are no class labels or pair information provided, and it is defined as $\mathbf{O}_u = [\mathbf{V}_u, \mathbf{T}_u]$, where $\mathbf{V}_u$ and $\mathbf{T}_u$ are the unlabeled image and text set. We also denote $\mathbf{V} = [\mathbf{V}_l, \mathbf{V}_u]$ and $\mathbf{T} = [\mathbf{T}_l, \mathbf{T}_u]$ where $\mathbf{V}$ and $\mathbf{T}$ are the whole image and text set.

The objective of CMGCNH is to represent $\mathbf{V}$ and $\mathbf{T}$ with a common set of binary codes $\mathbf{B} = [\mathbf{B}_l, \mathbf{B}_u]$ through learning modal-specific hash functions $\mathbf{F}_v(\mathbf{v})$ and $\mathbf{F}_t(\mathbf{t})$ for images and texts, respectively, where $\mathbf{B}_l$ and $\mathbf{B}_u$ represent the hash codes of supervised and unsupervised data points. $\mathbf{B}$ can be also denoted as $\mathbf{B} = \{\mathbf{b}_i\}_{i=1}^n \in \{+1, -1\}^{C \times n}$, where $\mathbf{b}_i$ is the C-bit hash code for the object $\mathbf{o}_i \in \mathbf{O}$. We learn $\mathbf{F}_v(\mathbf{v})$ and $\mathbf{F}_t(\mathbf{t})$ through a dual-path deep Asymmetric GCN architecture, i.e., to organize data into graph-based structures with a small number of anchors and implement convolution operations on these graphs. Specifically, for one modality, we model the data into an undirected graph where the nodes denote the data and anchor entities, and the edges connect the general data nodes and the anchor nodes and indicate if they are related, i.e., similar. The edges, i.e., similarity, between the data nodes and anchors, are defined as:

$$\mathbf{e}_{ij} = \begin{cases} 1, if((\mathbf{x}_i, \mathbf{a}_j) \in \mathbf{P})or(\mathbf{a}_j \in \mathbf{N}_{(\mathbf{x}_i)}) \\ \\ 0, otherwise \end{cases} \tag{2}$$

where $\mathbf{P}$ represents the set, in which a labeled data point $\mathbf{x}_i$ and an anchor $\mathbf{a}_j$ share at least one class label; $\mathbf{N}_{(\mathbf{x}_i)}$ denotes the set of k nearest anchor neighbors of an unlabeled data point $\mathbf{x}_i$. The constructed graph of images is denoted as $\mathbf{G}_v$ and the text graph is $\mathbf{G}_t$.

3.3   Dual-Branch Graph Convolutional Network Hashing

To implement convolution operations on the large-scale graphs, inspired by [28], we take full advantage of the anchors to build an asymmetric GCN architecture.

Suppose we have p pairs of anchors. We construct two anchor graphs for image and text modalities, respectively. The normalized graph adjacency matrix $\hat{\mathbf{A}}_v$ and $\hat{\mathbf{A}}_t$ with shape $p \times p$ are constructed as described in Sect. 3.1 and the relationships between anchors are defined as the same as labeled data. We also build $\hat{\mathbf{Z}}_v$ and $\hat{\mathbf{Z}}_t$ for $\mathbf{G}_v$ and $\mathbf{G}_t$, which are row-normalized asymmetric graph adjacency matrices that indicate the relationships with modality-specific anchors.

CMGCNH contains two modality-specific branches and each is built with two Asymmetric Graph Convolutional (AGC) layers and a group of typical Graph Convolutional (GC) layers between them. Here, for the sake of simplicity, we assume the number of GC layers is one. Take the image branch as an example, the branch architecture is as follows:

$$\mathbf{V}_g^1 = \sigma(\hat{\mathbf{Z}}_v^{\mathrm{T}} \mathbf{V} \mathbf{W}_v^1) \tag{3}$$

$$\mathbf{V}_g^2 = \sigma(\hat{\mathbf{A}}_v \mathbf{V}_g^1 \mathbf{W}_v^2) \tag{4}$$

$$\mathbf{U}_v = \varphi(\hat{\mathbf{Z}}_v \mathbf{V}_g^2 \mathbf{W}_v^3) \tag{5}$$

Here, $\mathbf{W}_v^1$, $\mathbf{W}_v^2$ and $\mathbf{W}_v^3$ are the weight matrices of the three layers, which are CMGCNH aims to learn. The first AGC layer (3) aggregates the filtered features of the neighbors to the anchor nodes through convolution operations, and $\mathbf{V}_g^1$ is the output of this layer. The middle GC layer (4) convolves the aggregated anchor data points $\mathbf{V}_g^1$ with their adjacency matrix $\hat{\mathbf{A}}_v$ and outputs $\mathbf{V}_g^2$. These two layers are followed by activation function σ (e.g., ReLU [14]). The last AGC layer (5) calculates the low-dimension features of each node with the weighted summation of anchors $\mathbf{V}_g^2$ and is followed by a Tanh function φ. $\mathbf{U}_v = [\mathbf{U}_{vl}, \mathbf{U}_{vu}]$ represents the final output of this branch. $\mathbf{U}_{vl}$ and $\mathbf{U}_{vu}$ denote the soft binary codes of labeled and unlabeled image data, respectively.

The other branch is built for text, which has the same architecture as the image-branch as shown below:

$$\mathbf{T}_g^1 = \sigma(\hat{\mathbf{Z}}_t^T \mathbf{T} \mathbf{W}_t^1) \tag{6}$$

$$\mathbf{T}_g^2 = \sigma(\hat{\mathbf{A}}_t \mathbf{T}_g^1 \mathbf{W}_t^2) \tag{7}$$

$$\mathbf{U}_t = \varphi(\hat{\mathbf{Z}}_t \mathbf{T}_g^2 \mathbf{W}_t^3) \tag{8}$$

Here, $\mathbf{U}_t = [\mathbf{U}_{tl}, \mathbf{U}_{tu}]$. We implement the two branches simultaneously and then merge $\mathbf{U}_{vl}$ and $\mathbf{U}_{tl}$ with coefficients λ_1 and λ_2 as follows:

$$\mathbf{U}_l = \lambda_1 * \mathbf{U}_{vl} + \lambda_2 * \mathbf{U}_{tl} \tag{9}$$

Then, $\mathbf{U}_l$ is relaxed to the unified hash code $\mathbf{B}_l$ through sign function. The third part employs a fully connected layer as a linear classifier, which takes the binary code $\mathbf{B}_l$ as the input and outputs the class label prediction of the data object $\mathbf{o}_i$. Furthermore, we perform L_2 norm penalty to force $\mathbf{U}_{lv}$ and $\mathbf{U}_{lt}$ to approximate to $\mathbf{B}_l$ as close as possible, so that $\mathbf{B}_l$ acts as the bridge of the two modalities to preserve the inter-modal similarity relationships. For the unlabeled data, the calculated $\mathbf{U}_{vu}$ and $\mathbf{U}_{tu}$ are constrained to be bit uncorrelated and balanced.

3.4   Objective Function

As depicted above, we expect to learn two sets of modality-specific hash functions $\mathbf{F}_v(\mathbf{v})$ and $\mathbf{F}_t(\mathbf{t})$ for images and texts to produce the unified binary codes $\mathbf{B}$ for $\mathbf{O}$ through projecting two modalities into a common Hamming space, i.e., the generated $\mathbf{U}_{lv}$ and $\mathbf{U}_{lt}$ are transformed to a common $\mathbf{B}$ through the sign function, therefore, we employ the quantization loss between the continuous $\mathbf{U}_{lv}$, $\mathbf{U}_{lt}$ and the discrete $\mathbf{B}_l$ as following:

$$\min_{\mathbf{B}_l, \mathbf{U}} \mathcal{L}_1 = \mu_{lv} \|\mathbf{B}_l - \mathbf{U}_{lv}\|^2 + \mu_{lt} \|\mathbf{B}_l - \mathbf{U}_{lt}\|^2 \tag{10}$$

in which μ_{lv} and μ_{lt} are the properly selected penalty parameters; $\|\cdot\|^2$ denotes the L_2 norm of vectors.

We also consider the original semantic structures, *i.e.*, similarity relationships. We strive to make the distance between the encoded objects with shared labels as close as possible, otherwise, far away from each other. Hence, we propose to minimize the classification error from the hash codes $\mathbf{B}_l$ of all labeled nodes. That is:

$$\min_{\mathbf{B}_l, \mathbf{W}} \mathcal{L}_2 = \|\mathbf{L}_l - \mathbf{B}_l \mathbf{W}_c\|^2 \tag{11}$$

where $\mathbf{W}^c$ is the weight matrix of a fully connected layer that acts as the classifier; $\mathbf{L}_l$ represents the label annotation matrix of the labeled data.

Since unlabeled data have no class constrain, we directly transform $\mathbf{U}_{uv}$ and $\mathbf{U}_{ut}$ to $\mathbf{B}_{uv}$ and $\mathbf{B}_{ut}$ through the element-wise sign function. To keep the code bits uncorrelation and balance, we add two constrains to maximize the information entropy:

$$\min_{\mathbf{B}} \mathcal{L}_3 = \eta(\left\|\mathbf{B}_{uv}^{\mathrm{T}}\mathbf{B}_{uv} - n_2\mathbf{I}_C\right\|^2 + \left\|\mathbf{B}_{ut}^{\mathrm{T}}\mathbf{B}_{ut} - n_2\mathbf{I}_C\right\|^2) \\ + \gamma(\left\|\mathbf{B}_{uv}^{\mathrm{T}}\right\|^2 + \left\|\mathbf{B}_{ut}^{\mathrm{T}}\right\|^2) \tag{12}$$

where η and γ are the trade-off hyper-parameters. The final objective function of CMGCNH is

$$\min_{\mathbf{B},\mathbf{U},\mathbf{W}} \mathcal{L} = \mathcal{L}_1 + \mathcal{L}_2 + \mathcal{L}_3 \tag{13}$$

3.5 Learning and Testing

Since we have three parameters, $\mathbf{B}, \mathbf{U}, \mathbf{W}$, to learn, we leverage the alternating learning strategy in training. Only one parameter is learned each time with the other parameters fixed.

In the test phase, given a query $\mathbf{q}$, the feature vector is sent into the well-trained corresponding branch. The graph asymmetric adjacency matrices are built as the way of training unsupervised data, which is based on the similarities between $\mathbf{q}$ and the anchors. Then we obtain the hash code $\mathbf{B}_q$ by forward propagation. That is

$$\mathbf{B}_q = sign(\varphi(\hat{\mathbf{Z}}_q(\sigma(\hat{\mathbf{A}}(\sigma(\hat{\mathbf{Z}}_q^{\mathrm{T}}\mathbf{q}^{\mathrm{T}}\mathbf{W}^1))\mathbf{W}^2))\mathbf{W}^3)) \tag{14}$$

The Hamming distances between $\mathbf{B}_q$ and hash codes of database are calculated and ranked, then we gain $\mathbf{q}$'s most similar data in the other modality.

4 Experiments

To verify the effectiveness of the proposed method CMGCNH, we conduct experiments on two widely-used cross-modal datasets: NUS-WIDE [2] and MIRFlickr-25K [6], and compare the testing results with 6 state-of-the-art work.

4.1 Datasets and Features

NUS-WIDE dataset [2] contains 269,498 images, each of which has a series of corresponding textual tags. In our experiment, each data entity has multiple of 10 most common labels selected from the total 81 concepts. The corresponding 181,364 entities form the dataset that consists of 2000 image-text pairs as the query set, and 179,364 pairs as the training set, in which, 1,000 randomly sampled pairs are used as labeled data, and the rest are unlabeled. We represent images with 4,09 6-D deep feature vectors extracted from the 19-layer VGGNet [16] and text with 1,392-D Bag-of-Visual-Words vectors.

Table 1. The MAP scores of two retrieval tasks on MIRFlickr-25K (a) and NUS-WIDE (b) with different lengths of hash codes.

(a) MIRFlickr-25K

Methods	image→text				text→image			
	16-bits	32-bits	64-bits	128-bits	16-bits	32-bits	64-bits	128-bits
CVH	0.602	0.587	0.578	0.572	0.607	0.591	0.581	0.574
PDH	0.623	0.624	0.621	0.626	0.627	0.628	0.628	0.629
CMFH	0.659	0.660	0.663	0.653	0.611	0.606	0.575	0.563
CCQ	0.637	0.639	0.639	0.638	0.628	0.628	0.622	0.618
CMSSH	0.611	0.602	0.599	0.591	0.612	0.604	0.592	0.585
SCM	0.585	0.576	0.570	0.566	0.585	0.584	0.574	0.568
CMGCNH (ours)	0.696	0.709	0.723	0.719	0.670	0.670	0.672	0.680

(b) NUS-WIDE

Methods	image→text				text→image			
	16-bits	32-bits	64-bits	128-bits	16-bits	32-bits	64-bits	128-bits
CVH	0.458	0.432	0.410	0.392	0.474	0.445	0.419	0.398
PDH	0.475	0.484	0.480	0.490	0.489	0.512	0.507	0.517
CMFH	0.517	0.550	0.547	0.520	0.439	0.416	0.377	0.349
CCQ	0.504	0.505	0.506	0.505	0.499	0.496	0.492	0.488
CMSSH	0.512	0.470	0.479	0.466	0.519	0.498	0.456	0.488
SCM	0.389	0.376	0.368	0.360	0.388	0.372	0.360	0.353
CMGCNH (ours)	0.575	0.578	0.589	0.596	0.576	0.578	0.602	0.613

MIRFlickr 25 K dataset [6] consists of 25,000 images. The images are associated with multiple textual tags and each belongs to at least one of the total 24 categories. Only the tags appearing at least 20 times are selected, hence we totally have 17,142 image-text pairs and randomly select 1,000 as the query set, and the rest form the training set, which includes 1,000 labeled and 15,142 unlabeled data. Images are represented with 4,096-D deep feature vectors from a 19-layer VGGNet [16] and text with 1,000-D BOW vectors.

4.2 Experiment Settings

Evaluation Metrics. We evaluate Hamming ranking and hash lookup procedures of CMGCNH and the baselines. The widely used metric Mean average precision (MAP) [11] is employed to measure the accuracy of Hamming ranking procedure, and the Precision-Recall Curve is used to measure the accuracy of the hash lookup.

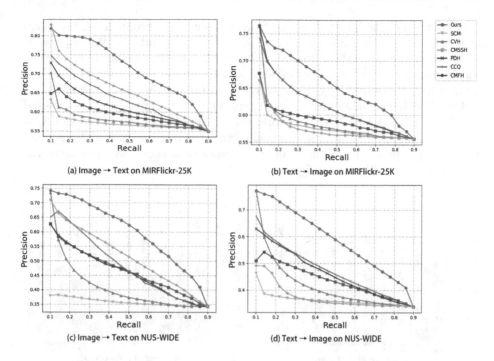

Fig. 2. Precision-recall curves on MIRFlickr (a, b) and NUS-WIDE (c, d) dataset. The code length is 64 bits.

Baselines. We compare CMGCNH with 6 state-of-the-art work. CVH [9] adapts the spectral hashing [19] to cross-view hashing with a generalized eigenvalue formulation. PDH [15] embeds proximity of original data and designs an optimized objective function based on block coordinate descent algorithm, to maintain the predictability of the generated binary code. CMFH [3] builds an undirected asymmetric graph to capture the fusion similarity among different modalities by collective matrix factorization. CCQ [12] proposes a seamless latent semantic analysis framework with multimodal correlation and composite quantization integrated, so that data in various modalities are encoded into an isomorphic latent space. CMSSH [1] solves a binary classification problem with learning a mapping which can be efficiently learned using boosting algorithms. SCM [24] proposes a semantic correlation maximization method based on semantic labels for improving the efficiency of cross-modal hashing.

4.3   Implementation Details

Our code is based on PyTorch. All experiments are conducted on a server with two GeForce GTX 2080 Ti GPUs.

As discussed in Sect. 2, the CMGCNH contains two branches and each branch consists of two AGC layers and a group of GC layers. The input of these two branches, *i.e.*, the input of the first AGC layer, is 4,096D embedding. The output of the first layer is in 2,048D. The input and output of the group of GC layers are set to 2,048D and the hash code length *i.e.*, 16, 32, 64 and 128. We implement experiments to explore the influence of the depth, *i.e.*, the number of GC layers. The two branches are implemented simultaneously and then merged based on the measure, $\mathbf{U}_l = \lambda_1 * \mathbf{U}_{vl} + \lambda_2 * \mathbf{U}_{tl}$. In the experiment, we use a validation set to choose the hyper-parameter λ_1 and λ_2 and find the best performance achieved with $\lambda_1 = 0.7$ and $\lambda_2 = 0.3$. Therefore, we set that λ_1 is fixed to 0.7 and λ_2 is 0.3. In the same way, we fix the loss coefficients μ_v, μ_t, η and γ at 1, 1, 1e-3 and 1e−4. For exploring the influence of the number of anchors, we implement the experiments with different anchor numbers.

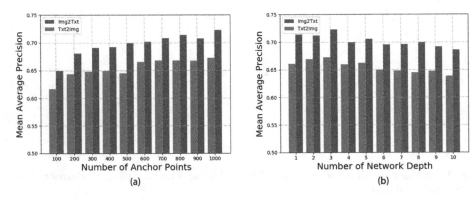

Fig. 3. Performance of cross-modal retrieval using different number of anchors (a) and network depth (b) on MIRFlickr dataset.

4.4   Experiment Results and Analysis

Comparisons with Baselines. The mAP results on different hash code lengths are listed in Table 1. The Precision-Recall curves (with 64-bit hash code) are plotted in Fig. 2. The experiment results show that CMGCNH performs the best in all methods. For MIRFlickr-25K dataset, CMGCNH keeps the best average mAP of 0.723 on image → text and 0.680 on text → image task. Compared with CMFH [3], which performs the best in all unsupervised methods, CMGCNH increases the mAP score by around 0.06 on 64-bits in two tasks. In comparison with the supervised method CMSSH, the mAP score of our method is about 1.00 higher in image → text task and about 0.08 higher on 128-bits in text → image. Likewise, in NUS-WIDE dataset, the performance of our method is satisfactory. For example, the mAP score of CMGCNH with 128-bits in the text → image task is about 0.1 higher than PDH [15] which performs the second best here.

From the Precision-Recall curves, it can be observed that CMGCNH outperforms all baselines, which means our method achieves a better precision-recall balance in the lookup procedural than other work. For instance, in image → text task on MIRFlickr-25K, with the same recall at 0.4, the precision of CMGCNH reaches 0.76, which is around 0.08 higher than the second best method CMFH

[3]. This indicates that CMGCNH can find the same number of relevant data candidates by retrieving less data in the database than other methods.

Effect of Anchor Selection. To explore influence of the number of anchors, we implement the experiment to calculate the mAP when this number changes from 100 to 1000 on 64-bits. In Fig. 3(a), it can be seen that the performance is getting better along with the number of anchors increase overall. This can be explained as that the more anchors used in the graph, the more information of the data nodes is preserved and propagated. It also demonstrates that the design of anchors used to keep and transfer semantic information is effective.

Effect of Model Parameters. For exploring how the depth of GC layers affects performance, we conduct an experiment to observe the changes of mAP when the depth rises from 1 to 10. From Fig. 3(b), we can see that the score reaches the peak at 3-depth and then starts to drop down. Hence, we suggest that the over-deep GC model will lose information during forward propagation, while over-shallow GC network cannot adequately aggregate and retrieve the node features. We fix the depth to 3 in experiments to achieve the best performance.

5 Conclusion

In this paper, we propose a novel semi-supervised cross-modal hashing framework, CMGCNH, which is the very first work of applying asymmetric graph convolutional network for scalable cross-modal retrieval. With the well designed graph anchors and asymmetric architecture, it implements cooperative multi-modal learning strategy to encode data into hash codes with the intra- and inter-modality correlations well preserved, and dramatically reduces the computation complexity. Experiments on two datasets demonstrate its superior performance.

References

1. Bronstein, M.M., Bronstein, A.M., Michel, F., Paragios, N.: Data fusion through cross-modality metric learning using similarity-sensitive hashing. In: CVPR, pp. 3594–3601 (2010)
2. Chua, T., Tang, J., Hong, R., Li, H., Luo, Z., Zheng, Y.: NUS-WIDE: a real-world web image database from national university of Singapore. In: CIVR, pp. 368–375 (2009)
3. Ding, G., Guo, Y., Zhou, J.: Collective matrix factorization hashing for multimodal data. In: CVPR, pp. 2083–2090. IEEE Computer Society (2014)
4. Hardoon, D.R., Szedmák, S., Shawe-Taylor, J.: Canonical correlation analysis: an overview with application to learning methods. Neural Comput. **16**(12), 2639–2664 (2004)
5. Hu, Y., Jin, Z., Ren, H., Cai, D., He, X.: Iterative multi-view hashing for cross media indexing. In: ACMMM, pp. 527–536 (2014)

6. Huiskes, M.J., Lew, M.S.: The MIR flickr retrieval evaluation. In: SIGMM, pp. 39–43 (2008)
7. Jiang, Q.Y., Li, W.J.: Deep cross-modal hashing. In: CVPR, pp. 3270–3278 (2017)
8. Kipf, T.N., Welling, M.: Semi-supervised classification with graph convolutional networks. In: ICLR (2017)
9. Kumar, S., Udupa, R.: Learning hash functions for cross-view similarity search. In: IJCAI, pp. 1360–1365 (2011)
10. Lin, Z., Ding, G., Hu, M., Wang, J.: Semantics-preserving hashing for cross-view retrieval. In: CVPR, pp. 3864–3872 (2015)
11. Liu, W., Mu, C., Kumar, S., Chang, S.: Discrete graph hashing. In: NeurIPS, pp. 3419–3427 (2014)
12. Long, M., Cao, Y., Wang, J., Yu, P.S.: Composite correlation quantization for efficient multimodal retrieval. In: SIGIR, pp. 579–588 (2016)
13. Luo, Y., Yang, Y., Shen, F., Huang, Z., Zhou, P., Shen, H.T.: Robust discrete code modeling for supervised hashing. Pattern Recogn. **75**, 128–135 (2018)
14. Nair, V., Hinton, G.E.: Rectified linear units improve restricted Boltzmann machines. In: ICML, pp. 807–814 (2010)
15. Rastegari, M., Choi, J., Fakhraei, S., Hal, D., Davis, L.S.: Predictable dual-view hashing. In: ICML, pp. 1328–1336 (2013)
16. Simonyan, K., Zisserman, A.: Very deep convolutional networks for large-scale image recognition. In: ICLR (2015)
17. Sun, L., Ji, S., Ye, J.: A least squares formulation for canonical correlation analysis. In: ICML (2008)
18. Wang, D., Cui, P., Ou, M., Zhu, W.: Learning compact hash codes for multimodal representations using orthogonal deep structure. IEEE Trans. Multimed. **17**(9), 1404–1416 (2015)
19. Weiss, Y., Torralba, A., Fergus, R.: Spectral hashing. In: NeurIPS, pp. 1753–1760 (2008)
20. Wu, G., et al.: Unsupervised deep hashing via binary latent factor models for large-scale cross-modal retrieval. In: IJCAI, pp. 2854–2860 (2018)
21. Wu, L., Wang, Y., Shao, L.: Cycle-consistent deep generative hashing for cross-modal retrieval. IEEE Trans. Image Process. **28**(4), 1602–1612 (2019)
22. Xu, X., Shen, F., Yang, Y., Shen, H.T., Li, X.: Learning discriminative binary codes for large-scale cross-modal retrieval. IEEE Trans. Image Process. **26**, 2494–2507 (2017)
23. Ye, Z., Peng, Y.: Multi-scale correlation for sequential cross-modal hashing learning. In: ACMMM, pp. 852–860 (2018)
24. Zhang, D., Li, W.J.: Large-scale supervised multimodal hashing with semantic correlation maximization. In: AAAI, pp. 2177–2183 (2014)
25. Zhang, J., Peng, Y., Yuan, M.: Unsupervised generative adversarial cross-modal hashing. In: AAAI, pp. 539–546 (2018)
26. Zhen, Y., Yeung, D.: Co-regularized hashing for multimodal data. In: NeuIPS, pp. 1385–1393 (2012)
27. Zhou, J., Ding, G., Guo, Y.: Latent semantic sparse hashing for cross-modal similarity search. In: SIGIR, pp. 415–424 (2014)
28. Zhou, X., et al.: Graph convolutional network hashing. IEEE Trans. Cybern. 1–13 (2019)

Typical Snapshots Selection for Shortest Path Query in Dynamic Road Networks

Mengxuan Zhang[✉], Lei Li, Wen Hua, and Xiaofang Zhou

School of Information Technology and Electrical Engineering,
The University of Queensland, Brisbane, Australia
mengxuan.zhang@uqconnect.edu.au, {l.li3,w.hua}@uq.edu.au,
zxf@itee.uq.edu.au

Abstract. Finding the shortest paths in road network is an important query in our life nowadays, and various index structures are constructed to speed up the query answering. However, these indexes can hardly work in real-life scenario because the traffic condition changes dynamically, which makes the pathfinding slower than in the static environment. In order to speed up path query answering in the dynamic road network, we propose a framework to support these indexes. Firstly, we view the dynamic graph as a series of static snapshots. After that, we propose two kinds of methods to select the typical snapshots. The first kind is *time-based* and it only considers the temporal information. The second category is the *graph representation-based*, which considers more insights: *edge-based* that captures the road continuity, and *vertex-based* that reflects the region traffic fluctuation. Finally, we propose the *snapshot matching* to find the most similar typical snapshot for the current traffic condition and use its index to answer the query directly. Extensive experiments on real-life road network and traffic conditions validate the effectiveness of our approach.

Keywords: Shortest path · Snapshot selection · Dynamic road network

1 Introduction

Shortest path query is a fundamental operation in road network routing and navigation. A road network can be denoted as a directed graph $G(V, E)$ where V is the set of road intersections, and $E \subseteq V \times V$ is the set of road segments. Each edge is associated with a numerical weight representing the length of a road segment or the time required to travel through. The road network is static if both the structure and the edge weights (i.e., V and E) do not change over time. As for the real-life road network, the traffic condition changes almost all the time, we model the road network as a dynamic graph. Here we treat this dynamic graph as a series of snapshots, with each snapshot is static by itself but dynamic between each other, and answer the path queries using their corresponding snapshot graphs.

© Springer Nature Switzerland AG 2020
R. Borovica-Gajic et al. (Eds.): ADC 2020, LNCS 12008, pp. 105–120, 2020.
https://doi.org/10.1007/978-3-030-39469-1_9

The shortest path problem has been extensively studied and the approaches can be grouped into two categories depending on if an index is created or not. The *index-free* methods like *Dijkstra's*, *A** [1,2], and *cache-based* [3], find the path only with the graph information. Therefore, they can adapt to the dynamic environment by simply running on the new graph. But they suffer from low query efficiency or inaccurate results, so various *index-based* methods [4–7] have been proposed to speed up the query answering. However, these indexes all take time to construct, and the traffic condition may have already changed before their construction finishes. Therefore, there are two extreme cases to use index on a dynamic graph. The first one is building an index for each snapshot, which is not space efficient and has much redundant information. The other one is creating a big time-dependent index [8] for the entire time domain like *TCH* [9] and *T2Hop* [10]. However, their index sizes are huge and they essentially require the graph to be static from the perspective of "change". Therefore, we aim to seek a balance between the two extremes by identifying some typical snapshots from the dynamic graphs and only build indexes for them. Given queries in a specific current traffic condition, we first match the traffic condition to the most similar typical snapshot and use its index to answer the queries. When none of the existing snapshots is similar enough, we regard the current road network as a new snapshot and construct an index for it.

However, it is unclear how to choose those typical snapshots and how to classify the current traffic condition. We try to represent multiple similar snapshot graphs as one typical graph and then process queries in it at the cost of query accuracy. There are two lines of studies focus on graph similarity measurement. The first one is the *graph edit distance* [11–13]. It uses the minimum edit operation number to transform one graph into another. The other one is the *feature-based distance* [14], where the similarity is not measured on the graph directly but on the abstraction of a graph. Existing methods in both these two lines consider either attribute similarity or structural similarity. However, the road network is a special graph where the topological structure does not evolve frequently because the road construction and closure are not very common. In addition, the edges and vertices in the road network are not associated with labels. It is the edge weight or the speed that varies with time, and we suppose that the structure remains stable for the road network. Therefore, the existing graph similarity measurement can hardly solve our problem. However, we also represent the graph as a feature vector but use the edge weight vector and vertex vector, and we focus on the speed profile change rather than the change of the topological structure or the associated labels. To the best of our knowledge, it is the first time to specify the representation and the similarity measurement of the road network. Then multiple snapshots are clustered, the representative snapshot in each cluster can be selected as the typical snapshot. When there comes a query, we classify the current road network as the most similar typical snapshot and process the shortest path on it.

To support accurate clustering and classification of the snapshots, three challenges must be addressed. The first challenge is that the original representation of the road network encounters the high-dimension curse. Various dimension reduction techniques such as *PCA* and *LDA* are proposed, but they are general methods and none are specified to the road network. Here, we reduce the dimension by calculating the covariance of each edge first and filtering the edges whose values are smaller than the threshold. Also, we propose another two representations with much lower dimension: *Edge-based* and *Vertex-based*. The second challenge is how to incorporate the road network features like region property and road network continuity into the selection. The two proposed graph representation methods focus on different aspects of the network feature. The *Edge-based* graph representation uses path to capture the continuity of the network. The *Vertex-based* representation selects the "hot spots" (typical vertices) in networking by evaluating the fluctuation of the traffic condition around the vertices. The third challenge is how to choose the typical graph given the current traffic condition. When there comes a query, we convert the graph in the two proposed ways and then match the current graph with one typical graph by using the classification algorithm. The contributions in this work can be summarized as follows:

- We formally study the problem of shortest path query in dynamic graphs.
- We propose two categories of the methods to select the typical snapshots: The *time-based* approaches that choose the snapshots directly, and the *graph-representation* approaches (*edge-based* and *vertex-based*) that consider the features like continuity, region condition.
- We present how to do the graph clustering and classification in our *graph-representation*.
- We conduct extensive evaluations using a large real-world road network and traffic condition. The experimental results verify the effectiveness of our approaches.

The remaining of this paper is organized as follows: We first discuss the current literature of the pathfinding and graph similarity measurement in Sect. 2. Section 3 introduces some common notions and defines the sub-problems: *Typical Snapshots Selection* and *Snapshot Matching*. For the first sub-problem, we propose two time-based approaches in Sect. 4, and present two graph representation-based methods in Sect. 5. The actual typical snapshot selection and the second matching sub-problem are discussed in Sect. 5.3. Evaluations of the proposed methods in a real-life dynamic road network are presented in Sect. 6. Finally, Sect. 7 concludes the paper.

2   Related Work

2.1   Shortest Path Algorithm

In the past decades, various techniques have been proposed for the shortest path calculation in road networks. The fundamental shortest path algorithms are *Dijkstra's* and *A** algorithms. The *Dijkstra's* is inefficient as it needs to traverse the entire network for the shortest path search. And the A^* improve the query efficiency by directing the traversal towards the destination with the help of the heuristic distance. Then there comes a line of research that accelerates the query answering by pre-calculating the index. Particularly, algorithms such as *Contraction Hierarchy* [4] prune the search space by referring to information stored in the index. Other algorithms like *2-Hop Labeling* [5] and *SILC* framework [6], attempt to materialize all the pairwise shortest path results in a concise or compressed manner such that a given shortest path query can be answered directly via a simple table-lookup or join. These index-based algorithms are usually efficient for query answering so as to return the query result within microseconds, but the major premise behind them is that the road network should be static. Since the index construction is often time-consuming and the road network evolves almost all the time, the rebuilt index cannot always fit the current refreshed network condition. Therefore, these algorithms do not adapt well to the dynamic environment.

Another line of research attempts to process the query in dynamic environment. It uses functions to describe the road condition directly [8,15,16]. However, the complexity of finding the fastest path is $\Omega(T(|V|\log|V| + |E|))$, where T is a large number related to the function. This complexity lower bound determines it is much slower to find a fastest path compared with the static environment. To further speed up the query efficiency, time-dependent indexes like *TCH* [17] and *T2Hop* [10] are proposed. However, these time-dependent algorithms essentially view the dynamic environment statically, because their time-dependent functions are stable. Any change of their function would result in the failure of the existing index and have to endure a time-consuming reconstruction process. Therefore, some works drop the time-dependent functions and run the query in the dynamic graph directly. Because it is hard to build an index for the dynamic graph, shared computation [1,2,18] is introduced to improve the query efficiency. Nevertheless, their efficiency is still not comparable with index-based approaches. In this work, we aim to bring the index back to the dynamic environment with the help of snapshots.

2.2   Graph Similarity Measurement

The graph distance can be measured mainly in two ways: *graph edit distance* [11,13] and *feature-based distance* [19,20]. *Graph edit distance* has been widely accepted for the graph similarity measurement, and two graphs whose distance is less than a similarity threshold is considered to be similar. It is a metric which can be used in various graphs such as directed or undirected, labeled or unlabeled, as well as single or multi-graphs. The distance is calculated as the minimal steps of graph edit operations including the insertion, deletion, or alteration of vertex or edge to transform one graph to another. In this way, this method can reflect the topological differences between graphs. However, it is not applicable to our problem because the topological structure of the road network does not change often and is supposed to be static here. For the *feature-based distance*, most of the existing works focus on the structure-based, attributed-based or structural/attribute distance. In [19], some labeled edges are selected as the features and one graph is represented as a feature vector where each dimension indicates the existence or the frequency of the corresponding edge. The neighborhood random walk model is proposed to combine the structural closeness and attribute similarity for the graph clustering [20]. However, in our scenario, the edges are associated with the length or travel time rather than the labels, and the structure is supposed to be static as mentioned above. In this work, we aim at distinguishing multiple snapshots by their speed profile, and we need to measure the graph similarity from the combination of edge weights and graph structure. Therefore, the existing graph similarity measurement is difficult to be applied here.

3   Problem Definition

Definition 1 *(Road network)*. *Road network is formalized as a dynamic weighted graph $G_D(V, E, W(T))$, where the vertex $v \in V$ (resp. edge $e \in E$) denoting road intersection (resp. segment) and the edge weight $w(e, t) \to \mathbb{R}, t \in T$ can change with time.*

If we take a snapshot of the dynamic graph at some time point t, then each edge on the snapshot $g_i = G_S(V, E, W(t_i))$ is associated with only one weight value. Suppose the road traffic condition is constant around a small time interval of the snapshot, then the dynamic graph can be treated as the set of multiple snapshots with the timestamp, that is $G_D = \{g_i = G_S(V, E, W(t_i)) | t_i \in T, \bigcup \{t_i\} = T\}$.

We focus on the shortest path query in the dynamic road network. Given k typical snapshots with their corresponding indexes, and the shortest path queries in the current road network, we try to match the current graph to the most similar typical graph and use its index for the query answering. Therefore, two sub-problems *typical snapshot selection* and *snapshot matching* appear and they are defined as followed.

Definition 2 *(Sub-Problem 1: Typical Snapshots Selection)*. *Given multiple snapshots $G = \{g_0, g_1, \ldots, g_{n-1}\}$ of a road network, typical snapshots selection puts them into k ($k < n$) clusters such that the snapshots in the same cluster are similar and those in different clusters are dissimilar. One representative snapshot is taken from each cluster as the typical snapshot.*

Definition 3 *(Sub-Problem 2: Snapshot Matching)*. *Given one snapshot g_i and k typical snapshots $G_T = \{g_1, g_2, \ldots, g_k\}$ of the road network, where g_i is not necessary in G_T, snapshot matching captures the snapshot g^* that is the most similar with g_i from G_T.*

Apparently, both of the two sub-problems need the graph similarity measurement. We measure the similarity of road networks by first abstracting the features and then use the distance between the feature vectors as the graph similarity.

To evaluate the difference or quality between the selected typical graph g_i and the actual graph g^*, we need an error measurement. We compute the traveling time $l_i(p)$ and $l^*(p)$ by using the edges of g_i and g^* for each $p \in P$. The error p is $error(p) = |l_i(p) - l^*(p)|/|l^*(p)|$, and the error between g_i and g^* is $error(g_i, g^*) = \dfrac{\sum error(p)}{|P|}$. Because the trajectories are collected from the taxi, this measurement focuses more on the actual impact on real-life traveling.

4   Time-Based Typical Snapshot Selection

The dynamic road network can be viewed as a time series of snapshots. Because the traffic on road network changes incrementally in real life and several continuous snapshots can be approximately the same. Based on the observation, we can select the typical snapshots by sampling on the time dimension. In the following, we present two baseline selection methods: *uniform sampling* and *non-uniform sampling*.

4.1   Uniform Sampling

Suppose the total snapshot number is n. The uniform sampling method selects the snapshots with the same step x starting from the yth snapshot ($y < x$). In other words, $G_T = \{g_i|i = y + kx, 0 \leq i < m\}$. When $x = 1$, all n snapshots are selected, and its error is 0; when $x = 2$, every odd or even snapshot is selected, and it has some error; when $x \geq \dfrac{n}{2}$, only one snapshot is selected, and it has the largest error. The number of the typical graph is $k = \lfloor m/x \rfloor$. Obviously, the error could be inversely proportional to the typical snapshot number k, and we test the performance of different k. This method can control the number of snapshots, but it cannot guarantee the worst case error. The time complexity is $O(n)$.

4.2   Non-uniform Sampling

The change rate of traffic conditions differs in each time period. For example, the road network is almost the same from midnight to the early morning because little traffic appears on road. But it can change dramatically during peak hours. Therefore, we select the typical snapshots non-uniformly according to how the traffic changes by time, which can be captured by the path-based error.

The sampling works in a sliding window fashion. First of all, an error threshold ϵ is set. After that, we visit the snapshots in the increasing order of timestamps and put the current visiting snapshot g_i into the current window G'. For each $g_j \in G'$, we compute its error $error'(g_j) = max(error(g_j, g_i))$, where $g_i \in G'$ and $g_j \neq g_i$. Then the g_j with the minimum $error'(g_j)$ is selected as the typical graph of the current window. If $error'(g_j) \leq \epsilon$, the windows keep expanding and test the next snapshot. Otherwise, a typical graph selected for the previous windows and a new window is created with g_i as the first snapshot. This procedure runs on until all the snapshots are visited. Apparently, this method can control the worst error, but it cannot determine the number of typical snapshots. The time complexity is $O(n^2)$.

5 Graph Representation-Based Selection

5.1 Edge-Based Representation

Suppose the road network structure does not change, which means V and E is steady, then only the weight vectors differ for multiple graphs. Therefore, in our first type of representation, we use the *weight vector* and the *delta weight vector* to denote one graph.

Single Edge Representation. If we denote one graph as the weight vector, then one snapshot G_i is directly represented as $W_i = [e_1, e_2, \ldots, e_{|E|}]$, which contains every edge's weight. And its variant is the delta weight vector, that is we can express one snapshot g_i as $\delta(W_i)$, where W_0 is the weight vector of g_0 (treated as referenced graph), and $\delta(W_i) = W_i - W_0 = [\delta e_1, \delta e_2, \ldots, \delta e_{|E|}]$. Because both of W_i and $\delta(W_i)$ has the same dimension number of $|E|$, which could be hundreds of thousands in real-life and suffers from the curse of dimension, we have to reduce the dimension number before computing the similarity.

The first approach of dimension reduction we apply is *PCA (Principal Component Analysis)*. However, it is a general dimension reduction algorithm and does not perform well in our scenario. In the road network, it is those edges that change dramatically over that distinguish a typical snapshot. Then we use the coefficient of variation cv (standard deviation divided by the mean) of each edge to measure how various an edge is and use a threshold to identify those various ones to construct a lower-dimensional weight vector.

Aggregated Edge Representation. The weight vector shows the weight of every edge in a graph, but it loses the information of the connection and continuity of road segments. Usually, it is the continuous road segments in some areas that are busy or congested rather than the individual road segments or all the road segments in one area. Therefore, we try to use the aggregated edge length of multiple paths to represent one graph and we call these paths as *typical paths*.

Each path p is a sequence of connected edges with $p = [e_0, e_1, \ldots, e_n]$ and the length of a path is $d(p) = \sum_{i=0}^{n} w(e_i)$. Suppose there are k typical paths, then one snapshot is represented as $g^{AE} = [d(p_0), d(p_1), \ldots, d(p_{k-1})]$.

To better represent a graph, the typical paths set should meet the following conditions: (1) The coverage of typical paths should be as large as possible to represent the graph completely; (2) The similarity between typical paths should be small to avoid the redundant representation; (3) The length (calculated as the total time passing through) of the same path should vary greatly so as to differ multiple snapshots . And according to the observation of traffic in daily life that the congested road segments are usually within local areas, such as the discontinuous red or yellow segments along one long path, we set the minimum static length l_{min} and the static maximum length l_{max} (calculated as the total length) of the candidate typical paths as 2 km and 3 km, respectively.

To meet the first condition of path selection, we partition the graph evenly into 4×4 regions $R = \{R_0, R_1, \ldots, R_{15}\}$. An example of the selected paths in each region is shown in Fig. 1. The selected paths number $pnum_i$ in region R_i is proportional to the vertices number in it with $pnum_i = pnum \times |V_i|/|V|$, where $pnum$ is the typical paths total number and $|V_i|$ is the vertices number in R_i. The paths generated at this step are the candidates. To meet the second condition, we compute the similarity between typical paths in a region and remove one of those that are larger than a threshold. The similarity here is the Jaccard Coefficient ($\frac{|p_i \cap p_j|}{|p_i \cup p_j|}$) over the edges. In the following, we present different ways to select the candidate typical paths.

Random Selection. The simplest way is to randomly select $pnum_i$ paths in each region R_i with path length between l_{min} and l_{max}. First of all, a length threshold η is determined randomly. After that, a starting edge is selected randomly, and we choose one of its neighbors randomly. The path keeps growing until the length is larger than η. Repeated edge is avoided for better coverage.

Edge-Constrained Selection. To increase the representativeness of the typical paths, we select those paths whose edges' coefficient of variations is no less than a threshold $thresh_{cv}$. However, it is inefficient to generate and validate candidates forwardly, so we do the coefficient of variation filtering first and construct a sub-graph only with the highly changing edges. After that, the candidates are generated on this sub-graph instead of the original graph.

Edge-Greedy Selection. The random selection ignores the weight variation totally so it suffers from generating the qualified candidates repeatedly, while the edge-constraint selection is limited to a small sub-graph so it faces the headache of high similarity between the candidates. Therefore, we propose a greedy method to generate the candidates considering both the weight variation and path distinction. This approach also runs on the original graph and select the starting edge randomly. As for growing the candidate path, the next selected out-edge is the one with the largest cv. To maintain the effectiveness of the path, a smaller threshold $thresh_{cv}$ is applied to validate the edge.

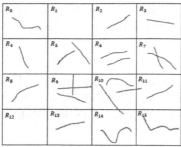

Fig. 1. Typical paths distribution   **Fig. 2.** Typical Vertex Selection

5.2   Vertex-Based Representation

In real life, there always exist some temporal hot spots in the road network, such as the inevitable road intersection during rush hour, the scenic spots on weekend, and the business area after work. Meanwhile, the traffic conditions in other "cold" areas stay normal at the same time. Then how about detecting these "key" vertices (called *typical vertices*) and use the aggregation of traffic conditions around them to represent the traffic condition on the whole road network? Consequently, two problems need to be solved: (1) how to find the typical vertices? (2) how to use the typical vertices to represent one snapshot for the similarity measurement among different snapshots?

Graph Representation. Suppose these typical vertices $V_T = \{v_i\}, v_i \in V$ in a road network have already been known in advance. Inspired by the *tree-based q-gram approach* for graph similarity join problem [11,21], we represent the traffic condition around each typical vertex v_i as the set of vertices that can be reached from v_i in a breath-first-search within a fixed time period (for example, 2 min). If a driver arrives at a hot spot, he or she is likely to be blocked by the traffic flow and could pass through fewer road intersections within the time period. Usually, the smoother the traffic condition around v_k in g_i is, the larger the value of $|S_{ik}|$ will be, and vice versa. Obviously we cannot learn much from the absolute value of $|S_{ik}|$, and we care more about the congestion than the smoothness of the traffic. We define the block coefficient of a vertex v_k in g_i as

$$b(v_{ik}) = max\{|S_{1k}|, |S_{2k}|, \ldots, |S_{nk}|\}/|S_{ik}| \tag{1}$$

where $max\{|S_{1k}|, |S_{2k}|, \ldots, |S_{nk}|\}$ represents the maximum reachable vertex number from v_k among multiple snapshots, and it reflects the non-block traffic condition around v_k in other words. The larger the block coefficient $b(v_{ik})$, the more congested around v_k at time period t_i.

In the first type of vertex-based representation, we denote one snapshot as the block coefficient of the typical vertices (called *vertex-bc representation*), that is $g_i = [b(v_{i0}), b(v_{i1}), \ldots, b(v_{i|V_T|})]$. We can also represent one snapshot as the vertex set of typical vertices (called *vertex-set representation*), that is

$g_i = [S_{i1}, S_{i2}, \ldots, S_{i|V_T|}]$ with S_{ik} denoting the vertex set reached from v_k within t_0 time in g_i. And the reachable vertex set from the vertex v_k in n snapshots can be denoted as $[S_{1k}, S_{2k}, \ldots, S_{nk}]$.

Typical Vertices Selection. The difference between the hot spots and the "cold" vertices is that the traffic condition fluctuates more dramatically around the hot spots. Hence, we define the traffic fluctuation $f(v_k)$ of v_k as the coefficient of variation of the block coefficient:

$$f(v_k) = \frac{\sigma\{b(v_{1k}), b(v_{2k}), \ldots, b(v_{nk})\}}{\mu\{b(v_{1k}), b(v_{2k}), \ldots, b(v_{nk})\}} \tag{2}$$

where σ and μ denotes the standard deviation and the mean of $\{b(v_{1k}), b(v_{2k}), \ldots, b(v_{nk})\}$..

To select the typical vertices, we visit the vertices in decreasing order of their traffic fluctuation and choose the top $|V_T|$ vertices. Besides, during the selection, we exclude the vertices that are close to the selected typical vertices because they are likely to capture the traffic condition of the overlapped local area or have the similar traffic fluctuation pattern.

Specifically, We first compute the vertex set S_{ik} for each vertex on each snapshot using *BFS*. However, the search does not stop at r but at $2r$ and also generates a larger coverage set S'_{ik}. S_{ik} is used to compute the block coefficient $b(v_{ik})$ and traffic fluctuation $f(v_k)$, while S'_{ik} is used to avoid the typical vertices being too close to each other. As shown in Fig. 2, the vertex coverage set of the selected vertices have no intersection with each other. The procedure stops when k typical vertices are selected. The time complexity is $O(|V||G_D| \times BFS(2r) + |V|\log|V|)$. Because the complexity of the *BFS* is dependent on a small radius $2r$, we use $BFS(2r)$ to denote its complexity.

5.3   Graph Clustering and Snapshot Matching

In this section, we discuss the methods to solve the two sub-problems. The previous section introduced two types of graph representations, and we present how to utilize them to select the typical snapshots. Section 5.3 presents how the typical snapshots are determined and Sect. 5.3 solves the *snapshot matching* sub-problem with graph classification.

Graph Clustering. Because the graphs are represented as low-dimensional vectors, we can utilize general clustering methods to put similar ones together. However, methods that tend to cluster arbitrary shapes like *DBSCAN* [22,23] are not suitable for tasks like this because of their errors are not guaranteed. Therefore, we use two types of methods: *adaptive K-means based clustering* and *agglomerative hierarchical clustering* [24] that have a distance threshold to do the clustering.

Graph Classification. When the traffic condition changes, we can receive a new snapshot g'. First of all, g' is converted into one of the graph representations. After that, it is compared with the existing typical snapshots and obtains the most similar one g^*. If the similarity between satisfies the threshold, we use the index of g^* directly to answer the path queries. Otherwise, g' is considered as a new typical snapshot, and a new index is also built for it.

6 Experiments

In this section, we experimentally evaluate the performance (in terms of the accuracy and efficiency) of the proposed *typical snapshot selection* and *snapshot matching* approaches using the real-life road network with real traffic condition.

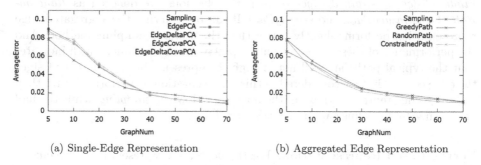

(a) Single-Edge Representation   (b) Aggregated Edge Representation

Fig. 3. Performance of edge-based representation

6.1 Experimental Setup

We execute the experiments on the Beijing road network with 31,2350 vertices and 40,3228 edges. Currently, there are 288 snapshots sampled every 5 min from the traffic condition in 1st April 2015. These snapshots are obtained from the taxi trajectories collected during that day. The original trajectory dataset contains 532,868 trajectories and 17,698,668 GPS points. We follow the same process of [15] to generate the speed profile.

All the algorithms are implemented in C++, compiled with full optimizations, and tested on a Dell R730 PowerEdge Rack Mount Server which has two Xeon E5-2630 2.2 GHz (each has 10 cores and 20 threads) and 378 G memory. The data are stored on a 12×4 TB Raid-50 disk.

6.2   Typical Snapshot Selection

Edge-Based Representation. Figure 3(a) shows the result of the *single-edge representation* test. These snapshots are clustered by *K-means*. The edge vector and the edge delta vector are denoted as *EdgePCA* and *EdgeDeltaPCA*, with the PCA dimension reduction. And we use *EdgeCovaPCA* and *EdgeDeltaCovaPCA* to denote the combine of coefficient of variant and PCA dimension reduction. The performance of *single-edge presentation* is better than the *uniform sampling* method only when the typical snapshot number is over 40. Because in this kind of representation, we only consider the weight of edge and ignore the connectivity of edges and the underlying topological structure. Although the graph structure stays the same for each snapshot, it has a great impact on the location of the shortest path.

Figure 3(b) shows the performance of the *aggregated-edge representation*. The *random/edge-constrained/edge-greedy* path selections are denoted as *Random-Path*, *ConstrainedPath*, and *GreedyPath*. It can be seen that the aggregated-edge representation performs slightly better than the uniform sampling method. And the performance of these three variants is pretty much the same, which indicates that the typical paths are still not enough to represent the snapshot. But since the edge connectivity is considered in this representation, it performs better than the singe-edge representation (all the lines are below the *sampling*, while the half of the single-edge's lines are above the *sampling*).

Vertex-Based Representation. For the *vertex-set* representation, we cluster the snapshots by *hierarchical clustering* and the testing performance is named as *vertex-set*. And we use both the *K-means* and *Hierarchical Clustering* in the *vertex-bc* representation and the results are denoted as *vertex-bc-Hier* and *vertex-bc-Kmeans* as shown in Fig. 4. In terms of vertex-based representation, it can be seen that the shortest path error of *vertex-set* representation is always smaller than that of the *vertex-bc* representation regardless of the clustering methods. In *vertex-bc* representation, we consider both the reachable vertex number and the vertex set distribution overlapping, which is proved reasonable in these experimental results. In terms of typical vertex number, the error decreases distinctly when the typical vertex number rise from 50 to 150. It makes sense because more typical vertices can represent the snapshot and show the traffic characteristics more completely so as to generate more accurate clustering results. When the typical vertex number increase from 150 to 200, the errors are almost the same for all three methods. This indicates that taking less than 150 typical vertices is enough to represent the snapshot. What's more, fewer typical vertices is good for improving the snapshot matching efficiency. It is interesting to find that the performance of selecting 50 typical vertices is almost the same as that of 200 typical vertices, which again shows the superiority of vertex-set representation.

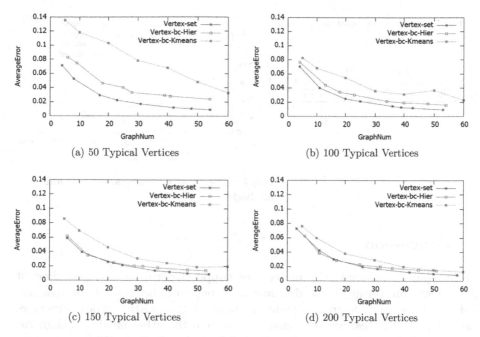

Fig. 4. Performance of vertex-based representation.

Time-Based Selection. In this section, we compare the performance of the *time-based* methods and the *graph representation-based* methods. For the representation method results, we choose *ConstrainedPath* from the *edge-based*, *vertex-set* from the *vertex-based* because they are the best of their own categories. The result is shown in Fig. 5. The worst method is the *uniform sampling*, followed by the *non-uniform sampling*. The three *graph representation-based* methods are all better than the *time-based* methods. Specifically, *vertex-based* is better than *edge-based*.

6.3 Snapshot Matching

In this section, we evaluate the running time of the *snapshot matching* procedure. Because the graph representation-based methods have higher accuracy than the time-based methods, we only show their results. The matching time is made up of the *representation time*, which convert the current snapshot into one of the representations, and the *similarity computation time*, which compares with the existing typical snapshots and finds the most similar one. Specifically, $matching\ time = t_r + k \times t_{Similarity}$, where k is the number typical snapshots.

The result is shown in Table 1. The *Edge-based* is the fastest to run because it only needs edge weight concatenation. The *Vertex-based* is slower because it has to run hundreds of *Dijkstra's* to collect the vertex set. Nevertheless, all of these methods can finish in one second, and the matching process like this only needs to run once when the traffic condition changes.

Table 1. Snapshot matching running time (sec)

	Edge-based	Vertex-based
Graph convert	6.012×10^{-6}	4.121×10^{-4}
Similarity	$k \times 10^{-8}$	$k \times 4.9 \times 10^{-5}$

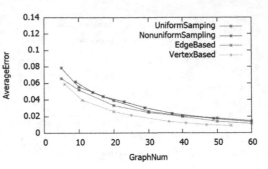

Fig. 5. Performance comparison of four methods

7   Conclusion

In this paper, we study the problem of supporting the index-based shortest path query answering in the dynamic road network. Because of the dynamic nature of the real-life traffic condition, none of the existing index structures can adapt to the real dynamic environment. On the other hand, although the traffic condition changes over time, it does not change dramatically in a short period. Therefore, we view the dynamic road network as a series of snapshots and only build the indexes on the typical ones. The first problem is how to determine if one snapshot is typical or not. We propose two sets of *time-based* and *graph representation-based* approaches to deal with it. After that, when facing a new traffic condition snapshot, we use the *snapshot matching* to find the most similar typical snapshot, and use its index to answer the path queries. Our extensive experiments use the real-life road network, traffic condition to validate the effectiveness of our methods.

References

1. Zhang, M., Li, L., Hua, W., Zhou, X.: Batch processing of shortest path queries in road networks. In: Chang, L., Gan, J., Cao, X. (eds.) ADC 2019. LNCS, vol. 11393, pp. 3–16. Springer, Cham (2019). https://doi.org/10.1007/978-3-030-12079-5_1
2. Zhang, M., Li, L., Hua, W., Zhou, X.: Efficient batch processing of shortest path queries in road networks. In: 2019 20th IEEE International Conference on Mobile Data Management (MDM), pp. 100–105. IEEE (2019)
3. Thomsen, J.R., Yiu, M.L., Jensen, C.S.: Effective caching of shortest paths for location-based services. In: Proceedings of the 2012 ACM SIGMOD International Conference on Management of Data, pp. 313–324. ACM (2012)
4. Geisberger, R., Sanders, P., Schultes, D., Delling, D.: Contraction hierarchies: faster and simpler hierarchical routing in road networks. In: McGeoch, C.C. (ed.) WEA 2008. LNCS, vol. 5038, pp. 319–333. Springer, Heidelberg (2008). https://doi.org/10.1007/978-3-540-68552-4_24

5. Ouyang, D., Qin, L., Chang, L., Lin, X., Zhang, Y., Zhu, Q.: When hierarchy meets 2-Hop-labeling: efficient shortest distance queries on road networks. In: Proceedings of the 2018 International Conference on Management of Data, pp. 709–724. ACM (2018)
6. Samet, H., Sankaranarayanan, J., Alborzi, H.: Scalable network distance browsing in spatial databases. In: Proceedings of the 2008 ACM SIGMOD International Conference on Management of Data, pp. 43–54. ACM (2008)
7. Wang, S., Xiao, X., Yang, Y., Lin, W.: Effective indexing for approximate constrained shortest path queries on large road networks. Proc. VLDB Endow. **10**(2), 61–72 (2016)
8. Li, L., Hua, W., Du, X., Zhou, X.: Minimal on-road time route scheduling on time-dependent graphs. Proc. VLDB Endow. **10**(11), 1274–1285 (2017)
9. Batz, G.V., Delling, D., Sanders, P., Vetter, C.: Time-dependent contraction hierarchies. In: Proceedings of the Meeting on Algorithm Engineering & Expermiments. Society for Industrial and Applied Mathematics, pp. 97–105 (2009)
10. Li, L., Wang, S., Zhou, X.: Time-dependent hop labeling on road network. In: 2019 IEEE 35th International Conference on Data Engineering (ICDE), pp. 902–913, April 2019
11. Zhao, X., Xiao, C., Lin, X., Wang, W.: Efficient graph similarity joins with edit distance constraints. In: 2012 IEEE 28th International Conference on Data Engineering, pp. 834–845. IEEE (2012)
12. Gouda, K., Hassaan, M.: CSI_GED: an efficient approach for graph edit similarity computation. In: 2016 IEEE 32nd International Conference on Data Engineering (ICDE), pp. 265–276. IEEE (2016)
13. Li, Z., Jian, X., Lian, X., Chen, L.: An efficient probabilistic approach for graph similarity search. In: 2018 IEEE 34th International Conference on Data Engineering (ICDE), pp. 533–544. IEEE (2018)
14. Chen, L., Gao, Y., Zhang, Y., Jensen, C.S., Zheng, B.: Efficient and incremental clustering algorithms on star-schema heterogeneous graphs. In: 2019 IEEE 35th International Conference on Data Engineering (ICDE), pp. 256–267. IEEE (2019)
15. Li, L., Zheng, K., Wang, S., Hua, W., Zhou, X.: Go slow to go fast: minimal on-road time route scheduling with parking facilities using historical trajectory. VLDB J.-Int. J. Very Large Data Bases **27**(3), 321–345 (2018)
16. Li, L., Kim, J., Xu, J., Zhou, X.: Time-dependent route scheduling on road networks. SIGSPATIAL Spec. **10**(1), 10–14 (2018)
17. Batz, G.V., Geisberger, R., Neubauer, S., Sanders, P.: Time-dependent contraction hierarchies and approximation. In: Festa, P. (ed.) SEA 2010. LNCS, vol. 6049, pp. 166–177. Springer, Heidelberg (2010). https://doi.org/10.1007/978-3-642-13193-6_15
18. Li, L., Zhang, M., Hua, W., Zhou, X.: Fast query decomposition for batch shortest path processing in road networks. In: 2020 IEEE 36th International Conference on Data Engineering (ICDE)
19. Yan, X., Yu, P.S., Han, J.: Substructure similarity search in graph databases. In: Proceedings of the 2005 ACM SIGMOD International Conference on Management of Data. ACM, pp. 766–777 (2005)
20. Zhou, Y., Cheng, H., Yu, J.X.: Graph clustering based on structural/attribute similarities. Proc. VLDB Endow. **2**(1), 718–729 (2009)
21. Wang, G., Wang, B., Yang, X., Yu, G.: Efficiently indexing large sparse graphs for similarity search. IEEE Trans. Knowl. Data Eng. **24**(3), 440–451 (2010)

22. Ester, M., Kriegel, H.-P., Sander, J., Xu, X., et al.: A density-based algorithm for discovering clusters in large spatial databases with noise. Kdd **96**(34), 226–231 (1996)
23. Gan, J., Tao, Y.: DBSCAN revisited: mis-claim, un-fixability, and approximation. In: Proceedings of the 2015 ACM SIGMOD International Conference on Management of Data, pp. 519–530. ACM (2015)
24. Defays, D.: An efficient algorithm for a complete link method. Comput. J. **20**(4), 364–366 (1977)

A Survey on Map-Matching Algorithms

Pingfu Chao, Yehong Xu[✉], Wen Hua, and Xiaofang Zhou

School of Information Technology and Electrical Engineering,
The University of Queensland, Brisbane, Australia
{p.chao,yehong.xu,w.hua}@uq.edu.au,
zxf@itee.uq.edu.au

Abstract. The map-matching is an essential preprocessing step for most of the trajectory-based applications. Although it has been an active topic for more than two decades and, driven by the emerging applications, is still under development. There is a lack of categorisation of existing solutions recently and analysis for future research directions. In this paper, we review the current status of the map-matching problem and survey the existing algorithms. We propose a new categorisation of the solutions according to their map-matching models and working scenarios. In addition, we experimentally compare three representative methods from different categories to reveal how matching model affects the performance. Besides, the experiments are conducted on multiple real datasets with different settings to demonstrate the influence of other factors in map-matching problem, like the trajectory quality, data compression and matching latency.

1 Introduction

Nowadays, the ubiquity of positioning devices enables the tracking of user/vehicle trajectories. However, due to the intrinsic inaccuracy of the positioning systems, a series of preprocessing steps are required to correct the trajectory errors. As one of the major preprocessing techniques, the map-matching algorithm finds the object's travel route by aligning its positioning data to the underlying road network. It is the prerequisite of various location-based applications, such as navigation, vehicle tracking, map update and traffic surveillance.

The map-matching problem has been studied for more than two decades. Despite hundreds of papers are proposed, to the best of our knowledge, only several works were conducted [4,8,14,19] surveying them. More importantly, even the most recent surveys [8] fail to categorise the existing methods comprehensively. They either classify them based on applications [8] that are not very distinctive to each other, or follow the previous categorisation [14] that is obsolete. Besides, various new techniques are introduced to the map-matching problem recently, including new models (weight-based [15], multiple hypothesis theory [16]), new tuning techniques (machine learning [12], information fusion

---

Y. Xu—Equal contribution.

© Springer Nature Switzerland AG 2020
R. Borovica-Gajic et al. (Eds.): ADC 2020, LNCS 12008, pp. 121–133, 2020.
https://doi.org/10.1007/978-3-030-39469-1_10

[5,9]), new data types (DGPS, inertial sensor, semantic road network) and new research topics (lane-level, parallel). Hence, it is about time to conduct a new survey to summarise existing solutions and provide guidance to future research.

Note that the existing map-matching problem covers various scenarios, ranging from indoor to outdoor and from pedestrian, vehicle to multimodal. However, to ensure a unified setting for survey and comparison, in this paper, we target the vehicle trajectory map-matching in an outdoor environment due to its popularity. We categorise the existing work from technical perspective. In addition, we discuss the main properties of the methods and future research directions according to the experiment results conducted on multiple matching algorithms. Overall, our contributions are listed as follows:

- We review the map-matching solutions proposed since the last comprehensive survey [14] and propose a new categorisation of the algorithms based on their methodology. Our proposed categorisation can better distinguish the existing methods from the technical perspective, which is beneficial for future study.
- We enumerate several map-matching challenges that are caused by low-quality trajectory data. The challenges are exemplified and explained concretely, which leads to future research directions.
- To further demonstrate the challenges, we implement three representative map-matching algorithms and conduct extensive experiments on datasets with different sampling rate, map density and compression level. Our claims about the relationship between data quality and map-matching quality are fully supported by the experiments.

The rest of the paper is organised as follows: In Sect. 2, we first formally define the map-matching problem and enumerate the existing surveys and their limitations. Then, we propose our new categorisation in Sect. 3. We further discuss the current challenges which are demonstrated through experiments in Sect. 4 and we draw conclusions in Sect. 5.

2   Preliminaries

2.1   Problem Definition

We first define the map-matching problem and relevant datasets, including trajectory (input), road network (input) and route (output):

Definition 1 *(Trajectory). A **trajectory** Tr is a sequence of chronologically ordered spatial points $Tr : p_1 \rightarrow p_2 \rightarrow ... \rightarrow p_n$ sampled from a continuously moving object. Each point p_i consists of a 2-dimensional coordinate $<x_i, y_i>$, a timestamp t_i, a speed spd_i (optional) and a heading θ_i (optional). i.e.: $p_i = <x_i, y_i, t_i, spd_i, \theta_i>$.*

Definition 2 *(Road Network). A **road network** (also known as map) is a directed graph $G = (V, E)$, in which a vertex $v = <x, y> \in V$ represents an intersection or a road end, and an edge $e = <o, d, l>$ is a directed road starting from vertices e.o to e.d (e.o, e.d $\in V$) with a polyline l represented by a sequence of spatial points.*

Definition 3 *(Route). A route R represents a sequence of connected edges, i.e.*
$R : e_1 \rightarrow e_2 \rightarrow ... \rightarrow e_n$, *where* $e_i \in G.E(1 \leq i \leq n)$ *and* $e_k.d = e_{k+1}.o$.

Definition 4 *(Map-Matching). Given a road network $G(V,E)$ and a trajectory Tr, the map-matching find a route $\mathcal{MR}_G(Tr)$ that represents the sequence of roads travelled by the trajectory.*

For simplicity, we omit the subscript G and use $\mathcal{MR}(Tr)$ instead to represent the matching result as different trajectories are usually map-matched on the same map. In general, the map-matching route is expected to be continuous as it represents the vehicle's travel history. However, it is quite often that $\mathcal{MR}(Tr)$ contains disconnected edges due to incorrect map-matching, which will be discussed in Sect. 4.

2.2 Related Work

Intuitively, since the vehicle usually runs on the roads, a fully accurate trajectory sampled from a vehicle should always lie on the map. Therefore, apart from some unexpected map errors, which happens less frequently and is addressed by map update process [2], the difficulty of map-matching problem solely depends on the quality of the input trajectories. As studied in many papers, the quality issues in trajectories are pervasive, which mainly caused by inaccurate measurement and low sampling rate. In terms of the *measurement error*, due to the unstable connection between GPS device and satellites, the location of GPS samples usually deviate from its actual position by a random distance. Meanwhile, the *sampling error* is mainly caused by lowering the sampling frequency.

To deal with the quality issues, the map-matching problem has been studied for more than two decades. In terms of the working scenarios and applications, the current map-matching solutions can be classified into online mode and offline mode. In online map-matching, the vehicle positions are sampled continuously and are processed in a streaming fashion, which means each time the map-matching is only performed on the current sample with a limited number of preceding or succeeding samples [3,21] as reference. The process is usually simple and fast for interactive performance. In contrary, the offline map-matching is performed after the entire trajectory is obtained, so it aims for optimal matching route with less constraint on processing time.

From the methodology perspective, Quddus et al. [14] first conducted a comprehensive review of the map-matching algorithms proposed before 2007. The paper classified the methods into four categories, namely *geometric*, *topology*, *probabilistic* and *advanced*. The *geometric* methods only focus on the distance between trajectory elements and the road network, while the *topology* methods take into consideration the connectivity and shape similarity. The *probabilistic* methods try to model the uncertainty of trajectory, including the measurement error and the unknown travel path between two samples, and they aim to find a path that has the highest probability to generate the given trajectory. The *advanced* category contains methods that are based on some advanced models, like Kalman Filter, particle filter and fuzzy logic. This categorisation shows the evolution of map-matching research, which starts from simple, fast but inaccurate geometric-based methods to more complicated but accurate probability/advanced solutions. It is by far the most comprehensive survey of this field. However, after more than ten years' development, most of the methods mentioned in the paper has been outperformed by their new successors and the previous categorisation also requires a revisit. Several surveys proposed afterwards reviewed the methods in certain perspectives. Hashemi et al. [4] targeted at the online map-matching scenario. Kubička et al. discussed the map-matching problem based on the applications [8], namely *navigation*, *tracking* and *mapping*. Other categorisations also appear recently (*incremental max-weight*, *global max-weight* and *global geometry*[19]) which shows that there is still no consensus on how to classify the algorithms technically. However, all of the existing categorisations inherit the same idea from Quddus' survey [14] with minor variations, which fail to categorise the recent methods for multiple reasons, explained in Sect. 3.

3   Survey of Map-Matching Algorithm

According to our study, previous categorizations fail to classify the current solutions due to three main reasons: (1) Categories for some primary methods, such as *geometric* category [14], are no longer the focus due to their weak performance. (2) Application-based classification [4,8] cannot fully distinguish the methods. Many of the map-matching algorithms, like the Hidden Markov Model (HMM) and Multiple Hypothesis Technique (MHT), apply to both online and offline scenarios for different applications. (3) Classifying algorithms by embedded mathematical tools are not feasible since many recent algorithms employ multiple mathematical tools. Furthermore, the same tool implemented in different algorithms may be used for different purposes, for example, an extended Kalman filter can be used to either estimate biases in GPS or fuse measurements from different sources [9].

Therefore, we establish a new classification that classifies the map-matching algorithms by their core matching model, which is employed to coordinate their techniques to finally achieve map-matching. In a map-matching algorithm, the map-matching model is the overall framework or matching principle for the map-matching process. A model usually consists of a set of computation components, like the calculation of distance, transition and user behaviour modelling, and a workflow connecting them. Those components are fixed while their definition and implementation vary among different methods. Existing map-matching models can be categorised into four classes: *similarity model*, *state-transition model*, *candidate-evolving model* and *scoring model*.

3.1   Similarity Model

The similarity model refers to a general approach that returns the vertices/edges that is *closest* to the trajectory geometrically and/or topologically. Intuitively, since a vehicle's movement always follows the topology of the underlying road network and the vehicle can never leap from one segment to another, the trajectory should also similar to those of the true path on the map. Therefore, the main focus in this category is how to define the *closeness*.

Distance-Based. Most of the earliest point-to-curve and curve-to-curve matching algorithms [14] follow this idea. Specifically, the point-to-curve solution projects each trajectory point to the geometric-closest edge, whereas the curve-to-curve matching algorithms project each trajectory segment to the closest edge where the *closeness* is defined by various similarity metrics. Fréchet distance is the most commonly-used distance function [18] since it considers the monotonicity and continuity of the curves. However, it is sensitive to trajectory measurement errors since its value can be dominated by the outliers. As an alternative, Longest Common Subsequence (LCSS)[23] divide a trajectory into multiple segments and find the shortest path on the map for each pair of start and end points of a trajectory segment. The shortest paths are then concatenated and form the final path while their corresponding LCSS scores are summed as the final score. Then, the path whose LCSS score is higher than a predefined threshold is regarded as the final matching result.

Pattern-Based. The pattern-based algorithms utilise the historical map-matched data to answer new map-matching queries by finding similar travel patterns [22]. The assumption is that people tend to travel on the same paths given a pair of origin and destination points. Therefore, by referring to the historical trajectories that are similar to the query trajectory, its candidate paths can be obtained without worrying about the sparseness of trajectory samples. Specifically, a historical trajectory or a trajectory obtained by concatenating multiple historical trajectories will be referred to if each point of this trajectory is in the safe region around the query trajectory. The algorithm finally uses a scoring function to decide the optimal route. However, due to the sparsity and disparity of historical data, the query trajectory may not be fully covered by historical trajectories especially in some rarely travelled regions, which leads to a direct matching process.

3.2 State-Transition Model

The state-transition models build a weighted topological graph which contains all possible routes the vehicle might travel. In this graph, the vertices represent the possible *states* the vehicle may be located at a particular moment, while the edges represent the *transitions* between states at different timestamps. Different from the road network, the weight of a graph element represents the possibility of a state or a transition, and the best matching results comes from the optimal path in the graph globally. There are three major ways of building the graph and solving the optimal path problem, namely Hidden Markov model (HMM), Conditional Random Field (CRF) and the Weighted Graph Technique (WGT).

Hidden Markov Model. HMM is one of the most widely used map-matching models as it simulates the road network topology meanwhile considers the reasonability of a path. HMM focuses on the case when states in the Markov chain are unobservable (hidden) but can be estimated according to the given observations associated with them. This model fits in the map-matching process naturally. Each trajectory sample is regarded as the observation, while the vehicle actual location on the road, which is unknown, is the hidden states. In fact, due to the trajectory measurement error, all the roads near the observation can potentially be the actual vehicle location (state), each of which with a probability (emission probability). As the trajectory travels continuously, the transition between two consecutive timestamps is concluded by the travel possibility (transition probability) between their candidate states. Therefore, the objective is to find an optimal path which connects one candidate in every timestamp. The final path is obtained by the Viterbi algorithm which utilises the idea of dynamic programming. The major difference between various HMM-based algorithms is their definition of emission probability and transition probability. Unlike the emission probability, which is defined identically in most papers, the definition of the transition probability varies since the travel preference can be affected by plenty of factors. Some works [11] prefers a candidate pair whose distance is similar to the distance between the observation pair, while others consider velocity changes [3], turn restriction [12], closeness to the shortest path, the heading mismatch and travel penalty on U-turns, tunnels and bridges. Besides, HMM is also applied to online scenario [3]. However, to build a reasonable Markov chain, online HMM-based algorithms usually suffer from latency problems, which means a point is matched after a certain delay.

Conditional Random Field. CRF is utilized in many areas as an alternative to HMM to avoid the selection bias problem [6]. As both CRF and HMM are statistic models, the major difference is that CRF models interactions among observations while HMM models only model the relation between an observation with the state at the same stage and its closest predecessor. Hunter et al. [6] proposed a CRF-based map-matching algorithm that can be applied to both online and offline situations with high accuracy. Its overall approach is similar to HMM-based algorithms but with different transition probability which considers the maximum speed limit and the driving patterns of drivers. However, the problem shared by both HMM and CRF is the lack of a recovery strategy for the match deviation. Since once a path is confirmed, it will be contained by all future candidate paths, which hurts the online scenarios especially.

Weighted Graph Technique. WGT refers to a model that infers the matching path from a weighted candidate graph, where the nodes are candidate road points of location measurements and edges are only formed between two nodes corresponding to two consecutive samples. In most WGT-based algorithms, candidate points are the closest points on road segments in a radius of measurements [5,10], which is similar to HMM. The process of the WGT can be summarized as three steps: (1) Initializing the candidate graph. (2) Weighting edges in the graph using a scoring function. (3) Inferring a path based on the weighted graph.

Algorithms fall in this category mainly differs from each other in weighting functions. Lou et al. [10] firstly propose the WGT. It weights an edge simply based on a spatial cost and a temporal cost, where the spatial cost is modelled on the distance between candidate c_i to its observed position p_i and the shortest length between c_i and c_{i+1} whereas the temporal cost is modelled on the velocity reasonability. Based on Lou's design, the following work further considers mutual influences between neighbouring nodes, road connectivity, travel time reasonability [5] and other road features (traffic lights, left turns, etc.).

3.3   Candidate-Evolving Model

Candidate-evolving model refers to a model which holds a set of candidates (also known as particles or hypotheses) during map-matching. The candidate set is initiated based on the first trajectory sample and keeps evolving by adding new candidates propagated from old ones close to the latest measurements while pruning irrelevant ones. Interpreting a candidate as a vote, by maintaining the candidate set, the algorithms are able to find a segment with the most votes, thereby, determining the matching path. Compare to the state-transition model, the candidate-evolving model is more robust to the off-track matching issue since the current matching is influenced not only by a previously defined solution, but also by other candidates. The particle filter (PF) and the Multiple Hypothesis Technique (MHT) are two representative solutions.

Particle Filter. PF is a state estimation technique that combines Monte Carlo sampling methods with Bayesian Inference. This technique has been utilized to support map-matching by the way of sensor fusion and measurement correction [17], while it is also applicable to directly address map-matching problem [1]. The general idea of the PF model is to recursively estimate the Probability Density Function (PDF) of the road network section around the observation as time advances. Here, the PDF is approximated by N discrete particles, each particle maintains a weight representing how consistent it is to the location observation. The process of a PF can be summarized as follows: Initially, N particles are sampled with the same weight representing different locations in the local road network. The weight of each particle keeps getting updated as new observations are received. Then the PDF for the road network section around the new observations is calculated and the area with the highest probability is determined as the matched region. A resampling stage starts afterwards, where a new set of particles are derived based on the current set. The particles with higher weights are more likely to propagate according to moving status to feed particles for the next cycle, while those with low weights are likely to die out.

Multiple Hypothesis Technique. Similar to PF, the MHT also tries to maintain a list of candidate road matches for the initial trajectory point and the list is expected to be as large as possible to ensure correct result coverage. However, different from the PF which iterate through all possibilities over time, the MHT is a much simpler model that inherits the idea of maintaining hypotheses but manages to reduce computation during the process. An MHT evaluates each candidate road edge (or point) based on a scoring function instead of trying to approximate the complicated PDF for the neighbour map area. Thereby, the computation cost of the MHT is dramatically reduced. According to the intuition, the MHT can be easily adopted in online scenario [16]. Moreover, since it possesses all the possibility of previous hypotheses, Taguchi et al. [16] propose a prediction model which extends the hypotheses to further predict the future route, which can achieve better online map-matching accuracy without introducing latency.

3.4   Scoring Model

Naïve Weighting. A group of algorithms [13,15] apply the weight without using a particular model. Instead, they simply assign a group of candidates to each trajectory segment (or location observation) and find a road edge from each group that maximizes the predefined scoring function. The found segment in every timestamp is either returned if applied to the online scenario or waited to be joint with other matched segments if applied in the offline scenario. Most recent work in this category [15] achieves a lane-level map-matching performance. The algorithm first identifies lanes in each road by utilising the road width information in the map and partition them into grids accordingly. The algorithm then finds candidate lane grids around the observed location and scores these grids at each timestamp. The grid results in the maximum score are then returned. The scoring function is a linear combination of four features, i.e. the proximity between the grid and trajectory sample, the estimated location of the vehicle at the next time stage, the reachability from the grid and the intention of a turn. These features are modelled individually, their scores can be obtained from the corresponding models in every timestamp. In addition, feature scores are weighted differently in the scoring function whose coefficients are computed by a training process before map-matching starts.

4   Challenges and Evaluations

Despite various of map-matching models are proposed to deal with trajectory quality issues, the current solutions still fail to achieve decent matching quality in all scenarios. Therefore, in this section, we will discuss several major challenges caused by data quality issues that are affecting the map-matching results. We will demonstrate them both visually and experimentally to exemplify their significance.

4.1   Experimental Settings

As listed in Table 1, we use four datasets for our experiments. The *Global*[7] dataset is a public dataset for map-matching evaluation. It contains 100 GPS trajectories sampled from 100 different areas all over the world, each of which is provided with a dedicate underlying map. Besides, we extract three sub-areas, namely *Beijing-U*, *Beijing-R* and *Beijing-M*, from a commercial dataset which contains taxi trajectories in Beijing. The reason for choosing these four datasets is their diversity in terms of trajectory quality and map density. The *Global* dataset has the best trajectory accuracy and its maps are also very sparse. The *Beijing-U* and *Beijing-R* represent two maps extracted from urban and rural areas, respectively. They have roughly the same size but different map density ($27.3 vs 13.9$), so they can be used to evaluate the influence of map density to map-matching results. *Beijing-M* is a larger map area with more trajectories for large-scale performance test.

Table 1. Summary of experiment datasets

Name	Input trajectory			Road network			
	Trajectory count	Trajectory point count	Sampling rate (sec)	# of vertices + mini nodes	# of edges	Map size (km²)	Map density (km/km²)
Global	100		1	N/A	N/A	N/A	N/A
Beijing-U	7,905	247,544	11.0	7,672	4,484	9.9	27.3
Beijing-R	3,106	119,612	8.6	3,927	1,326	9.9	13.9
Beijing-M	73,072	3,285,934	10.3	41,353	22,580	57.0	24.2

Our experiments are performed on a single server with two Intel(R) Xeon(R) CPU E5-2630 with 10 cores/20 threads at 2.2 GHz each, 378 GB memory and Ubuntu 16.04. Both the route matching result $\mathcal{MR}(Tr)$ and the corresponding ground-truth are regarded as sets of road edges and are evaluated by F-measure, which is commonly used in map-matching evaluation [15,19]. The candidate map-matching algorithms used in the experiments include the most popular offline HMM map-matching [11], the most-recent offline WGT algorithm [20] and an online Scoring method [13].

4.2 Data Quality Challenges

According to our observations from the experiments, the current data quality issues affect the map-matching in three major ways: the unnecessary detours, the matching breaks and the matching uncertainty.

Unnecessary Detour. As an example shown in Fig. 1a, the matching result sometimes may contain unnecessary detours, which happens more frequently when the trajectory sampling rate is very high. In most scenarios, the detour is caused by two consecutive trajectory samples being too close to each other so that the succeeding point happens to be matched to the upper stream of its preceding point. Therefore, the shortest path between these two points has to

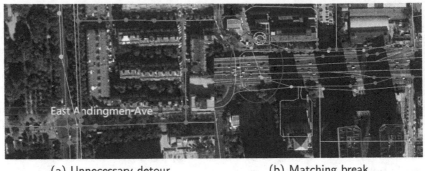

(a) Unnecessary detour   (b) Matching break

Fig. 1. Example of map-matching challenges (Color figure online)

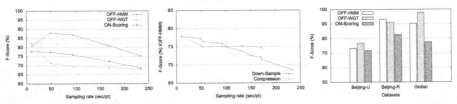

(a) Accuracy over different (b) Down-sample v.s. com- (c) Influence of map density
sampling rate   pression   and trajectory quality

Fig. 2. Experimental results

go through a long detour. To avoid such issue, the measurement error should be considered when finding the shortest path, which means a certain degree of backtrace should be allowable. Alternatively, instead of simply project trajectory samples to the candidate roads to find candidate points, the actual matching point should follow a distribution, according to the trajectory measurement error, along the candidate road.

In general, as depicted in Fig. 2a, the detour problem strongly affects the matching quality when the sampling rate is high. The result shows that it is not always the case that a higher sampling rate leads to higher matching quality especially when the measurement error becomes the major problem. Therefore, a better way of modelling the measurement error is still required.

Matching Break. The matching break is a common problem in map-matching, which is mainly caused by trajectory outliers. This happens more frequently in the state-transition matching model when the correct state falls out of the candidate range of the outlier. In this case, the states of two consecutive observations may be unreachable, leading to disconnected matching route, as shown in the green circled area in Fig. 1a. Currently, most of the solutions [11] try to overcome this problem by identifying and removing the outliers to remedy the broken route. In Fig. 2b, we apply online scoring method on *Beijing-M* with random down-sample and trajectory compression (Douglas-Peucker algorithm), respectively. The result shows that simple trajectory compression fails to prune outliers as they are usually preserved as outstanding point, which means more preprocessing step is required to remove such outliers. However, considering the detour problem in high sampling rate data, the trajectory compression achieves better performance compared with simply down-sample the trajectory as it better preserve the shape of the trajectory, which is still beneficial.

Matching Uncertainty. Although the main goal of map-matching algorithms is to reduce the uncertainty of trajectory, the matching uncertainty varies in different scenarios. One of the main factor, which is not mentioned by any of previous work, is the map density. Intuitively, the map-matching of trajectory is much harder when the map area is full of roads compared with an emptier region. As shown in Fig. 2, the map density can significantly affect the matching quality as the *Beijing-U* has much worse performance than *Beijing-R* given both of them have a similar trajectory quality. On the other hand, the trajectory quality also plays an important role since the performance on *Global* is better than on *Beijing-U* with similar map density. Therefore, achieving decent performance on dense map area is still a challenging task for future map-matching research.

5 Conclusion

In this paper, we conduct a comprehensive survey of the map-matching problem. We reveal the inability of all previous surveys in classifying new map-matching solutions. On top of that, we propose a new categorisation of existing methods from the technical perspective, which consists of similarity model, state-transition model, candidate-evolving model and scoring model. In addition, we list three major challenges (unnecessary detour, matching break and matching uncertainty) that the current map-matching algorithms are facing. To exemplify and demonstrate their influence on the current map-matching algorithms, we conduct extensive experiments over multiple datasets and map-matching algorithms. Overall, this paper concludes the current state of the map-matching problem and provides guidance to future research directions.

References

1. Bonnifait, P., Laneurit, J., Fouque, C., Dherbomez, G.: Multi-hypothesis map-matching using particle filtering. In: 16th World Congress for ITS Systems and Services, pp. 1–8 (2009)
2. Chao, P., Hua, W., Zhou, X.: Trajectories know where map is wrong: an iterative framework for map-trajectory co-optimisation. World Wide Web, 1–27 (2019)
3. Goh, C.Y., Dauwels, J., Mitrovic, N., Asif, M.T., Oran, A., Jaillet, P.: Online map-matching based on hidden markov model for real-time traffic sensing applications. In: 2012 15th International IEEE Conference on Intelligent Transportation Systems, pp. 776–781. IEEE (2012)

4. Hashemi, M., Karimi, H.A.: A critical review of real-time map-matching algorithms: current issues and future directions. Comput. Environ. Urban Syst. **48**, 153–165 (2014)
5. Hu, G., Shao, J., Liu, F., Wang, Y., Shen, H.T.: If-matching: towards accurate map-matching with information fusion. IEEE Trans. Knowl. Data Eng. **29**(1), 114–127 (2017)
6. Hunter, T., Abbeel, P., Bayen, A.: The path inference filter: model-based low-latency map matching of probe vehicle data. IEEE Trans. Intell. Transp. Syst. **15**(2), 507–529 (2014)
7. Kubička, M., Cela, A., Moulin, P., Mounier, H., Niculescu, S.I.: Dataset for testing and training of map-matching algorithms. In: 2015 IEEE Intelligent Vehicles Symposium (IV), pp. 1088–1093. IEEE (2015)
8. Kubicka, M., Cela, A., Mounier, H., Niculescu, S.I.: Comparative study and application-oriented classification of vehicular map-matching methods. IEEE Intell. Transp. Syst. Mag. **10**(2), 150–166 (2018)
9. Li, L., Quddus, M., Zhao, L.: High accuracy tightly-coupled integrity monitoring algorithm for map-matching. Transp. Res. Part C: Emerg. Technol. **36**, 13–26 (2013)
10. Lou, Y., Zhang, C., Zheng, Y., Xie, X., Wang, W., Huang, Y.: Map-matching for low-sampling-rate GPS trajectories. In: Proceedings of the 17th ACM SIGSPATIAL International Conference on Advances in Geographic Information Systems, pp. 352–361. ACM (2009)
11. Newson, P., Krumm, J.: Hidden Markov map matching through noise and sparseness. In: Proceedings of the 17th ACM SIGSPATIAL International Conference on advances in Geographic Information Systems, pp. 336–343. ACM (2009)
12. Osogami, T., Raymond, R.: Map matching with inverse reinforcement learning. In: Twenty-Third International Joint Conference on Artificial Intelligence (2013)
13. Quddus, M., Washington, S.: Shortest path and vehicle trajectory aided map-matching for low frequency GPS data. Transp. Res. Part C: Emerg. Technol. **55**, 328–339 (2015)
14. Quddus, M.A., Ochieng, W.Y., Noland, R.B.: Current map-matching algorithms for transport applications: state-of-the art and future research directions. Transp. Res. Part C: Emerg. Technol. **15**(5), 312–328 (2007)
15. Sharath, M., Velaga, N.R., Quddus, M.A.: A dynamic two-dimensional (D2D) weight-based map-matching algorithm. Transp. Res. Part C: Emerg. Technol. **98**, 409–432 (2019)
16. Taguchi, S., Koide, S., Yoshimura, T.: Online map matching with route prediction. IEEE Trans. Intell. Transp. Syst. **20**(1), 338–347 (2018)
17. Wang, X., Ni, W.: An improved particle filter and its application to an INS/GPS integrated navigation system in a serious noisy scenario. Meas. Sci. Technol. **27**(9), 095005 (2016)
18. Wei, H., Wang, Y., Forman, G., Zhu, Y.: Map matching by Fréchet distance and global weight optimization. Technical Paper, Departement of Computer Science and Engineering, p. 19 (2013)
19. Wei, H., Wang, Y., Forman, G., Zhu, Y.: Map matching: comparison of approaches using sparse and noisy data. In: Proceedings of the 21st ACM SIGSPATIAL International Conference on Advances in Geographic Information Systems, pp. 444–447. ACM (2013)
20. Yang, C., Gidofalvi, G.: Fast map matching, an algorithm integrating hidden Markov model with precomputation. Int. J. Geogr. Inf. Sci. **32**(3), 547–570 (2018)

21. Yin, Y., Shah, R.R., Wang, G., Zimmermann, R.: Feature-based map matching for low-sampling-rate GPS trajectories. ACM Trans. Spat. Algorithms Syst. (TSAS) **4**(2), 4 (2018)
22. Zheng, K., Zheng, Y., Xie, X., Zhou, X.: Reducing uncertainty of low-sampling-rate trajectories. In: 2012 IEEE 28th International Conference on Data Engineering, pp. 1144–1155. IEEE (2012)
23. Zhu, L., Holden, J.R., Gonder, J.D.: Trajectory segmentation map-matching approach for large-scale, high-resolution GPS data. Transp. Res. Rec. **2645**(1), 67–75 (2017)

Gaussian Embedding of Large-Scale Attributed Graphs

Bhagya Hettige$^{(\boxtimes)}$, Yuan-Fang Li, Weiqing Wang, and Wray Buntine

Monash University, Melbourne, Australia
{bhagya.hettige,yuanfang.li,teresa.wang,wray.buntine}@monash.edu

Abstract. Graph embedding methods transform high-dimensional and complex graph contents into low-dimensional representations. They are useful for a wide range of graph analysis tasks including link prediction, node classification, recommendation and visualization. Most existing approaches represent graph nodes as point vectors in a low-dimensional embedding space, ignoring the uncertainty present in the real-world graphs. Furthermore, many real-world graphs are large-scale and rich in content (e.g. node attributes). In this work, we propose GLACE, a novel, scalable graph embedding method that preserves both graph structure and node attributes effectively and efficiently in an end-to-end manner. GLACE effectively models uncertainty through Gaussian embeddings, and supports inductive inference of new nodes based on their attributes. In our comprehensive experiments, we evaluate GLACE on real-world graphs, and the results demonstrate that GLACE significantly outperforms state-of-the-art embedding methods on multiple graph analysis tasks.

Keywords: Graph embedding · Link prediction · Node classification

1 Introduction

Much real-world data can be expressed as graphs, e.g. citation networks [1,6,13], social-media networks [8], language networks [12,13], and knowledge graphs [9]. Graph embedding methods transform graph nodes with highly sparse, high-dimensional content into low-dimensional representations. They are effective in capturing complex latent relationships between nodes [4,6,11,13] and have been successfully employed in a wide array of graph analysis tasks such as link prediction, node classification, recommendation and visualization. The effective embedding of graph data faces a number of challenges.

Uncertainty modelling: Most of the previous work [4,6,11,13] on graph node embedding represents nodes as point vectors in the embedding space, which fails to capture the uncertainty in node representations. Furthermore, graphs constructed from real-world data can be very complex, noisy and imbalanced. Therefore, a mere point-based representation of the nodes may not be able to capture the variability of the graph and so some hidden patterns [1]. **Scalability:**

© Springer Nature Switzerland AG 2020
R. Borovica-Gajic et al. (Eds.): ADC 2020, LNCS 12008, pp. 134–146, 2020.
https://doi.org/10.1007/978-3-030-39469-1_11

Many real-world graphs are very large, containing millions of nodes and edges. The efficient embedding of such large graphs is thus important but challenging. LINE [13] is handling large-scale graphs using an optimized loss function they develop based on local and global network structure, but it does not consider node attributes. **Inductiveness:** Most existing graph embedding approaches are transductive and cannot infer embeddings for nodes unseen at training time. In practice, however, graphs evolve with time, and new nodes and edges can be added into the graph. There are a few recent studies [1,6] which tried to provide a solution to this limitation. However, these methods either do not scale up to large graphs, or require additional information about the graph structure.

In this paper, we propose GLACE, **G**aussian representations for **L**arge-scale **A**ttributed graph **C**ontent **E**mbedding, a novel graph embedding method that addresses all of the above challenges. GLACE learns node embeddings as probability distributions from both node attributes and graph structure information in an end-to-end manner: we use node attributes to initialize the structure-based loss function, and update and transfer the learning back to the encoding function to minimize the loss. We use a proximity measure to quantify graph properties to be preserved in the embedding space, i.e. first-order proximity to learn from observed relations and second-order proximity to learn from a node's neighbourhoods. We learn from node attributes by a non-linear transformation function (encoder), and then define Gaussian embedding functions to model the uncertainty of the embedding by feeding the encoded representation. Therefore, the mean vector of the representation denotes the position of the node in the embedding space, while the covariance matrix gives the uncertainty of the node embedding. We deal with new nodes by learning from node attributes, so that a learned model can be used to infer embeddings for new nodes based on their attributes. The combination of node attributes and local sampling allows GLACE to be scalable, being able to support graphs of hundred thousand nodes with hundred thousand attributes and half a million edges on modest hardware. GLACE derives embeddings from node attributes, which allows it to converge faster during training. The main contributions of this work: **(1)** we propose a novel, end-to-end method to embed nodes as probability distributions to model **uncertainty** of the embedding, **(2)** our model is **inductive** as it can infer embedding for unseen nodes using node attributes, **(3)** our model is **scalable** and **efficient**, and supports graphs with hundreds of thousands of nodes on modest hardware with a fast convergence rate, while other methods require significantly more memory, more time, or both, and **(4)** we perform extensive experiments on real-world datasets for link prediction, node classification, induction, and visualization, and GLACE significantly outperforms the baselines.

2   Related Work

Below we give a brief overview of recent graph embedding techniques. A more extensive introduction to the area can be found in these recent survey studies [2,3,5].

Unsupervised graph embedding approaches attempt to preserve graph properties in the embedding space. Random walk-based methods such as Deep-Walk [11] and node2vec [4] generate random walks for each node, and learn embeddings using these node sequences with a technique similar to Skip-Gram [10]. LINE [13] learns from proximity measures considering first- and second-order proximity. SDNE [16] proposes a semi-supervised model, in which they learn first-order proximity in the supervised component and second-order proximity in the unsupervised component. Graph2Gauss [1] proposes a personalized ranking scheme such that for a given anchor node, nodes in the immediate neighborhood are closer in the embedding space, while nodes multiple hops away are placed increasingly more distant to the node. Variational graph auto-encoders (VGAE) [7] is also an unsupervised learning method for undirected graphs.

Learning *uncertainty* of embeddings has been shown to produce meaningful representations [1,15]. Word2gauss [15] proposes a Gaussian embedding space to model word embeddings. Graph2Gauss [1] captures uncertainty of graph nodes similarly. Both methods show that capturing embedding uncertainty learns more meaningful representations in their evaluation tasks. Another recent study [17] proposes to learn node embeddings as Gaussian distributions using the Wasserstein metric rather than KL divergence, as the former preserves edge transitivity.

Graphs can vary greatly in *size* (i.e. number of nodes and edges). Some methods are designed to be scalable while others do not scale well due to high space and/or time complexities. LINE [13] is a method designed to handle large-scale graphs efficiently using negative sampling and edge sampling optimization strategies. Graph2Gauss [1], on the other hand, exhibits poor scalability as it needs to compute hops for each node up to a predefined number. This process is not only time consuming, but also consumes significant memory.

3   GLACE Methodology

3.1   Notations and Problem Definition

Homogeneous Graph: Let $G = (\mathcal{V}, E, \mathbf{X})$ be an attributed homogeneous graph, where $\mathcal{V}$ is the set of nodes, E is the set of edges between nodes in $\mathcal{V}$, where each ordered pair of nodes $(i, j) \in E$ is associated with a weight $w_{ij} > 0$ for edge from i to j, and $\mathbf{X} \in \mathbb{R}^{|\mathcal{V}| \times D}$ is the attribute matrix of the nodes which represents an attribute matrix of $\mathcal{V}$, where $\mathbf{x}_i \in \mathbf{X}$ is a D-dimensional attribute vector of node i.

GLACE Embedding: GLACE aims to represent each node $i \in \mathcal{V}$ as a low-dimensional Gaussian distribution embedding, $\mathbf{z}_i = \mathcal{N}(\mu_i, \Sigma_i)$, where $\mu_i \in \mathbb{R}^L$, $\Sigma_i \in \mathbb{R}^{L \times L}$ where L is the embedding dimension with $L \ll |\mathcal{V}|, D_k$, in embedding space $\mathbb{R}^L$, such that nodes close to each other in the original graph are also close in the embedding space. We learn Σ_i as a diagonal covariance vector, $\Sigma_i \in \mathbb{R}^L$, instead of a covariance matrix to reduce the number of parameters to learn.

3.2   Overall Architecture

GLACE is an end-to-end framework for learning node embeddings using both node attributes and graph structure in an efficient manner. Node attributes are first fed through a non-linear transformation function and then through two non-linear transformation functions to obtain a mean vector and diagonal covariance vector which represent a Gaussian embedding. GLACE is flexible in handling different node attribute formats, such as text and images, since we can define the encoder architecture accordingly. Our unsupervised loss function is defined based on graph structure. We learn local and global graph structure using our proximity measure, since we can optimize the function using negative sampling [10] to achieve scalability. Local structure is learnt with first-order proximity, i.e. based on edge weight between nodes [2], and global structure is learnt with second-order proximity, i.e. based on similarity between neighborhoods of a pair of nodes [2]. GLACE learns in an end-to-end manner: **forward learning:** we use encoded node attributes as input to the optimization function of Graph Structure Encoding, and **back-propagation:** we minimize the optimization function of Graph Structure Encoding by updating the node embeddings, and then propagating the update back to the Node Attribute Encoding part.

3.3   Node Attribute Encoding

We learn node attributes using two levels of transformations, encoding and Gaussian embedding. At the first level, we use a multi-layer perceptron (MLP) to encode the node attribute information and generate an intermediate vector from node attribute information. We use a feed-forward encoder, $f : \mathcal{V} \rightarrow \mathbb{R}^m$ which takes an attribute vector $\mathbf{x}_i \in \mathbf{X}$ as input for node i, and outputs a m-dimensional intermediate vector.

$$\mathbf{u}_i = f(\mathbf{x}_i) = \mathbf{W}\mathbf{x}_i + \mathbf{b} \tag{1}$$

The attribute encoder of the model is expressed using weight matrix $\mathbf{W} \in \mathbb{R}^{D \times m}$ and bias vector $\mathbf{b} \in \mathbb{R}^m$ where m is the dimension of the hidden representation. Note here that, we can easily alter the encoder architecture such that it aligns and captures different types of inputs (e.g. images, text). But for efficiency purposes we have only considered an MLP architecture. This intermediate vector $\mathbf{u}_i$ is then used as input to two encoders f_μ and f_Σ to learn $\boldsymbol{\mu}$ and $\boldsymbol{\Sigma}$ in the Gaussian distributions. The final latent representation of node i of type k is $\mathbf{z}_i = \mathcal{N}(\boldsymbol{\mu}_i, \boldsymbol{\Sigma}_i)$, where $\boldsymbol{\mu}_i = f_\mu(f(\mathbf{x}_i))$ and $\boldsymbol{\Sigma}_i = f_\Sigma(f(\mathbf{x}_i))$.

$$\boldsymbol{\mu}_i = f_\mu(\mathbf{u}_i) = \mathbf{W}_\mu \mathbf{u}_i + \mathbf{b}_\mu \tag{2}$$

$$\boldsymbol{\Sigma}_i = f_\Sigma(\mathbf{u}_i) = ELU(\mathbf{W}_\Sigma \mathbf{u}_i + \mathbf{b}_\Sigma) + 1 \tag{3}$$

The two functions defined in Eq. 2 with $\mathbf{W}_\mu \in \mathbb{R}^{m \times L}$ and $\mathbf{b}_\mu \in \mathbb{R}^L$, and in Eq. 3 with $\mathbf{W}_\Sigma \in \mathbb{R}^{m \times L}$ and $\mathbf{b}_\Sigma \in \mathbb{R}^L$ denote the Mean Encoder and Covariance Encoder respectively. Note that, as the difference between different node types have been caught by $\mathbf{u}_i$ generated by f_k, all the node types share the same Mean Encoder and Covariance Encoder in GLACE to achieve good scalability. Here for the uncertainty representation, we constrain the covariance matrix to be diagonal to reduce the number of parameters to learn. The exponential linear unit (ELU) is used as the activation function in the Covariance Encoder. An ELU can have negative values as well, and it drives the mean of the activation outputs be closer to zero which makes learning and convergence much faster. We add 1 to obtain positive covariance.

Note that, even inside the Node Attribute Encoding component, GLACE also learns the parameters in an end-to-end manner. Through the shared parameter $\mathbf{u}_i$, GLACE forwards the updating inside Encoder f_k to Gaussian Encoders f_μ and f_Σ, and propagates the updating inside Gaussian Encoders back to f_k automatically during the optimization process.

3.4   Graph Structure Encoding

GLACE aims at capturing both local (first-order) and global (higher-order) proximity information in graphs. But considering the scalability to large-scale graphs, for the global information, GLACE only encodes second-order proximity. For each node i, the learned Gaussian distributions, $\mathbf{z}_i$, in Sect. 3.3 are used as the input to the Graph Structure Encoding component in this section.

Dissimilarity Measure: Let $d(\mathbf{z}_i, \mathbf{z}_j)$ be the dissimilarity measure between latent representations of two nodes $i, j \in \mathcal{V}$. Since $\mathbf{z}_i$ and $\mathbf{z}_j$ are Gaussian distribution embedding, we should select a dissimilarity measure to be a function to *measure the dissimilarity between two probability distributions*. Therefore, the dissimilarity measure between two latent representations is calculated using asymmetric KL divergence, $d(\mathbf{z}_i, \mathbf{z}_j) = D_{KL}(\mathbf{z}_j || \mathbf{z}_i)$. Alternatively, we could also use a Wasserstein metric instead of KL divergence as in [17]. Since KL divergence is asymmetric, for undirected graphs we extend the distance to a symmetric dissimilarity measure as:

$$d(\mathbf{z}_i, \mathbf{z}_j) = \frac{1}{2}(D_{KL}(\mathbf{z}_i || \mathbf{z}_j) + D_{KL}(\mathbf{z}_j || \mathbf{z}_i)) \qquad (4)$$

First-Order Proximity: We learn first-order proximity of nodes, by modelling local pairwise proximity between two connected nodes in the graph. The empirical probability for first-order proximity measure observed in the original graph between nodes i and j is defined as the ratio of the weight of the edge (i, j) to the total of the weights of all the edges in the graph. For each *undirected* edge (i, j) we define the joint probability as a sigmoid function between node i and j. These two functions can be defined as respectively:

$$\hat{p}_1(i,j) = \frac{w_{ij}}{\Sigma_{(\hat{i},\hat{j})\in E}w_{\hat{i}\hat{j}}} \text{ and } p_1(i,j) = \frac{1}{1 + \exp\left(d(\mathbf{z}_i, \mathbf{z}_j)\right)} \quad (5)$$

We preserve the first-order proximity by minimizing the distance between the two distributions, $O_1 = D_{KL}(\hat{p}_1 || p_1)$, for all edges. Motivated by this function, we use the following objective function as in LINE [13] for first-order proximity:

$$O_1 = - \sum_{(i,j)\in E} w_{ij} \log p_1(i,j) \quad (6)$$

Second-Order Proximity: Nodes which have more similar neighbourhoods should be closer in embedding space with respect to the nodes with less similar neighbourhoods. The empirical probability of second-order proximity observed for edge (i,j) can be defined as the ratio of the weight of edge (i,j) to the total weight of edges from node i to its immediate neighborhood, $N(i)$. Similarly to LINE, each node is represented with two complementary embeddings, the first embedding $\mathbf{z}_i$, is as defined previously, and the second is the context embedding, h'_i, defined in Eqs. 10 and 11. For each *directed* edge (i,j) (if the edge is undirected, it can be treated as two edges with equal weights and opposite directions) we define the probability of *context* j generated by node i as a softmax function. The two probability distributions are defined as follows:

$$\hat{p}_2(j|i) = \frac{w_{ij}}{\Sigma_{\hat{i}\in N(i)}w_{ii}} \text{ and } p_2(j|i) = \frac{\exp\left(-d(\mathbf{z}_i, \mathbf{z}'_j)\right)}{\Sigma_{\hat{i}\in V}\exp\left(-d(\mathbf{z}_i, \mathbf{z}'_{\hat{i}})\right)} \quad (7)$$

We preserve the second-order proximity by minimizing the distance between the two distributions, $O_2 = \sum_{i\in V}\lambda_i D_{KL}(\hat{p}_2(.|i)||p_2(.|i))$, where λ_i is the prestige of node i. Motivated by this [13] we preserve the second-order proximity:

$$O_2 = - \sum_{(i,j)\in E} w_{ij} \log p_2(i,j) \quad (8)$$

When we define the second-order proximity measure, the neighbourhood nodes are considered as contexts for the anchor node. Therefore, we should define another set of node attribute encoding functions to model the context representations used for neighbourhood nodes, similarly to the Eqs. 1, 2 and 3. The encoder for context nodes is $f' : V \rightarrow \mathbb{R}^m$. The latent representation of context node i is $\mathbf{z}'_i = \mathcal{N}(\boldsymbol{\mu}'_i, \boldsymbol{\Sigma}'_i)$, where $\boldsymbol{\mu}'_i = f'_\mu(f'(\mathbf{x}_i))$ and $\boldsymbol{\Sigma}'_i = f'_\Sigma(f'(\mathbf{x}_i))$.

$$\mathbf{u}'_i = f'(\mathbf{x}_i) = \mathbf{W}'\mathbf{x}_i + \mathbf{b}' \quad (9)$$
$$\boldsymbol{\mu}'_i = f'_\mu(\mathbf{u}_i) = \mathbf{W}'_\mu\mathbf{u}_i + \mathbf{b}'_\mu \quad (10)$$
$$\boldsymbol{\Sigma}'_i = f'_\Sigma(\mathbf{u}_i) = ELU(\mathbf{W}'_\Sigma\mathbf{u}_i + \mathbf{b}'_\Sigma) + 1 \quad (11)$$

3.5 Model Optimization

The objective function in Eq. 8 is a bottleneck as it requires evaluation on the entire set of nodes for the optimization of one single edge as shown in Eq. 7. Based on the negative sampling approach [10,13], we sample several negative edges (i.e., defined as N) for each edge in the training set to optimize the objective function. With negative sampling our objective function O_2 in Eq. 8 becomes:

$$\sum_{(i,j)\in E} \left(\log \sigma(-d(\mathbf{z}_i, \mathbf{z}'_j)) + \sum_{n=1}^{N} \mathbb{E}_{v_n \sim P_n(v)} \log \sigma(d(\mathbf{z}_i, \mathbf{z}'_{v_n})) \right) \tag{12}$$

Similarly, we can efficiently compute O_1 in Eq. 6 with negative sampling:

$$\sum_{(i,j)\in E} \left(\log \sigma(-d(\mathbf{z}_i, \mathbf{z}_j)) + \sum_{n=1}^{N} \mathbb{E}_{v_n \sim P_n(v)} \log \sigma(d(\mathbf{z}_i, \mathbf{z}_{v_n})) \right) \tag{13}$$

where we draw negative edges from the noise distribution $P_n(v)$ with negative node probability distribution, $P_n(v) \propto out\_degree(v)^{3/4}$ for $v \in V$. Similarly, we can optimize objective function O_1 in Eq. 6, replacing $\mathbf{z}'_j$ and $\mathbf{z}'_{v_n}$ in Eq. 12 with $\mathbf{z}_j$ and $\mathbf{z}_{v_n}$ respectively. We further optimize our training process by implementing early stopping for training algorithm using a validation set and assessing the performance at each iteration.

Table 1. Statistics of the real-world graphs.

Dataset	$|\mathcal{V}_1|$	$|E|$	D_1	#Labels
Cora-ML	2,995	8,416	2,879	7
Cora	19,793	65,311	8,710	70
Citeseer	4,230	5,358	2,701	6
DBLP	17,716	105,734	1,639	4
Pubmed	18,230	79,612	500	3
ACM	115,772	539,910	124,856	–

3.6 Complexity Analysis

Training of GLACE takes $O(T \times b \times (dN + (N + 2) \times (Dm + mL + L))) = O(T \times b \times N \times (d + Dm + mL + L))$, where T is the maximum number of iterations, b is the batch size, d is the maximum node degree, N is the number of negative samples, D is the attribute vector dimension, m is the intermediate vector dimension (hidden layer of Node Attribute Encoder), and L is the embedding dimension. For each edge in the batch, fetching N negative samples takes $O(dN)$ time. For each of the $(N + 2)$ nodes, i.e., i, j and $\{v_n\}_{v_n \in Neg(i)}$, we compute and update parameters in the Node Attribute Encoder with two levels of transformations (i.e., f_{enc}, f_μ and f_Σ) in $O(Dm) + O(2mL) + O(2L) = O(Dm + mL + L)$ time. Since GLACE initializes node embeddings using encoded node attribute information, it can achieve faster convergence in optimization (in practice we can see that GLACE starts to reach optimization point at $T = 100$. We will discuss further our method's scalability over LINE in the experiments section).

4 Experiments

We evaluate our method with state-of-the-art baselines on: link prediction, node classification, inductive learning and visualization. In addition, we demonstrate the scalability and inductiveness of our model. Source code for GLACE is publicly available at https://github.com/bhagya-hettige/GLACE.

4.1 Datasets

We use six publicly available real-world attributed graphs (Table 1). These are citation networks in which nodes denote papers and edges represent citation relations. For each paper, we have TF-IDF vectors of the paper's abstract as attributes. Cora-ML is a subset extracted from the Cora citation network. The larger ACM network is constructed using Aminer data [14].

4.2 Compared Algorithms and Setup

All the experiments were performed on a MacBook Pro laptop with 16 GB memory and a 2.6 GHz Intel Core i7 processor. For each of the following models, we give maximum of 5 h as a threshold for training.

Attributes: for evaluation tasks, we use raw node attributes as input features instead of node embeddings. **node2vec** [4]: is a random walk based node embedding method that maximizes the likelihood of preserving nodes' neighbourhood using biased random walks starting from each node. Therefore, node2vec considers only second-order proximity. **LINE** [13]: is for large-scale non-attributed graphs and uses first-order and second-order proximity information. **GraphSAGE** [6]: is an inductive learning approach for attributed graphs which learns an embedding function by sampling and aggregating features of local neighbourhoods of nodes. We use the unsupervised version of GraphSAGE with the pooling aggregator (which performed best for citation networks according to [6]). Since we use node class labels in the node classification task, supervised version of GraphSAGE is not considered in evaluation. **Graph2Gauss (G2G)** [1]: produces Gaussian node embeddings using node attributes and graph structure, which introduces a personalized ranking of nodes based on neighbouring hops. G2G is applicable to homogeneous graphs with plain/attributed nodes and (un)directed and unweighted edges.

We also include a non Gaussian representation model to assess the effectiveness of uncertainty modelling. **LACE** (without Gaussians): We use a version of our method in which we represent nodes as vectors in an embedding space using node attributes and graph structure. **GLACE** (with Gaussians): This is the complete version of our method which produces Gaussian distribution representations for graph nodes using node attributes and graph structure.

For LINE and GLACE, we consider first-order (1st), second-order (2nd) and a concatenated representation of first- and second-order proximities $(1^{st} + 2^{nd})$. Accordingly, the concatenated representation would have both local and global information. For all the models, we use 128 as the dimension of the embedding. Since GLACE learns two vectors for mean and variance respectively, we set $L = 64$ to conduct a fair comparison with other methods, so the number of dimensions learned for each node still remains the same.

4.3   Link Prediction

For all the methods we extract a test set containing 20% randomly selected edges from the graph and an equal number of non-edges which are not present in the graph. For all datasets we use the same splits for all the methods. The remaining 80% of the edges are used for training the embedding models. In probability distribution based embedding methods (G2G and GLACE) we use negative KL divergence to rank the Gaussian embeddings. For other embedding methods (attributes, node2vec, LINE and LACE), we use dot product similarity of node embedding to ranking. We consider both 1st-order and 2nd-order proximity. We also consider joint embedding performance by concatenating the resulting embedding from the two proximity. For LINE, we record the concatenated embedding of the two proximities, which is identified as the best-performing setting for LINE [13]. AUC and AP scores of link prediction task are shown in Table 2.

Table 2. Link prediction performance. Experiments not completed within threshold settings are marked with "-".

Algorithm	Cora		Citeseer		DBLP		Pubmed		ACM	
	AUC	AP	AUC	AP	AUC	AP	AUC	AP	AUC	AP
Attributes	82.98	77.71	81.53	75.60	75.89	69.56	82.98	77.71	-	-
node2vec	87.86	87.19	79.91	82.08	87.03	84.36	88.74	86.58	91.18	91.49
LINE	75.23	77.96	71.20	72.11	80.01	83.09	79.97	82.86	75.32	76.81
GraphSAGE	85.30	84.72	83.33	85.38	89.63	90.12	89.43	90.90	-	-
G2G	97.87	98.03	96.28	96.54	96.35	96.79	95.75	95.65	-	-
LACE$_{(1^{st})}$	96.59	96.66	94.21	94.95	91.91	92.68	83.89	84.26	95.14	95.07
LACE$_{(2^{nd})}$	96.83	96.67	94.29	94.61	93.30	93.37	93.72	92.80	94.37	93.91
LACE$_{(1^{st}+2^{nd})}$	97.51	97.40	95.35	95.76	93.82	94.14	89.53	89.85	96.01	95.79
GLACE$_{(1^{st})}$	_98.54_	_98.46_	96.41	96.40	_98.48_	_98.33_	_97.69_	_97.42_	_98.00_	97.94
GLACE$_{(2^{nd})}$	98.43	98.31	_97.22_	_97.20_	98.16	97.95	97.02	96.56	97.94	97.79
GLACE$_{(1^{st}+2^{nd})}$	**98.60**	**98.52**	**98.43**	**98.37**	**98.55**	**98.40**	**97.82**	**97.49**	**98.34**	**98.24**

A number of important observations can be made from the tables. **(1)** GLACE clearly outperforms the state-of-art embedding methods by a significant margin in both homogeneous and bipartite graphs. The introduction of uncertainty modelling in GLACE improves performance considerably when compared to models without Gaussian embedding, i.e. node2vec, LINE and LACE. **(2)** In homogeneous graphs, GLACE$_{(1^{st}+2^{nd})}$, which learns from both the explicit edges in the graph and neighbourhood similarities, is the best performing model. **(3)** G2G shows a very competitive performance to GLACE in smaller graphs (Cora, DBLP and Pubmed) due to its hop-based node ranking scheme, but it does not scale up for large-scale graphs, ACM and Stackoverflow. **(4)** GLACE's better scalability is also shown, as it is the only attributed graph embedding model that completes the largest dataset, ACM.

4.4 Multi-class Node Classification

The node embeddings are obtained using the complete node set from the evaluated models. Similarly to [1,13], we randomly sample different percentages of labeled nodes from the graph for training a logistic regression classifier to predict class label, and use the rest of the nodes for evaluation. The percentages of nodes used for training the classifier for node classification task are $10\%, 20\%, \ldots, 90\%$. The evaluation metric we report is F1-score, and the results are averaged over 10 trials. We performed this experiment on all the evaluated graphs, and we report the results for Cora-ML, Citeseer, and DBLP datasets in Fig. 1.

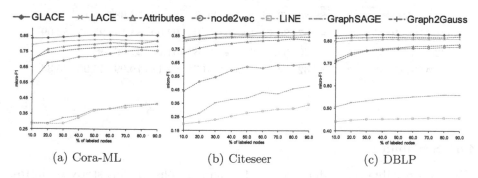

(a) Cora-ML   (b) Citeseer   (c) DBLP

Fig. 1. Node classification performance. Improvements of GLACE are statistically significant for $p < 0.01$ estimated by a paired t-test.

Based on the results, it can be seen that GLACE again consistently outperforms the baseline methods. This is clearly due to uncertainty modelling of the representations. As can be seen in the figures, there is a clear separation of node classification performance between the methods that consider node attributes and the methods that do not. An exception to this observation is GraphSAGE, which considers attributes but has a considerably poorer performance than GLACE, G2G and LR. This can be due to its aggregation process which magnifies any error. LACE (without Gaussians) is able to outperform some of the baseline methods, and this is due to the incorporation of node attributes.

4.5   Inductive Learning

We have evaluated the inductive property by training the models with 10% and 50% nodes hidden from the original graph. Then we evaluate how well the models can infer embeddings for unseen nodes on the link prediction task, comparing our model against G2G [1], which also takes attributes into account. Although GraphSAGE [6] is also an inductive node embedding method, it is not applicable in this scenario as it requires unseen nodes to be connected to existing nodes. We perform this task on Cora-ML, Citeseer, Pubmed and ACM graphs. Table 3 summarizes the results.

As can be seen from the table, GLACE outperforms G2G across all the datasets over the two hidden percentage values. It can also be observed that, GLACE suffers considerably less performance degradation than G2G when more nodes are hidden (i.e. from 10% to 50%). Since G2G requires constructing hops and keeping them in memory, we could not run experiments for G2G (with maximum number of hops to consider > 1) on the ACM dataset, which also demonstrates the scalability advantage of GLACE.

Table 3. Link prediction performance with inductive learning.

Algorithm [hidden %]	Cora-ML		Citeseer		Pubmed		ACM	
	AUC	AP	AUC	AP	AUC	AP	AUC	AP
G2G [10%]	88.83	79.34	87.96	80.39	88.96	77.08	–	–
GLACE [10%]	93.07	86.72	90.76	85.03	93.00	84.19	95.05	89.09
G2G [50%]	57.26	34.70	61.71	43.87	51.22	27.39	–	–
GLACE [50%]	87.62	74.64	83.69	70.74	92.18	79.99	93.96	85.33

4.6   Scalability

LINE is a scalable embedding method for plain graphs. In this study we introduced GLACE as an improved scalable embedding method for attributed graphs. In this section we evaluate the efficiency of our method against the large-scale embedding method, LINE, and see how the introduction of attributes and uncertainty modelling assist GLACE in converging faster for optimization. We report the validation AUC for link prediction task in ACM dataset against time. The trend is similar in other datasets. It is worth noting that even though LINE is designed for large-scale graphs, it takes a much longer time to converge (Fig. 2). This is due to the fact that the number of iterations required by LINE for convergence is proportional to the number of edges [13]. On the other hand, taking advantage of node attributes and uncertainty modelling, GLACE achieves convergence substantially faster. GLACE achieves a significant performance boost even after 1 min of training.

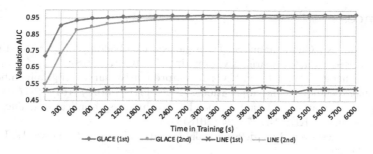

Fig. 2. GLACE's faster convergence. Link prediction performance in ACM training.

4.7 Visualization

We evaluate the ability to visualize the Cora-ML citation network. First, each model learns 128-dimensional node embeddings ($L = 64$ for Gaussians). Then, the dimensions are reduced to 2 dimensions using t-SNE. Figure 3 shows the visualizations from the models which produced the best layouts. The color of a node (i.e. a paper) represents one of the seven research areas. G2G produces moderately good clustering, but papers belonging to different areas are still not clearly separated. LACE and GLACE learn node embeddings that can clearly separate different classes. GLACE produces the best result in terms of tightly clustered papers of the same area with clearly visible boundaries.

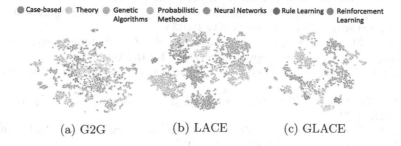

(a) G2G   (b) LACE   (c) GLACE

Fig. 3. Visualization of Cora-ML graph (L = 64).

5   Conclusion

We present GLACE, an unsupervised learning approach to efficiently learn node embeddings as probability distributions to capture uncertainty of the representations. GLACE learns from both node attributes and graph structural information, and is efficient, scalable and easily generalizable to different types of graphs. GLACE has been evaluated with respect to several state-of-the-art embedding methods in different graph analysis tasks, and the results demonstrate that our method significantly outperforms all the evaluated baselines.

References

1. Bojchevski, A., Günnemann, S.: Deep gaussian embedding of attributed graphs: unsupervised inductive learning via ranking. In: ICLR (2018)
2. Cai, H., Zheng, V.W., Chang, K.C.: A comprehensive survey of graph embedding: problems, techniques, and applications. IEEE TKDE **30**(9), 1616–1637 (2018)
3. Goyal, P., Ferrara, E.: Graph embedding techniques, applications, and performance: a survey. KBS **151**, 78–94 (2018)
4. Grover, A., Leskovec, J.: node2vec: scalable feature learning for networks. In: ACM SIGKDD (2016)
5. Hamilton, W.L., Ying, R., Leskovec, J.: Representation learning on graphs: methods and applications. IEEE Data Eng. Bull. **40**(3), 52–74 (2017)
6. Hamilton, W.L., Ying, Z., Leskovec, J.: Inductive representation learning on large graphs. In: NIPS (2017)
7. Kipf, T.N., Welling, M.: Variational graph auto-encoders. In: NIPS Workshop on Bayesian Deep Learning (2016)
8. Liao, L., He, X., Zhang, H., Chua, T.: Attributed social network embedding. IEEE TKDE **30**(12), 2257–2270 (2018)
9. Lin, Y., Liu, Z., Sun, M., Liu, Y., Zhu, X.: Learning entity and relation embeddings for knowledge graph completion. In: AAAI (2015)
10. Mikolov, T., Sutskever, I., Chen, K., Corrado, G., Dean, J.: Distributed representations of words and phrases and their compositionality. In: NIPS (2013)
11. Perozzi, B., Al-Rfou, R., Skiena, S.: Deepwalk: online learning of social representations. In: ACM SIGKDD (2014)
12. Tang, J., Qu, M., Mei, Q.: PTE: predictive text embedding through large-scale heterogeneous text networks. In: ACM SIGKDD (2015)
13. Tang, J., Qu, M., Wang, M., Zhang, M., Yan, J., Mei, Q.: LINE: large-scale information network embedding. In: WWW (2015)
14. Tang, J., Zhang, J., Yao, L., Li, J., Zhang, L., Su, Z.: Arnetminer: extraction and mining of academic social networks. In: ACM KDD (2008)
15. Vilnis, L., McCallum, A.: Word representations via gaussian embedding. In: ICLR (2015)
16. Wang, D., Cui, P., Zhu, W.: Structural deep network embedding. In: ACM SIGKDD (2016)
17. Zhu, D., Cui, P., Wang, D., Zhu, W.: Deep variational network embedding in wasserstein space. In: ACM SIGKDD (2018)

Geo-Social Temporal Top-k Queries in Location-Based Social Networks

Ammar Sohail[✉], Muhammad Aamir Cheema, and David Taniar

Faculty of Information Technology, Monash University, Melbourne, Australia
{ammar.sohail,aamir.cheema,david.taniar}@monash.edu

Abstract. With recent advancements in location-acquisition techniques and smart phone devices, social networks such as Foursquare, Facebook and Twitter are acquiring the location dimension while minimizing the gap between physical world and virtual social networking. This in return, has resulted in the generation of geo-tagged data at unprecedented scale and has facilitated users to fully capture and share their geo-locations with timestamps on social media. Typical location-based social media allows users to *check-in* at a location of interest using smart devices which then is published on social network and this information can be exploited for recommendation. In this paper, we propose a new type of query called *Geo-Social Temporal Top-k* ($GSTT_k$) query, which enriches the semantics of the conventional spatial query by introducing social relevance and temporal component. In addition, we propose three different schemes to answer such a query. Finally, we conduct an exhaustive evaluation of proposed schemes and demonstrate the effectiveness of the proposed approaches.

1 Introduction

The increasing use of smart phones, location-based services and recent advancements in location-acquisition technologies such as GPS, have made location information an essential part of social networks such as Facebook and Foursquare. In location-based social network (LBSN), a relationship (edges) between two entities (nodes) is not only limited to friendship, but can also be of another type such as works-at, lives-in and studies-at etc. [1]. The nodes and edges may also contain spatial and temporal information respectively such as a user's check-ins at different locations. Consider an example of a Facebook user Alice who was born in Germany, works at Monash University and checks-in at a particular restaurant [1]. Facebook records this information by linking Facebook pages of *Monash University* and *Germany* with Alice [2], e.g., Alice and Monash University are connected by an edge labelled works-at and Alice and Germany are connected with an edge labelled born-in.

Social connections assist us in making right decisions in various activities and events and thus impose some influence on us [3]. In the past few years, a large body of work has studied a wide variety of queries on location-based social networks to enable various applications. For example in [1,3], top-k queries were studied that return k places based on their distances from query as well as their

R. Borovica-Gajic et al. (Eds.): ADC 2020, LNCS 12008, pp. 147–160, 2020.
https://doi.org/10.1007/978-3-030-39469-1_12

popularity among the friends of the query user (e.g., are frequently visited by the friends). A major limitation of the existing work on top-k queries is that they ignore the temporal aspects, e.g., the popularity of a place is defined based on the whole time dimension. In real world scenarios, the users may be interested in the places that are popular during a specific time period (e.g., during Christmas holidays, or within last six months etc.). Inspired by this, in this paper, we study the problem of finding *top-k* places considering their distance from the query q and popularity of a place in q's social circle during given time interval. Consider an example of a visitor from Switzerland visiting Melbourne and wants to find a nearby *café* which serves *Rösti* (a traditional Swedish hot cake) with coffee and has become popular (e.g., frequently visited) among people from Switzerland during last year. This involves utilizing spatial information (i.e., nearby *café*, check-ins), social information (i.e., people who were born-in Switzerland) as well as temporal information (i.e., *cafés* that are visited during last year).

The applications of such queries are not limited to traditional location-based social services and can also be used in disaster management, public health, security, tourism etc. For example, in disease monitoring, we may want to find frequently visited places (top-k) in last 6 months by people infected by Ebola virus [3]. Consider a health-based social network where each health risk (e.g., Ebola) is an entity and people affected by it are connected to it via an edge. One can issue a query to find the top-k frequently visited places in the last 6 months by the one-hop neighbors of the Ebola entity.

Although several types of queries have been investigated on LBSNs [4], to the best of our knowledge, none of the existing methods are applicable to answer the queries similar to the above; that aim at finding nearby places that are popular among a particular group of users satisfying social and temporal constraint. Motivated by this, in this paper, we formalize this problem as a *Geo-Social Temporal Top-k* ($GSTT_k$) query and propose efficient query processing techniques. Specifically, a $GSTT_k$ query retrieves top-k places (points of interest) ranked according to their spatial, social and temporal relevance to the query user. A formal definition is provided in Sect. 3.1 and we make the following contributions in this paper.

- To the best of our knowledge, we are the first to study the $GSTT_k$ query that retrieves nearby places popular among a particular group of users in the social network during specified time interval.
- At first, we present two different approaches i.e., *Social-First* and *Spatial-First* to solve our problem and then we propose our main algorithm called *Hybrid*.
- We conduct an exhaustive evaluation of the proposed schemes using real dataset and demonstrate the effectiveness of the proposed approaches. Our experiments show that our main algorithm outperforms the other two.

2   Related Work

Geo-Social queries recently became more visible to researchers due to the emergence of handheld technology [4,5]. In [5], they study *skyline operator* and introduce a new type of query. In skyline queries, a query user does not need to have adequate domain knowledge to be able to decide upon the balance factor which is mandatory for top-k queries. They adopted grid-based partitioning schemes to quickly filter the places that cannot be the part of candidate objects. However, their techniques cannot handle the temporal component and thus, cannot be exploited to answer our work. Also, nearest neighbour queries have been widely utilized in location-based social networks [6,7].

Top-k queries fetch top-k objects based on a user defined scoring function and have been extensively studied [1,3,8]. In [3], they introduce a new type of group query where a group of users may want to plan an activity and are looking for a suitable venue based on its popularity among users' social circles. However, their work cannot be applied to answer our work which includes temporal information. The work presented in this paper builds on our previous work [1,3] which study top-k and skyline queries on LBSNs by considering social and spatial aspects. However, the major difference is the temporal aspect which is addressed in this paper.

Temporal queries retrieve query results based on given temporal properties. It is noteworthy that time dimension has strong influence in many domains for example, Topic Detection and Tracking, Spatial queries, Information retrieval, Top-k queries, Geo-Textual queries [9,10]. Recently, researchers started investigating periodic patterns of user preferences (e.g., weekend night interests). One solution is to add a time dimension to user-item matrix and apply techniques introduced in [11]. Work proposed in [12] offers time-aware recommendations using a user-based collaborative filtering method. However, none of the proposed works exploit user's social circle to recommend point of interests (POIs).

In an early attempt on bulk insertion for an R-tree, the data items to be inserted are first sorted by their spatial proximity and then packed into blocks of B rectangles [13]. There is another work on the bulk insertion which uses a STLT (small-tree-large-tree) approach [14]. If a small tree covers a large area, the node of a large tree into which a small tree is inserted needs to be enlarged to enclose it. This means the STLT only works well for highly skewed data sets [15]. However, this suffers with the same problem of the R-trees being inserted may increase the overall overlap of the target R-tree. To the best of our knowledge, none of existing techniques can be applied or trivially extended to solve $GSTT_k$ query.

3   Preliminaries

3.1   Problem Definition

Location Based Social Network (LBSN): A *location-based social network* consists of a set of entities U (e.g., users, Facebook Pages etc.) and a set of places P as defined in our previous work [5].

Score of a Place p: Given a query user q, a range r and a temporal interval $I[st, et]$ (where st denotes start time and et denotes end time), the score of a place $p \in P$ is 0 if $||q, p|| \geq r$ where $||q, p||$ is the Euclidean distance between query location and p. If $||q, p|| \leq r$, the score of p is a weighted sum of its spatial score ($p_{spatial}$) and its social score (number of q's friends check-ins in the given temporal interval I) (p_{social}).

$$p.score = \alpha \times p_{spatial} + (1 - \alpha) \times p_{social} \tag{1}$$

where α is a parameter used to control the relative importance of spatial and social scores. The social score p_{social} is computed as in our previous work [5]. Let's take the one-hop neighbors of the query user (denoted as F_q) considering a particular relationship type for example, if the relationship is works-at and the query entity is a Facebook Page for the company Samsung, then F_q is a set of users who work at Samsung. Although our techniques can handle any type of relationship, for the ease of presentation, in the rest of the paper we only consider the friendship relationships [3]. In this context, F_q contains the friends of the query user q. Let $p.visitors$ denotes the set of all users that visited (i.e., checked-in at) the place p during given temporal interval $I(st, et)$. The social score p_{social} of place p is computed as follows:

$$p_{social} = \frac{|F_q \cap p.visitors|}{|F_q|} \tag{2}$$

where $|X|$ denotes the cardinality of a set X and the spatial score $p_{spatial}$ is based on how close the place is to the query location. Formally, given a range r, $p_{spatial} = 0$ if the place does not lie in the range r. Otherwise, $p_{spatial} = (r - ||q, p||)$ where $||q, p||$ indicates Euclidean distance between query location and p. Note that p_{social} is always between 0 to 1 and we normalize $p_{spatial}$ such that it is also within the range 0 to 1, e.g., the data space is normalized such that $||q, p|| \leq 1$ and $r \leq 1$ [3].

Geo-Social Temporal Top-k ($GSTT_k$) Query: Given an LBSN, a $GSTT_k$ query q returns k places with the highest scores where the score $p.score$ of each place p is computed as described above.

Example 2.1: We extend the example given in [3] and Fig. 1(a) illustrates the locations of a set of places $P = \{p_1, p_2, p_3, p_4\}$ and a query q. Let's assume that the query q is with $k = 2$, range $r = 0.15$, temporal interval I is *"during last year"* and has a set of friends $F_q = \{u_1, u_2....u_9, u_{10}\}$. The number in bracket next to each place is the number of friends of q who visited the place during last year. Figure 1(b) shows the Euclidean distances and visitors (from the friends of q i.e., F_q) of each place during all times (column 3) as well as during last year (column 4). Let's assume $\alpha = 0.5$, the spatial score of p_2 is $p_{spatial} = 0.07$, the social score of p_2 is $p_{social} = 0.30$ and by applying Eq. 1, we get the score of p_2 i.e., $p_2.score = 0.5 \times 0.07 + (1 - 0.5) \times 0.30 = 0.185$.

Similarly, for p_1, the spatial score is $p_{spatial} = 0.05$, the social score of p_1 is $p_{social} = 0.0$ and by applying the same equation, we get the score of p_1 i.e., $p_1.score = 0.5 \times 0.05 + (1 - 0.5) \times 0.0 = 0.025$. For p_3 and p_4, their scores will be $Score(p_3) = 0.205$ and $Score(p_4) = 0.115$ respectively. The result of the query q is (p_2, p_3) according to scoring function in Eq. 1.

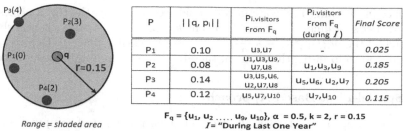

P	$\|q, p_i\|$	P_i.visitors From F_q	P_i.visitors From F_q (during I)	Final Score
P_1	0.10	u_3, u_7	-	0.025
P_2	0.08	u_1, u_3, u_9, u_7, u_8	u_1, u_3, u_9	0.185
P_3	0.14	$u_3, u_5, u_6, u_2, u_7, u_8$	u_5, u_6, u_2, u_7	0.205
P_4	0.12	u_5, u_7, u_{10}	u_7, u_{10}	0.115

Range = shaded area

$F_q = \{u_1, u_2 \ldots u_9, u_{10}\}$, $\alpha = 0.5$, $k = 2$, $r = 0.15$
I = "During Last One Year"

(a) A Query q (b) Sample Dataset

Fig. 1. Temporal Top-k Query Example

3.2 Framework Overview

The proposed framework consists of three techniques to answer $GSTT_k$ query: (I) Social-First, (II) Spatial-First and (III) Hybrid. The *Social-First* approach first processes the social component (e.g., friendship relations and their check-ins) for given temporal interval I and then processes spatial component (e.g., places in given range). The *Spatial-First* approach initially processes the spatial component followed by processing the social component. In contrast, *Hybrid approach* is capable of processing both social and spatial components simultaneously to answer the query [3]. It utilizes two types of pre-processed information related to each user $u \in U$, her check-ins and summary of her friends' check-in and; the summary of visitor's check-ins for each place p.

Precisely, we index places, users' check-in information and visitor's check-in information by exploiting R-tree [16]. We create Facility R-Tree where all places ($p \in P$) in a given dataset are indexed based on their location coordinates and Friendship Index where for each user, her friends are indexed using B^+-*Tree* sorted on their IDs. This is used to efficiently retrieve the friends based on their IDs [1].

3D Check-In R-Tree: For each user u, we create a *3D Check-In R-Tree* which indexes all the check-ins of the u. This is a 3 dimensional R-tree where two dimensions belong to the location coordinates of the check-in and the third dimension corresponds to the time of the check-in.

4 Proposed Techniques

4.1 Social-First Based Approach

In this approach, scores of the places in given range r are computed by considering the check-ins of each friend $u \in F_q$. Specifically, for each friend $u \in F_q$, its *3D Check-In R-Tree* is traversed to obtain the places in the range where u has checked-in during given temporal interval I. The social score of each checked-in place by any friend is updated. When every user $u \in F_q$ is processed, we have the final social score of each place in the range. Next, the algorithm considers each place in the range and computes its final score. Finally, the top-k places are returned. Let's assume, the score of current k_{th} place p is $Score_k$, it was shown in [1] that if the $||q, p|| \geq (r - \frac{Score_k}{\alpha})$, we can prune that place p. Due to space limitation, we skip in-depth details of the algorithm including its pseudocode.

4.2   Spatial-First Based Approach

Initially, this approach retrieves all places in given range r and computes spatial score of each place p in ascending order of distance from q [1]. For each accessed place, its social score is computed by exploring the visitors of the place and the friends of the query user q. For each unaccessed place p, an upper bound is computed using its distance from q and assuming its social score to be 1 (the maximum possible). The algorithm terminates if the upper bound score of the next place is smaller than the score of k_{th} place found so far. Let's assume, the score of current k_{th} place p is $Score_k$, it was shown in [1] that if the $||q, p|| \geq (r - \frac{(Score_k - (1-\alpha))}{\alpha})$, the process stops since every subsequent place p in the priority queue is further than the current place p from q. Due to space limitation, we skip in-depth details of the algorithm including its pseudocode.

4.3   Hybrid Approach

This section focuses on our third approach (i.e., Hybrid) to process $GSTT_k$ queries which is capable of processing social, spatial and temporal components simultaneously. Before presenting the technique in detail, we describe our index and space partitioning techniques.

3D Friends Check-Ins R-Tree: In addition to the previous indexes, for each user u, we introduce another index called *3D Friends Check-Ins R-tree (3DFCR-Tree)* which maintains the summary of check-ins of the user u's friends. Specifically, *3DFCR-Tree* stores check-in information of each friend of u by indexing a few MBRs for each friend. Thus, it represents the summary of all friends check-ins.

One approach is to use the root MBR of each of u's friends *3D Check-In R-Tree* and index them in *3DFCR-Tree*. The problem with indexing root MBR is that, many root nodes may be too big (e.g., consider a user who has checked-in in every continent) and this would result in huge overlap among the MBRs affecting the effectiveness of the R-tree. To overcome the shortcoming, we propose to index the children of the root nodes instead of the root nodes. Let's assume a query $q \in U$ where the friends of q are $F_q = \{u_1, u_2, u_3 \ldots u_{19}, u_{20}\}$. Figure 2(a) illustrates the idea of the *3DFCR-Tree* of q. Similarly, Fig. 2(b) shows one of the leaf nodes of a *3DFCR-Tree* which indexes child entries of root MBR of few friends' (e.g., u_1, u_3, u_7) *3D Check-In R-Trees*.

Visitors Check-Ins R-Tree (*VCRTree*): As described earlier, for each user, we maintain her friends' summary to prune irrelevant friends when a query arrives. Similarly, each place p has visitors (*p.visitors* containing their IDs) and their check-ins information during different times. To maintain this information,

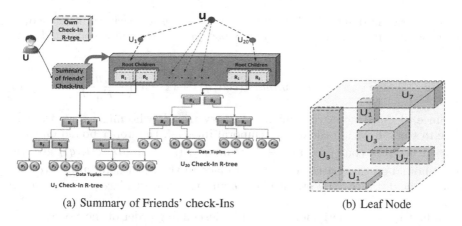

(a) Summary of Friends' check-Ins   (b) Leaf Node

Fig. 2. 3D Friends Check-Ins R-Tree

we create an R-tree (denoted as *VCRTree*) and each indexed point is a two-dimensional point where one dimension is visitor ID and other dimension is check-in time.

4.3.1   Algorithm Overview

Initially, when a query arrives, we create a two dimensional grid (which covers given range r) on the fly. For each cell of the grid, we compute an upper bound on score for each place that may lie in the cell (to be explained later) and based on the upper bound, we access places in the order to prune unnecessary places and friends which are not relevant. Secondly, by employing *VCRTree* for remaining candidate places, we further prune the irrelevant ones based on social and temporal criteria. Below, we explain the pruning criteria in detail with pseudocode given in Algorithm 1.

Using Range Grid: In this step, we construct the on the fly 2D-Grid to prune two kind of objects based on *3DFCR-Tree* as follows.

1. Pruning Friends: If an MBR of *3DFCR-Tree* does not overlap with the grid or with given temporal interval I, we can prune it which in return, prunes that particular friend. The pruned friends are the friends of the query who have not checked-in in given range r during given temporal interval I. Specifically, to compute the upper bound on social score of a cell c_{ij} of range grid, the algorithm traverses *3DFCR-Tree* of a query user q to compute number of objects (child nodes of root of friends' Check-In R-trees) intersecting with the cell. Let's consider an example in Fig. 3(a) where we have a range grid cell c_{ij} and some *3DFCR-Tree* objects belonging to q's friends ranging from u_1 to u_5. Since only u_1, u_4 and u_5 overlap with c_{ij}, they might have checked-in at any place p in the cell. Therefore, the maximum number of friends who might have visited a place in the cell is 3, which can be used to obtain the upper bound on social score.

2. Pruning Places: Each cell c_{ij} in the grid contains a list of places P_c that lie inside it and a list of overlapping MBRs of *3DFCR-Tree* (denoted as V_{cell})

based on criteria described above. Once the list V_{cell} for each cell is fetched, an upper bound on the score (denoted as $Score_{cell}$) of each cell is computed using Eq. 3.

$$Score_{cell} = \alpha(r - mindist(cell, q)) + (1 - \alpha)\left(\frac{|V_{cell}|}{|F_q|}\right) \quad (3)$$

Since, $|V_{cell}|$ denotes the number of query friends who might have visited a place in the cell within the query temporal interval, the upper bound on social score of a cell is computed as $\frac{|V_{cell}|}{|F_q|}$. Similarly, $(r - mindist(cell, q))$ gives an upper bound on the spatial score of any place in the cell where $mindist(cell, q)$ denotes the distance between the query q and the nearest place p to the q in the cell.

In first loop (at line 1), for each cell in descending order of the $Score_{cell}$, the algorithm accesses each place p in the cell (at line 4) to compute score of the place while maintaining the current k_{th} place score (at line 7). If the current k_{th} place score is greater than the next cell's $Score_{cell}$, the algorithm stops since all the subsequent cells can not contain a place with higher score than current k_{th} place's score (at line 3). Below, we describe how to compute the score of a candidate place efficiently.

Algorithm 1. Hybrid Algorithm

---
1 **foreach** *Range Grid cell c_{ij} in descending order of upper bound scores* **do**
2   **if** $Score_{cell} \leq Score_k$ **then**
3 | return top-k results;
4   **foreach** *place p in cell c_{ij}* **do**
5 | $ComputeScore(p)$;   // Algorithm 2
6   **end**
7   Update top-k results and $Score_k$;
8 **end**

4.3.2 Computing Score of a Candidate Place

Intuition: A naïve approach: Let's consider a query q with a list of friends and their check-ins, and a place p with a list of visitors. To compute score of the place, we have to traverse through whole friends' list and visitors' list to see if a friend has visited the place during given temporal interval I. In general, the above approach is not efficient since in many applications, the size of F_q may be huge e.g., people born-in Germany. To speed-up the query processing, we employ an R-Tree (*VCR-Tree*) to index visitor IDs and their check-in times (as described earlier).

Let's consider an example where we have three MBRs of *VCR-Tree* (R_1, R_2 and R_3) shown in Fig. 3(b) along with given temporal interval $I(20, 45)$ (shaded area) and a list of friends F_q. Clearly, MBR R_2 neither intersects with any user in F_q (see the broken lines) nor with given temporal interval I. Therefore, we can prune the MBR. Note that, MBR R_3 does overlap with given temporal interval I. However, it does not intersect with any user in F_q and can also be pruned. Similarly, we can prune user U_{11} since none of the three MBRs intersect with it. Since MBR R_1 intersects with both the F_q and given temporal interval I, it might contain check-ins of the friends. In Fig. 3(b), the relevant users of the query q are U_{14}, U_{18} and U_{21} (shown in solid) who visited the place during given temporal interval I. Next, we explain the technique in Algorithm 2 with pseudocode given below.

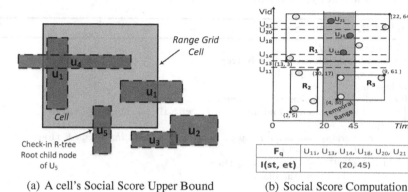

(a) A cell's Social Score Upper Bound   (b) Social Score Computation

Fig. 3. Social Score

To compute the score of a candidate place p, the algorithm starts finding the friends of q who visited the place p by traversing the F_q in ascending order of friend IDs (at line 1). For this purpose, it accesses MBRs of *VCRTree* of the place p based on their minimum visitor ID by first initializing a *min-heap* with root MBR of *VCRTree* with *minimum visitor ID* as sorting key (at line 2). Then, in first loop (at line 3), the algorithm starts de-heaping entries iteratively and examines whether or not it intersects with the remaining number of friends in F_q (to be verified as visitors and denoted as $F_{q.remaining}$) and given temporal interval I (at line 7). If the entry E intersects with either of the two and is also an object (i.e., check-in belongs to a friend in the F_q), the algorithm either updates the social score of the place p or prunes it based on an upper bound on the score of the place p (denoted as $P_{maxScore}$) using Eq. 4.

$$P_{maxScore} = \alpha \times p_{spatial} + (1 - \alpha) \times P_{maxSocial} \qquad (4)$$

To choose from one of the two options, the algorithm first computes $P_{maxScore}$ of the place p using maximum possible social score of the place p (denoted as $P_{maxSocial}$) which is computed as described in Eq. 5. Let $F_{q.traversed}$ denotes a subset of the F_q which has been traversed so far to find friends in the F_q who visited the place p and assuming all the remaining friends in the $F_{q.remaining}$ have visited the place p.

$$P_{maxSocial} = \frac{|F_{q.traversed} \cap p.visitors| + |F_{q.remaining}|}{|F_q|} \qquad (5)$$

Intuitively, $P_{maxSocial}$ is the maximum possible social score of a place p at any point during the computation of final score of the place p. Consequently, if $P_{maxScore}$ of the place p is less than the current k_{th} place score, the algorithm terminates without computing the final score and prunes the place p (at line 10) since it cannot be in top-k places. Otherwise, it updates the social score of the place p (at line 12). Similarly, if the entry E does not overlap either with the $F_{q.remaining}$ or given temporal interval I, it is instantly pruned and consequently, its child entries are not en-heaped.

Algorithm 2. ComputeScore(p)

---

1 $F \leftarrow$ *first friend in F_q*;
2 Initialize min-heap with Root of VCR-Tree;
3 **while** *min-heap is not empty* **do**
4 | De-heap entry E;
5 | **if** $F < $ *Minimum Visitor ID of E* **then**
6 | | $F \leftarrow$ binary search to find first F in F_q with ID $>=$ minimum visitor ID of E;
7 | **if** *(E overlaps with given temporal interval I or with the friend F* **then**
8 | | **if** *E is an object* **then**
9 | | | **if** $P_{maxScore} < Score_k$ **then**
10 | | | | Prune the place p;
11 | | | **else**
12 | | | | Update Social score ;
13 | | **else**
14 | | | Insert child entries of E into min-heap with minimum visitor ID as a key;
15 **end**
16 Return $Score(p)$;

4.3.3   Handling Updates

Now, we provide a very high level idea of how to update the indexes. For this purpose, we index last month data using a separate data structure in addition to the data structure that maintains all previous months data and during query processing, we use both the data structures. Similarly, to update the data structures, a periodic bulk update is performed.

5   Experiments

5.1   Experimental Setup

To the best of our knowledge, this problem has not been studied before and no previous algorithm can be trivially extended to answer $GSTT_k$ queries. Therefore, we evaluate the proposed algorithms on their performance by comparing them with each other.

Each method is implemented in C++ and experiments are run on Intel Core $I5$ 2.4 GHz PC with 8 GB memory running on 64-bit Ubuntu Linux. We use real dataset of *Gowalla* [17] and various parameters such as *number of queries, range (km)*, *temporal interval (months)*, *grid size*, *average number of friends and k*. The default values of the parameters used are 100, 100, 6, 16, 600 and 10 respectively. *Gowalla* dataset contains 196,591 users, 950,327 friendships, 6,442,890 check-ins over the period of February 2009 - October 2010 and 1,280,956 checked-in places across the world [3]. The node size of *Facility R-Tree* index is set to 4096 Bytes and 1024 Bytes for *3D Check-In R-Tree*, *3DFCR-Tree* and *VCR-Tree* indexes because they have fewer objects as compared to *Facility R-Tree*. For each experiment, we randomly choose 100 users and consider them as query users.

5.2   Performance Evaluation

Index Size: Figure 4(a) compares the index sizes of five different subsets of the real dataset. To obtain these datasets, we randomly selected $100,000$ to $500,000$ places and we extracted their corresponding social networks based on visitors of the places. The input data contains *places, check-in information, friends and their relationship information* in few simple text files (without indexing). The value on top of each Bar denotes how many times bigger the respective index size is compared to the input data. For example, for $100,000$ places, the size of indexes utilized by the *Social-First* algorithm is 2.29 times bigger than the input data. Note that the size of all our indexes is linear to the input data for all datasets (e.g., *Hybrid* is 3–4 times bigger than the input data). As expected, *Hybrid* index is the largest index.

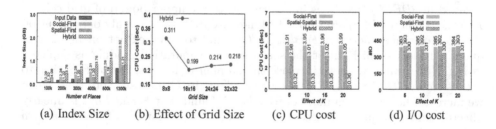

| (a) Index Size | (b) Effect of Grid Size | (c) CPU cost | (d) I/O cost |

Fig. 4. Index and Grid Size; and Effect of k

Effect of Grid Size: In Fig. 4(b), we study the effect of different number of cells in which grid is partitioned in *Hybrid* technique. The CPU cost also depends on the number of cells because it affects grid partitioning and grid cells' upper bound computation which plays a vital role in pruning phase. In our study, we found that the best CPU performance can be achieved by splitting the region covering given range r into grid of 16×16 cells for the default parameters.

Effect of k: In this evaluation, we test our proposed techniques for various values of k. As shown in Fig. 4(c), *Hybrid* is up to 15 times faster and the performance is not significantly affected by the value of k. The reason is that, the main cost depends on creating the grid and then computing upper bounds of the cells and this dominant cost is not affected by k. Similarly, I/O cost remains unaffected to much extent as illustrated in Fig. 4(d) for all the three algorithms since the higher value of k does not incur more disk access. Note that, *Hybrid* performs better than the other two even though it processes more indexes. However, due to efficient pruning techniques, it incurs less I/O cost.

Effect of Range: Next, we evaluate the performance of our techniques for range between 50 to 400 km in Fig. 5. The region in which we want to find top-k places is defined by the given range r containing average number of places between $5,000$ *to* $100,000$. Note that, *Spatial-First* is linearly affected as we increase the range r due to linear growth in number of places as shown in Fig. 5(a). Similarly, *Social-First* shows a steady growth in CPU cost with the increase in range r. Although it accesses the *3D Check-In R-Tree* for each friend but the cost is increased because the cost of range query on these R-trees is affected with the range r. Note that, *Hybrid* performs several times better than the other two. Further, in terms of I/O cost, as we increase the range r, *Social-First* again shows a steady growth since the number of *3D Check-In R-Trees* which need to be processed, is independent of the range r as illustrated in Fig. 5(b). Note that, *Spatial-First* is most affected since as we increase the range r, it has to process more places which in return, incurs more disk access.

Effect of Average Number of Friends: In this experiment, we study the effect of number of friends on the three techniques in Fig. 5. Note that the size of *3DFCR-Tree* relies on number of query q's friends and the distribution of each friend's check-ins in search space which determines the number of objects to be indexed in *3DFCR-Tree*. This in return affects the upper bound of grid cells in *Hybrid* technique. In *Spatial-First* technique, CPU cost is mainly dependent on the cost of range query on *Facility R-Tree* and to some extent on number of query q's friends which affect the social score computation module as depicted in Fig. 5(c). Similarly, as we increase the number of friends, *Social-First* has to process more *3D Check-In R-Trees* which affects its CPU cost. Note that, when we increase the average number of friends, we found that *Social-First* is linearly affected since it requires to access *3D Check-In R-Tree* for each friend as shown in Fig. 5(d).

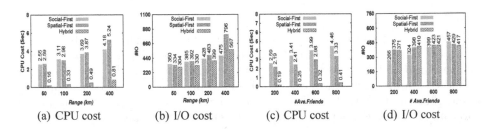

(a) CPU cost   (b) I/O cost   (c) CPU cost   (d) I/O cost

Fig. 5. Effect of varying Range and number of Friends

Effect of Concurrent Number of Queries: Next, we compare the performance of our techniques for various number of queries. Figure 6(a) shows average CPU cost of the techniques which slightly varies depending on the number of query q's friends and query location. *Social-First* technique has higher CPU cost for any number of queries than the other two because it accesses *3D Check-In R-Tree* for each friend and issues a range query as illustrated in the figure. Similarly, *Spatial-First* has slightly different CPU cost because of different query and number of places in range r. Note that, *Hybrid* algorithm performs several times better and the cost for different number of queries is slightly affected by the query location, number of friends and number of places in range r. Similarly, for all the three algorithms, the average I/O cost is mainly independent of the number of queries and is slightly affected by the query location, number of friends and number of places in range r as depicted in Fig. 6(b).

Effect of Temporal Interval: In Fig. 6, we evaluate the effect of size of temporal interval I to test the performance of the three methods. *Social-First* algorithm has higher CPU cost even for smaller temporal intervals because most of *3D Check-In R-Trees* overlap with the temporal interval as shown in Fig. 6(c). Similarly, the CPU cost of *Spatial-First* method remains high specifically for bigger temporal intervals due to more number of places to be processed. On the other hand, in *Hybrid* technique, temporal interval affects cells' upper bound computation and consequently, the pruning phase gets affected. Note that, *Hybrid* performs several times better than the others. Further, in terms of I/O cost, as we increase the temporal interval I, *Social-First* shows a steady growth since the number of *3D Check-In R-Trees* which need to be processed, slightly depends on the temporal interval I as illustrated in Fig. 6(d). Note that, *Spatial-First* is most affected since as we increase the temporal interval I, it has to process more places and is the main cause of high disk access.

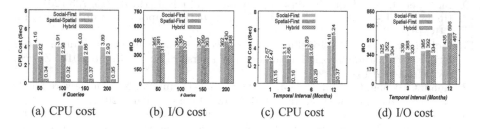

(a) CPU cost   (b) I/O cost   (c) CPU cost   (d) I/O cost

Fig. 6. Effect of varying number of Queries and Temporal Interval

5.3 Conclusions

In this work, we are the first to formalize the problem of *Geo-Social Temporal Top-k* $(GSTT_k)$ query and propose efficient query processing techniques. First, we present two different approaches i.e., *Social-First* and *Spatial-First* to solve our problem and then, we propose our main algorithm called *Hybrid*.

Hybrid technique is capable of processing social, spatial and temporal components simultaneously by utilizing a hybrid index specifically designed to handle $GSTT_k$ queries. Results of empirical studies demonstrate the effectiveness of our main algorithm (i.e., *Hybrid*).

Acknowledgements. Muhammad Aamir Cheema is supported by DP180103411 and FT180100140.

References

1. Sohail, A., Murtaza, G., Taniar, D.: Retrieving top-k famous places in location-based social networks. In: Cheema, M.A., Zhang, W., Chang, L. (eds.) ADC 2016. LNCS, vol. 9877, pp. 17–30. Springer, Cham (2016). https://doi.org/10.1007/978-3-319-46922-5_2
2. Curtiss, M., et al.: Unicorn: a system for searching the social graph. PVLDB **6**(11), 1150–1161 (2013)
3. Sohail, A., Hidayat, A., Cheema, M.A., Taniar, D.: Location-aware group preference queries in social-networks. In: Wang, J., Cong, G., Chen, J., Qi, J. (eds.) ADC 2018. LNCS, vol. 10837, pp. 53–67. Springer, Cham (2018). https://doi.org/10.1007/978-3-319-92013-9_5
4. Armenatzoglou, N., Ahuja, R., Papadias, D.: Geo-social ranking: functions and query processing. VLDB J. **24**(6), 783–799 (2015)
5. Sohail, A., Cheema, M.A., Taniar, D.: Social-aware spatial top-k and skyline queries. Comput. J. **61**(11), 1620–1638 (2018)
6. Gao, H., Liu, H.: Data analysis on location-based social networks. In: Chin, A., Zhang, D. (eds.) Mobile Social Networking. CSS, pp. 165–194. Springer, New York (2014). https://doi.org/10.1007/978-1-4614-8579-7_8
7. Cheema, M.A., et al.: Efficiently processing snapshot and continuous reverse k nearest neighbors queries. VLDB J. **21**(5), 703–728 (2012)
8. Cheema, M.A., et al.: A unified approach for computing top-k pairs in multidimensional space. In: ICDE 2011, Hannover, Germany, pp. 1031–1042 (2011)
9. Li, F., et al.: Top-k queries on temporal data. VLDB J. **19**(5), 715–733 (2010)
10. Hoang-Vu, T.-A., et al.: A unified index for spatio-temporal keyword queries. In: CIKM (2016)
11. McInerney, J., et al.: Modelling heterogeneous location habits in human populations for location prediction under data sparsity. In: UbiComp 2013, Zurich, Switzerland (2013)
12. Yuan, Q., Cong, G., Ma, Z., Sun, A., Magnenat-Thalmann, N.: Time-aware point-of-interest recommendation. In: SIGIR 2013, Dublin, Ireland (2013)
13. Kamel, I., Khalil, M., Kouramajian, V.: Bulk insertion in dynamic r-trees. In: Proceedings of the International Symposium on Spatial Data Handling, vol. 4, pp. 31–42 (1996)
14. Chen, L., et al.: Bulk-insertions info r-trees using the small-tree-large-tree approach. In: ACM-GIS (1998)
15. Choubey, R., Chen, L., Rundensteiner, E.A.: GBI: a generalized r-tree bulk-insertion strategy. In: Güting, R.H., Papadias, D., Lochovsky, F. (eds.) SSD 1999. LNCS, vol. 1651, pp. 91–108. Springer, Heidelberg (1999). https://doi.org/10.1007/3-540-48482-5_8
16. Guttman, A.: R-trees: a dynamic index structure for spatial searching. In: SIGMOD, Boston, Massachusetts. IEEE, New York (1984)
17. Cho, E., Myers, S.A., Leskovec, J.: Friendship and mobility: user movement in location-based social networks. In: SIGKDD 2011, San Diego, CA, USA (2011)

Effective and Efficient Community Search in Directed Graphs Across Heterogeneous Social Networks

Zezhong Wang[1], Ye Yuan[1], Xiangmin Zhou[2(✉)], and Hongchao Qin[1]

[1] School of Computer Science and Engineering, Northeastern University,
Shenyang, China
zezhong_wang@sina.cn, yuanye@mail.neu.edu.cn, qhc.neu@gmail.com
[2] School of Science, RMIT University, Melbourne, VIC 3000, Australia
xiangmin.zhou@rmit.edu.au

Abstract. Communities in social networks are useful for many real applications, like product recommendation. This fact has driven the recent research interest in retrieving communities online. Although certain effort has been put into community search, users' information has not been well exploited for effective search. Meanwhile, existing approaches for retrieval of communities are not efficient when applied in huge social networks. Motivated by this, in this paper, we propose a novel approach for retrieving communities online, which makes full use of users' relationship information across heterogeneous social networks. We first investigate an online technique to match pairs of users in different social network and create a new social network, which contains more complete information. Then, we propose k-Dcore, a novel framework of retrieving effective communities in the directed social network. Finally, we construct an index to search communities efficiently for queries. Extensive experiments demonstrate the efficiency and effectiveness of our proposed solution in directed graphs, based on heterogeneous social networks.

Keywords: Community search · User identity linkage · Direction of relationships

1 Introduction

Today, billions of users are now engaged in multiple online social networks, such as Facebook, Twitter, Foursquare, and Weibo. Communities in social networks, are useful for many real applications (product recommendation [1–4] and setting up social events [5] and so on). A great deal of research has been conducted on discovering communities. Classical methods [6,7] aim to extract all the communities for a social network. For one thing, they are not customized for a query request and are not suitable for quick retrieval of communities. For another, these solutions do not make full use of user's relationship information. Meanwhile, the

© Springer Nature Switzerland AG 2020
R. Borovica-Gajic et al. (Eds.): ADC 2020, LNCS 12008, pp. 161–172, 2020.
https://doi.org/10.1007/978-3-030-39469-1_13

users' information in one single social network is not enough to retrieve cohesive communities for the query user.

We study effective and efficient solutions for community search across heterogeneous social networks. Three key issues need to be addressed. First, we need to find a way to make full use of users' information in multiple social networks. We propose a method to create a new social network in a short time, which contains the users' all information in multiple social networks. A given user often simultaneously register in several social networks. Each social network platform contains different and rich information of the person. Failing to utilize users' all information could lead to the community discovery results with low quality. Considering we retrieve communities in an "online" manner, we are supposed to match pairs of users and create a new social networks in a short time. Second, we need to construct a model based on query user, which can perform well in directed graphs. This is vital, as users' relationships is of significance for understanding the social network's structure. The direction of the relationship are often meaningful and unsymmetrical [8,9]. Consider Trump, the president of USA, has around 30 millions of followers in Twitter, but he only follows less than 100 persons. If we ignore the direction of relationships and further simplify the social networks' structure into undirected graphs, we could get communities with low cohesiveness and even wrong ones [10]. Finally, we need find a way to save the user information processing time. We should further develop an index to decrease the time cost.

To overcome these problems, we propose a framework (CS-HSN) for community search by utilizing the users' relationships in multiple social networks. We first design algorithms to supplement the users' relationships between vertices based on information in multiple social networks. Then we build a novel model, called k-Dcore(k-core in directed graphs). The contributions of the article are highlighted as follows:

- We design a novel k-Dcore model, which measures the "goodness" of communities according to the relationships between the vertices. The communities we generate could perform better the others.
- We propose a solution to match pairs of users in a short time and combine multiple social networks into one. In this way, the users' information could be enriched greatly.
- We develop an index by using some compression techniques. Based on the indexes, the query performance can be improved significantly.

The remainder of the paper is organized as follows. We briefly review the related work in Sect. 2. We introduce problem definition in Sect. 3. In Sects. 4 and 5, we describe our approach of user identity linkage and the algorithm for retrieving communities in directed graphs, respectively. In Sects. 6 and 7, we show the approach's cost analysis and report extensive experimental results. Finally, Sect. 8 concludes the paper.

2   Related Work

In this section, we review the existing research on two problems closely related to our work, including the community search and user identity linkage across heterogeneous social networks.

2.1   Community Search

Community search methods aim to retrieve communities in an "online" manner, based on a query request. Sozio et al. [5] proposed the first algorithm Global to find the k-core containing q. Cui et al. [1] proposed Local, which uses local expansion techniques to enhance the performance of Global. We will compare the two kind of solutions in our experiments. Some recent work [11–13] finds communities in attributed graphs. Some others focus on topological structure, including k-clique [14], k-truss [15], and spectral cluster [16]. However, these community search algorithms overlook direction of edges, which contains the rich information and is meaningful in the social networks. Wang [10] proposed a method to retrieve communities in directed graphs based on query user. Nevertheless, the method ignores the information across heterogeneous social networks.

2.2   User Identity Linkage

According to the model construction of user identity linkage, we summarize existing models into three groups: supervised [17], semi-supervised [18] and unsupervised models [19]. In order to math the users, Vosecky [17] proposes a supervised method, which uses distance-based profile features and a supervised aggregating method to link user identities. Liu [18] proposes a semi-supervised multiobjective framework jointly modeling heterogeneous behaviors and structure consistency. Considering the high cost to obtain matching users by using supervised and semi-supervised methods, we cannot apply these models into our online search. TLabitzke's [17] algorithm tries to compare neighborhood based network features for user identity linkage. The model is a typical aligning algorithm, which is an "online" method. However, this method is not based on the query user, which is not suitable for community search.

3   Problem Definition

This section provides a formal problem definition and describes our proposed approach briefly.

Definition 1 *(k-Dcore). Given a directed graph G and an integer k $(k \geq 1)$, a* **k-Dcore** *is a strongly connected directed component of G, satisfying that, $\forall v \in$ k-Dcore, in-degree and out-degree's minimum of $v \geq k$.*

Definition 2 *(Heterogeneous social network).* *A heterogeneous social network can be modeled as a directed graph* $G = (V, E, N)$*, where* $V = v_1, v_2 ... v_n$ *represents all vertices, E is the set of all the edges in the graph, which represents the relationships between the vertices, and N is the set of all vertices' name strings.*

Problem 1 **(User identity linkage of social networks).** Given heterogeneous social networks $G_1 = (V, E, N)$ and $G_2 = (V, E, N)$, it identifies and match users $v_{G_1 1} ...$ and $v_{G_2 1} ...$ in G_1, G_2, as the same natural people across the social networks, and combines the two social network into a new linked social network Gl.

Definition 3 *(Communities in the linked social network).* *The communities* Gl_q *is the k-Dcores we get in the linked social network Gl, which should hold the following properties:*

1. **Strong Connectivity.** $Gl_q \subseteq Gl$ *is strongly connected and contains q;*
2. **Structure cohesiveness.** $v \in Gl_q$*,* $mindeg_{Gl_q}(v) \geq$ *the threshold k;*

Problem 2 **(CS-HSN).** Given heterogeneous social networks $G_1(V, E, N)$, $G_2(V, E, N)$ and the vertex query q, **CS-HSN** (community search across heterogeneous social networks) returns a set of communities $Gl_q \in Gl$.

4   Our User Identity Linkage Approach

We aim to match users, by comparing their profiles from different social networks. We proceed as follows.

4.1   Retrieval of Valid User Sets

To retrieve right match, it is supposed to compare all the users. However, we observe that there are often many users which are not meaningful for the search. We thus investigate a pruning algorithm to get valid user sets.

Given the query user's two accounts in SN_1, SN_2, we get **1-Dcores** of SN_1 and SN_2, which we call V_{SN_1} and V_{SN_2}. We only compare the users in V_{SN_1} and V_{SN_2}, because they are valid for the query. For one thing, our search is based on the query user and retrieves communities from **1-Dcores** (the process will be introduced in Sect. 5). For another, the users in V_{SN_1} and ones in V_{SN_2}, which are closely related to each other, are more possibly matched with each other. In this way, we only compare the users in V_{SN_1} and V_{SN_2}, which significantly saves time cost.

4.2   Comparisons of Users

In order to match the users, we should compare users' profiles in V_{SN_1} with the ones' in V_{SN_2}. If V_p is one user in V_{SN_1} and there are totally n users in V_{SN_2}, we compare the profile of V_p with n profiles (1:n) and get a comparison set. We illustrates the concept of comparison sets and get k comparison sets in Fig. 1(a).

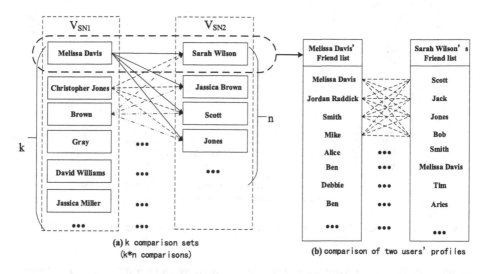

Fig. 1. Comparison of users

Then, we choose the comparison sets' friend lists as the character of the profile to compare. We all known that, most of users do not share all the private information, such as, job, hometown and contact, in every social network, and some methods of retrieving users' information waste a lot of time, for example, face recognition. In view of this, we choose the friend list. For one thing, friends lists are publicly available. For another, comparisons of the users can be done via simple string comparisons, which is suitable for online query. Then, we choose users' friends list, FL_1 and FL_2, to compare. Figure 1(b) depicts one single comparison between Melissa Davis and Sarah Wilson.

4.3   Matching Users

In order to match users, we refer to the number of the intersection of FL_1 and FL_2 ($FL_1 \cap FL_2$) as overlap. We choose largest overlaps and distinction distance as a correlation metric to judge whether two compared users belong to the same natural person. As shown in Fig. 2, the gap between the target comparison' overlap value and the next lower one is called the distinction distance and quantifies how distinct the target comparison stands from the other comparisons. Only if the two compared users' overlap is maximum and distinctive distance is greater than the threshold θ, we get the match.

4.4   Combination of Social Networks

Based on the result that pairs of users in different social networks are matched as the same natural person, we can create a new social network which contains all the information. As shown in Algorithm 1, we supplement vertices and relationships

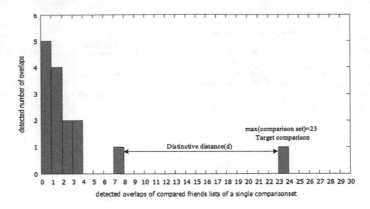

Fig. 2. Histogram of detected comparison overlaps for a comparison set (1:15)

between vertices in G_1 from ones in G_2. In this way, we can get a new social network containing more information and search communities in the new one.

Algorithm 1 Combination of social networks

1: Match(m) is the function that get the user n in the other social network, which is matched with m.

Input: graphs of social networks $G_1 = (V, E, N)$ and $G_2 = (V, E, N)$, sets of matching users M_{SN1} and M_{SN2};

Output: the graph of the new social networks G_n;

2:   $G_n := G_1$;

3: **for** each $i \in M_{SN1}$ **do**

4:     **for** each $j \in Match(i).friendlist$ **do**

5:         **if** $j \in M_{SN2}$ **then**

6:             $i.friendlist.add(Match(j))$;

7:         **else**

8:             $G_1.add(j)$;

9:             $i.friendlist.add(Match(j))$;

10:        **end for**

11:    **end if**

12: **end for**

13: **return** G_n;

---

5   Our Community Search Approach

In this section, we demonstrate how to get k-Dcore in the directed graphs and construct an index for querying efficiently.

5.1   Cores Decomposition

For the question of retrieving communities in the directed graph, we define the k-Dcore based on min-degree, which is minimum of the vertices' in-degree value and out-degree in the directed graph.

Vladimir Batagelj present [20] an algorithm for k-core, which determines the cores hierarchy, for implementing both functions and running in a constant time ($O_{(m)}$). For one thing, we improve the $O_{(m)}$ algorithm based on min-degree, as shown in Algorithm 2 (line 2), which guarantees that the vertex is closely linked with other vertices. For another, we apply strongly connected algorithm for extract strongly connected subgraphs. Strong connectivity guarantees that each member of the community is reachable to others. Tarjan's strongly connected components algorithm [20] takes a directed graph as input, and produces a partition of the graph's vertices into the l strongly connected components with different core numbers (line 6). At meanwhile, Tarjan's algorithm runs in linear time, which is suitable for online search. In this way, we could avoid the effect of celebrities and zombie fans as discussed in Sect. 1. Christos propose a method called D-core [21], which is based on in-degree and out-degree. However, it is not meaningful to set threshold for vertices' in-degree and out-degree, respectively. Vertices' in-degree and out-degree are both of importance. If the threshold of in-degree or out-degree is greater the other, it could cause the effect of celebrities and zombie fans. Furthermore, it raises the complexity of time and space, which is not suitable for online search.

In Fig. 3(a), given a graph G, we order the vertices in an increasing sequence of their min-degree and get a strongly connected subgraph. We first get the strongly connected component of G(A, B, C, D, E, F, G, H, I, J) (line 6), and record them with core number 1. We move away F, G step by step (line 19), which own lowest min-degree 1. In this way, we recount the min-degree of F and G's neighbors and reorder the rest, accordingly. Then, just as the process of core number 1, we verify the strong connectivity again, and find that H, I, J and A, B, C, D, E are two strongly connected components, $v_{2,1}$ and $v_{2,2}$. We move them away and recount their neighbors' min-degree. Finally, we get a 1-Dcore, two 2-Dcores, and a 3-Dcore.

5.2   Index Construction

In order to search communities efficiently, we construct a C-tree(Core tree) according to the result of core decomposition. As shown in Fig. 3(b), we choose F, G with lowest core number as root ($r_{1,1}$). The vertices H, I, J($r_{2,1}$), are not strongly connected with A, B, C, D, E($r_{2,2}$), so the two are the child nodes of ($r_{1,1}$). A, B, C, D, as ($r_{3,1}$), is the child node of ($r_{2,2}$). If A is the query vertex and structure cohesiveness threshold is 2, we will find the community in the subtree, which consists of ($r_{2,2}$) and ($r_{3,1}$).

Algorithm 2 Cores Decomposition

Input: Graph G = (V,E,N);
Output: strongly connected subgraphs with its core number;
1: initialize $V_{0,0}, V_{0,1}, V_{1,0}...V_{k_{max},k_{max}}$ as empty sets;
2: order the set of vertices V in increasing order of their min-degree;
3: CoreNum := $Deg_{min}(V.head)$;
4: **for** each $v \in V$ in the order **do**
5:     **if** $Deg_{min}(v) \geq$ CoreNum || v=V.head **then**
6:         $V_{CoreNum,l}$:= Tarjan(V);
7:         CoreNum := $Deg_{min}(v)$;
8:     **end if**
9:     **for** each u$\in Neighbour_{in}(v)$ **do**
10:         **if** u $\in$ V **then**
11:             $Deg_{out}(v)$:= $Deg_{out}(v)$-1;
12:         **end if**
13:     **end for**
14:     **for** each u$\in Neighbour_{iout}(v)$ **do**
15:         **if** u $\in$ V **then**
16:             $Deg_{in}(v)$:= $Deg_{in}(v)$-1;
17:         **end if**
18:     **end for**
19:     delete v from V;
20:     reorder V accordingly
21: **end for**
22: **return** $V_{0,0}, V_{0,1}, V_{1,0}...V_{k_{max},k_{max}}$

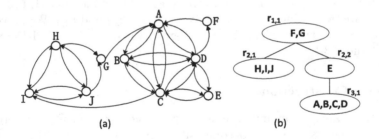

(a)   (b)

Fig. 3. Process of index construction

6   Cost Analysis

In the process of user identity linkage, we match the users on the basis of simple string comparisons of provided data rather than on the use of complex correlation algorithms, so we can regard that the work is done in constant time a. Combination of the two social network can be done in $O(m)$. What's more, the k-core decomposition [20] can be done in $O(m)$ and Tarjan's algorithm used to verify strongly connected component costs $O(m+n)$. Besides, the C-tree could be constructed in $O(l \cdot n)$. We apply Tarjan's algorithm in the subgraphs with different core numbers. If maximum of structure cohesiveness is k_{max}, the total time cost is $O((k_{max} + 1) \cdot m + (l + 1) \cdot n)$.

7   Experiment Evaluation

This section demonstrates the effectiveness and efficiency of our proposed approach, community search across heterogeneous social networks (CS-HSN).

7.1   Experimental Setup

We gather and select the data sets of Twitter and Foursquare in Singapore, from 2014.11 to 2016.01. The data set consists of user profiles, follow relationships, contents and so on (Table 1).

Table 1. Datasets of the networks

Dataset	Vertices	Edges
Twitter	160,338	2,405,628
Foursquare	76,503	1,531,357

We randomly selected 200 query vertices, of which core numbers are higher than 5. We calculate the averages of the 200 queries. Our methods were implemented on a machine with CPU Inter(R) Core(TM)i7-2600, 8.00 GB memory, 3.40 GHz frequency, 500 GB hard disk. All programs are coded in Java.

7.2   Evaluation Methodology

In this part, we conduct experiments of classical algorithm in several different data sets, and compare CS-HSN with other outstanding CS methods: Local search [5], Global search [1].

To measure similarities, we apply a classical measure, the Jaccard index, and develop the measure in our circumstance, called CMF (community member frequency). Given algorithms $A = \{A_1, A_2, ..., A_\psi\}$, $CMF(A(q))$, which ranges from 0 to 1, states that two vertices are considered to be highly similar if they share some common neighbors. The higher their value, the more cohesive is a community. $Nbr(v)$ is the set of v's neighbours and C denotes the set of vertices in a community.

– CMF: $CMF(A_\psi) = \frac{1}{|C_i|^2} \sum_{u \in C} \sum_{v \in C} \frac{Nbr(u) \cap Nbr(u)}{Nbr(u) \cup Nbr(u)}$

Global search is based on the undirected graph and retrieves a connected subraph which contains the query vertex, q. Local search also overlooks direction of the relationships. The algorithm explores from q, until it forms a cohesive subgraph. The three methods all adopt minimum degree measurement to guarantee the structure cohesiveness of communities. However, the algorithms and the graphs they work on are different, which result in different effectiveness of retrieved communities.

7.3   Effectiveness Evaluation

In Fig. 4, we compare CS-HSN with other CS methods about cohesiveness of communities specifically, about CMF value for the two given datasets. The figure shows that CS-HSN outperform in cohesiveness of communities, because CS-HSN mainly considers the users' information in other social networks, while Global search and Local search do not. Furthermore, CS-HSN also show better performance than others, since CS-HSN takes advantage of the relationships' direction, by working on directed networks without any simplification. As we discuss in Sect. 1, using undirected edges to represent unidirectional and bidirectional relationships could leave negative influence on topological structure and further produce wrong results. Notice that the CMF values for Twitter and Foursquare are same, because we match the users in Twitter and Foursquare, and compare the two to a new social network, in which we extract communities.

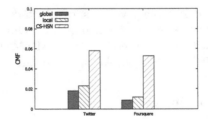

Fig. 4. Effectiveness of the algorithms

7.4   Efficiency Comparison

In this part, we compare the query efficiency with other CS methods for the two given datasets, under different k, which is the threshold of community cohesiveness. A lower k renders a larger subgraph of the graphs simplified from networks for all the algorithms. Extensive experiments were conducted to verify the efficiency of CS-HSN. In Fig. 5, we can see Local search outperforms than Global search in general, and it is apparent that CS-HSN executes more efficiently than others because of index construction. The index we use to find communities for a large number of queries, is not reconstructed in each time. Hence, there is a little additional time on average, which could be ignored.

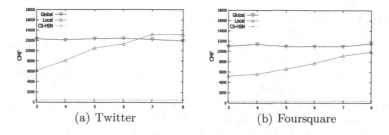

(a) Twitter   (b) Foursquare

Fig. 5. Efficiency of the algorithms about different k

8   Conclusion

In this paper, we investigate the problem of community search in directed graphs and propose a novel framework CS-HSN to retrieve effective community with strongly connected structure cohesiveness. To the best of our knowledge, this is the first work on community search in directed graphs, across heterogeneous social networks. We can also apply CS-HSN in undirected graphs, which shows its wide applicability. As shown in experiments, CS-HSN method is efficient and more effective than other methods.

References

1. Cui, W., Xiao, Y., Wang, H., Wei, W.: Local search of communities in large graphs. In: SIGMOD (2014)
2. Zhou, X., Chen, L., Zhang, Y., Cao, L., Huang, G., Wang, C.: Online video recommendation in sharing community. In: SIGMOD, pp. 1645–1656 (2015)
3. Zhou, X., et al.: Enhancing online video recommendation using social user interactions. VLDB J. **26**(5), 637–656 (2017)
4. Zhou, X., Qin, D., Chen, L., Zhang, Y.: Real-time context-aware social media recommendation. VLDB J. **28**(2), 197–219 (2019)
5. Sozio, M., Gionis, A.: The community-search problem and how to plan a successful cocktail party. In: SIGKDD (2010)
6. Newman, M.E.J., Girvan, M.: Finding and evaluating community structure in networks. Phys. Rev. E Stat. Nonlinear Soft Matter Phys. **69**(2), 026113 (2004)
7. Yang, J., Mcauley, J., Leskovec, J.: Community detection in networks with node attributes. In: ICDM (2013)
8. Zhang, J., Wang, C., Wang, J.: Who proposed the relationship?: recovering the hidden directions of undirected social networks. In: WWW (2014)
9. Fang, Y., Wang, Z., Cheng, R., Wang, H., Hu, J.: Effective and efficient community search over large directed graphs. IEEE Trans. Knowl. Data Eng. **PP**(99), 1 (2018)
10. Wang, Z., Yuan, Y., Wang, G., Qin, H., Ma, Y.: An effective method for community search in large directed attributed graphs. In: Zhu, L., Zhong, S. (eds.) MSN 2017. Communications in Computer and Information Science, vol. 747, pp. 237–251. Springer, Singapore (2018). https://doi.org/10.1007/978-981-10-8890-2_17
11. Fang, Y., Cheng, R., Luo, S., Jiafeng, H.: Effective community search for large attributed graphs. Proc. VLDB Endowment **9**(12), 1233–1244 (2016)

12. Huang, X., Lakshmanan, L.V.S.: Attribute-driven community search. Proc. VLDB Endowment **10**(9), 949–960 (2017)
13. Chen, L., Liu, C., Liao, K., Li, J., Zhou, R.: Contextual community search over large social networks. In: ICDE, April 2019
14. Cui, W., Xiao, Y., Wang, H., Lu, Y., Wei, W.: Online search of overlapping communities. In: SIGMOD (2013)
15. Huang, X., Cheng, H., Qin, L., Tian, W., Yu, J.X.: Querying k-truss community in large and dynamic graphs. In: SIGMOD (2014)
16. Li, Y., Jing, C., Liu, R., Wu, J.: A spectral clustering-based adaptive hybrid multi-objective harmony search algorithm for community detection. In: Evolutionary Computation (2012)
17. Vosecky, J., Dan, H., Shen, V.Y.: User identification across multiple social networks. In: International Conference on Networked Digital Technologies (2009)
18. Liu, S., Wang, S., Zhu, F., Zhang, J., Krishnan, R.: Hydra: large-scale social identity linkage via heterogeneous behavior modeling (2014)
19. Nie, Y., Yan, J., Li, S., Xiang, Z., Li, A., Zhou, B.: Identifying users across social networks based on dynamic core interests. Neurocomputing **210**, S0925231216306178 (2016)
20. Zaversnik, M., Batagelj, V.: An o(m) algorithm for cores decomposition of networks. arXiv preprint, p. 0310049 (2003)
21. Giatsidis, C., Thilikos, D.M., Vazirgiannis, M.: D-cores: measuring collaboration of directed graphs based on degeneracy. Knowl. Inf. Syst. **35**(2), 311–343 (2013)

Entity Extraction with Knowledge from Web Scale Corpora

Zeyi Wen[1]([⊠]), Zeyu Huang[2], and Rui Zhang[2]

[1] The University of Western Australia, Perth, Australia
zeyi.wen@uwa.edu.au
[2] The University of Melbourne, Melbourne, Australia
z.huang56@student.unimelb.edu.au, rui.zhang@unimelb.edu.au

Abstract. Entity extraction is an important task in text mining and natural language processing. A popular method for entity extraction is by comparing substrings from free text against a dictionary of entities. In this paper, we present several techniques as a post-processing step for improving the effectiveness of the existing entity extraction technique. These techniques utilise models trained with the web-scale corpora which makes our techniques robust and versatile. Experiments show that our techniques bring a notable improvement on efficiency and effectiveness.

Keywords: Entity extraction · String matching · Pre-trained model

1 Introduction

Entity extraction is widely used in text mining and natural language processing. For example, it can be used for pre-processing unstructured text: tagging and highlighting the named entities of interest. A common approach for approximate entity extraction is by comparing a substring against an entity. The approach identifies the candidate substrings from free text that match a given list of named entities. For ease of presentation, we use "dictionary" to refer to the list and "entities" to refer to the named entities. Our previous work [16] developed the "2ED" algorithm, which this paper is built on, represents a string matching approach for entity extraction. 2ED is based a distance that considers both character-level edit-distance and token-level edit-distance between a substring from the text and an entity from the dictionary.

Although 2ED reaches a high F_1 score with improved efficiency compared to other techniques, the limitation of 2ED is that 2ED is based on lexical evidence of the text and the dictionary, which lacks the ability to catch syntactical and semantical evidence within the text and the dictionary. To improve 2ED, we propose multiple techniques including (i) using web-scale corpora for distinguishing a typo from an intended token in the substring, (ii) estimating word similarity using word embedding, and (iii) other improvements including more advanced tokenisation. We implement our proposed techniques as a post-processing step

© Springer Nature Switzerland AG 2020
R. Borovica-Gajic et al. (Eds.): ADC 2020, LNCS 12008, pp. 173–185, 2020.
https://doi.org/10.1007/978-3-030-39469-1_14

for the 2ED algorithm. According to our evaluation, the post-processing brings 47% improvement measured by area under the Receiver Operating Characteristic (ROC) curve, in predicting whether a matched substring represents a valid entity in the dictionary.

2   Related Work

Another widely adopted approach to entity extraction is machine Learning such as Recurrent Neural Networks (RNN) [15], Convolutional Neural Networks (CNN) [2] and SVMs [17]. Most of the machine learning based approaches do not require a dictionary consisting of entities of interest. In this paper, we mainly focus on the string matching approach which finds the nearest neighbour of an entity [6]. There have been various research in the area of entity extraction. Chiu et al. [2] used an architecture combining Long Short-Term Memory (LSTM) and CNN for named entity extraction, which can utilise both token-level and character-level evidence. Wei et al. [15] applied an RNN to entity extraction tasks in the medical domain. Besides the machine learning approaches, there are also researches focused on string matching for entity extraction, like the concept recognition system in [14] which implemented a dictionary based entity extraction tool as a component of an NLP pipeline.

Recent works in language models also inspired our work in this paper. Heafield [5] proposed an efficient language model enabling fast queries which also uses space-efficient data structures like TRIE. The BerkeleyLM project [5] enables the storage of large n-gram language models with a fast and small data structure. Progress in the research of word embedding has facilitated many text mining tasks. Mikolov et al. [12] explored the performance of representations of words in a vector-space and demonstrated that these vectors captures various features and rules in the language without human intervention during the training phase. Whitelaw et al. [18] proposed an spell-checking and autocorrection method that utilises the web as a noisy corpus. The approach used shares some common features with our method in this paper as it makes use of the web as a source for training a language model. One major difference is that in their approach a machine learning based classifier was further used while we rely on a rule-based method for classification.

3   The 2ED Algorithm

The previous 2ED algorithm proposed a novel method for estimating the distance (similarity) between a candidate substring and an entity called FuzzyED [16]. The novelty of FuzzyED is in that it proposed a function for measuring similarity between two strings that consist of a sequence of tokens, by taking into consideration both the character-level and the token-level edit-distances. Together with the function is a series of techniques for improving the performance by producing highly promising candidate sub-strings in an efficient way [16]. We will first introduce some key features of the 2ED algorithm which are related to the post-processing work that we will discuss in this paper. We will also point out some potential weaknesses of this previous work that enlightened the improvements we will propose.

3.1   Features of the 2ED Algorithm

Using IDF to Assign Weights to Tokens: One important idea that is exploited throughout the process of 2ED is that tokens in an entity should have discriminated weights. The algorithm proposed using (normalised) Inverted Document Frequency (IDF) as the weight for each token [16], which makes use of information from the dictionary. The IDF of a token in the dictionary is a representation of its relative importance in an entity. If a token is rarely seen in the dictionary, the 2ED algorithm assumes it is more substantial in a named entity. Such tokens are called "core" tokens and should form an essential part of an entity [16]. The weights of tokens are widely used in several steps of the algorithm including the sub-string generation step, where "core" tokens are used as the starting point for spanning; the spanning step, for determining the point for terminating spanning of the sub-string; the shrinking step, for updating the lower bound dissimilarity; and finally the computation of FuzzyED.

Pruning and Filtering: Since the computation of FuzzyED is relatively expensive, multiple methods for reducing the number of candidates are proposed. The algorithm uses sophisticated spanning and shrinking techniques for generating candidate substrings from the text which is proven to be more efficient than enumeration based substring generation algorithms [16]. In addition, some general filters utilizing information from IDF are used to further reduce the candidates for FuzzyED computation.

Calculation of FuzzyED Score: The final step for determining whether a candidate matches an entity is to calculate similarity between the two strings by applying the FuzzyED algorithm. The formal definition is $FuzzyED(E, S) = C_D(S) + C_I(E) + C_S(E, S)$, were E and S denotes the entity and the substring respectively. $C_D(\cdot)$ denotes the deletion cost of removing a token; $C_I(\cdot)$ denotes the insertion cost of inserting a token; $C_S(\cdot)$ denotes the substitution cost of substituting a token in S with a similar token in E.

As we can see, both character-level and token-level edit-distances are considered. The character-level edit-distance is in the substitution cost part, where the cost of substituting a token with another is related to the edit-different of the two tokens. The token-level edit-distance is calculated in a way similar to the character-level version, which is a well studied dynamic programming problem. The resulting FuzzyED score is in the range of [0, 1] representing the similarity between the substring and the entity, where a score of 1 means exact match. The pairs with a FuzzyED score greater or equal to the threshold will be added to the extracted entity list.

Parameters in 2ED: The 2ED algorithm features hyper-parameters that can be used to tune the thresholds for two levels of similarities [16]. The hyper-parameters include δ for token-level similarity threshold and τ for character-level similarity thershold. The two hyper-parameters are in domain [0, 1].

3.2   Drawbacks of the 2ED Algorithm

Applicability of IDFs as Token Weights: As described above, the 2ED algorithm uses the dictionary as the source for obtaining Inverted Document Frequency. The intuition of this approach is to assign different weights to the tokens within an entity so that they can reflect their relative importance in the entity. Such weights are finally used to calculate the FuzzyED score as in formula (1). However, the approach for weighing different tokens directly from the dictionary may have some potential vulnerabilities. Suppose a data analysis practitioner is interested in Australian educational institutes on Wikipedia and a dictionary specifically designed for this purpose is used. Then the IDF of tokens such as "Australian" and "University" can be much smaller than desired. In this case, IDF from a more comprehensive corpus might be a better fit. In fact, the experimental data sets used in the validation of the 2ED algorithm contain dictionaries of millions of named entities, which makes it more appropriate to use IDF as token weights.

Effectiveness of Token-Level Edit-Distance: The proposed function for FuzzyED calculates the cost of token-level edit by the sum of three operations: insertion, deletion and substitution. Thus the cost of transforming "Alpha Beta" to "Beta Alpha" is one deletion and one insertion, which is the sum of weights of the two words. This is because the same operations are used for token-edit and character-edit. But as an observation from the English language, token-edit and character-edit are different. In the above example, we might have over estimated the distance between "Alpha Beta" and "Beta Alpha". Consequently, more operations on the token level needs to be introduced and their costs should be studied to reflect the linguistic "distance". Another concern about including token-level edit-distance in the FuzzyED algorithm is its significance in real world use cases, i.e. how many matched pairs (between a substring and an entity) truly incur a token-level edit operation. We will show that this concern is valid for the corpus and dictionary we have chosen in the next section where statistics of the validation of the current 2ED algorithm will be presented.

4   Improvement on 2ED

The effectiveness of the 2ED algorithm in terms of precision and recall was studied in previous works [16]. The metrics used are listed in the Table 1 below.

Table 1. Metrics used for evaluating 2ED

Notation	Description	Definition
tp	True positive count	# of correctly returned entities
fp	False positive count	# of wrongly returned entities
fn	False negative count	# of missed entities
p	Precision	$p = \frac{tp}{tp+fp}$
r	Recall	$r = \frac{tp}{tp+fn}$

According to the study in [16], 2ED reached a recall of above 96% when token-level threshold is set to 0.9, and above 99% when is set to 0.85 on some data sets. While the results above are impressive, we also explored the previous 2ED algorithm in greater detail by focusing on its performance on two kinds of edit-distances respectively. We use a lower threshold of at 0.8 to allow us to observe as many matched pairs of substrings and entities (hereafter "matched pairs") as reasonably possible. The data set used at this stage is a corpus of IMDb reviews [8] and a dictionary of movie titles obtained from the IMDb website [4]. The results of running 2ED algorithm on this data set are as follows: (i) the number of sub-strings matched (with $\delta = \tau = 0.8$) is 39908, and (ii) the number of sub-strings approximately matched (score < 1) is 7540.

The Table 2 below shows a summary of the labelled matched pairs.

Table 2. Summary of the labelled matched pairs from 2ED

Summary of labelled matched pairs	Total	fp	tp
Number of matched pairs labelled	200	47	154
Matched pairs with token-level edit-distance	42	20	22
Matched pairs with character-level edit-distance	156	27	129
Matched pairs with both levels of edit-distance	2	0	2

Although the number of substrings labelled is relatively small, we can still draw some qualitative conclusions: First, the number of approximately matched substrings (score < 1) takes a considerable proportion of the number of all matched substrings when the threshold δ is set to 0.8. Secondly, the true positive matches takes up over 75% of the manually labelled sample. Thirdly, out of the manually labelled sample, substrings with character-level edit-distance takes a dominant majority and also contributes to the biggest proportion of the true positive matches. Lastly, substrings with both levels of edit distance takes a little proportion in the sample. According to the analysis above, we will focus on improving the effectiveness of the previous work for extracting substrings with character-level edit-distance.

4.1 Distinguishing a Typo from an Intended Token

Limitation of Lexical Edit-Distances. Previous experimental studies of the 2ED algorithm provided some intuitions for our improvement work. For example, the following two matched pairs have a very close 2ED score but pair #1 is an invalid match while pair #2 is valid (Table 3).

Table 3. Examples from 2ED

#	Substring	Entity	2ED
1	About the premise	About the promise	0.844754
2	Code of honor	Code of honour	0.862025

To be more general, 2ED measures the similarity of two tokens by lexical edit-distance. In example #1, the difference between this matched pair is within the word pair "premise" and "promise". 2ED measures the distance between the word pair by number of character-level operations including insertion, deletion and substitution. Thus, the difference is represented by a substitution operation that turns the letter "e" in word "premise" into the letter "o" in word "promise". Similarly in example #2, the distance is represented by an insertion operation that turns the word "honor" into "honour". However, the validity of the two matched pairs is not represented by the lexical edit-distance within these pairs. The pair in example #2 is valid because token "honor" is an variation of token "honour" in English; while the pair in example #1 is not valid because "premise" and "promise" are two different words that share little similarity in their grammatical position and semantical meaning. In fact, the lexical edit-distance between two tokens is more applicable as a representation of their similarity (distance) when one of them is a mis-spelled version (typo) of the other. It is common that words that look similar may or may not have close meanings and grammatical position (e.g. part-of-speech). Thus, some criteria for distinguishing a typo from an intended token should be introduced to help us judge whether it is appropriate to apply the FuzzyED which is based on lexical edit-distance.

4.2 Using Language Models

We propose the following conditions for identifying a typo based on the above analysis: suppose the substring contains a token ts that has a close lexical edit-distance with the corresponding token te in the entity. We assume ts is not a typo if and only if (i) ts is a valid word in the language and (ii) ts fits in the context in the substring. The next step is to model these two conditions in a feasible way. In fact, the conditions (i) and (ii) above can both be judged with a corpus of its language, where the validity of a single token can be measured by its frequency in the corpus and the validity of its context by the frequency of word phrases or (token-level) n-grams. Since single tokens are just (token-level) 1-grams, the above conditions can be simplified as judging whether the n-grams generated around ts are valid n-grams in the language, where n is in range $[1, k]$ and $k \geq 2$. N-grams and language models. The application of (token-level) n-grams in NLP tasks is versatile, one of them being a statistical language model. A language model can help us tell (i) how likely a given n-gram will appear in a language or (ii) the conditional probability that an n-gram is followed by a certain word. According to the analysis above, we are using statistics of the n-grams in a language without domain-specific knowledge or linguistic rules. Thus it is appropriate to use a statistical language model trained from a large corpus.

Utilising Web-Scale Corpora: Since our task is to specifically use the language model as a comprehensive corpus of a language, it is critical to find a source where we can obtain large scale n-grams. In 2012, Lin et al. [7,8] published the second version of the "Google Books Ngram Corpus, where frequencies of n-grams in the Google Books collection are collected with historical statistics. The corpus "reflects 6% of all books ever published" [7]. Considering the scale and coverage of the corpus, we find it a great source for our purpose. Training from such a large corpus consisting of hundreds of gigabytes of data is not trivial. Even if we leave out all historical information and use n-gram frequencies collectively, maintaining a map of n-grams and their frequencies is still a memory consuming task to be executed on a single machine. Besides memory consumption of the training process, the complexity of the model is another concern. Based on the above complexity analysis, we adopt a relatively simple model in this paper, the BerkeleyLM [13], which features a trained n-gram based model using the Google Books Ngram Corpus. The model provides interfaces for querying (i) the (conditional) log-probability of an n-gram and (ii) the raw count of an n-gram in the Google Books Ngram Corpus. The trained model uses stupid back-off for estimating the (conditional) probability of an n-gram as follows $P(w_i|w_1, w_2, ..., w_{i-1}) = \frac{count(w_1, w_2, ..., w_i)}{count(w_1, w2, ..., w_{i-1})}$.

4.3 Estimating Word Similarity

As discussed in Sect. 4.1, we are interested in the case where an unmatched token in the substring is not a typo and thus the applicability of the previous 2ED algorithm needs to be carefully reviewed. Here, the method we propose is to use word embedding for measuring the distance between two tokens. From the experimental results in Sect. 4.1, an observation is that the unmatched tokens in a matched pair can belong to various cases. For example, (i) ts and te may be variations of each other (e.g. "honour" and "honour"); (ii) ts may be the plural form of te or vice versa (e.g. "survivors" and "survivor"). A word embedding will help us capture the "distance" between the unmatched tokens. The word embedding adopted in this paper is Google's word2vec [1] which represents words in a corpus by vectors of floats. According to Mikolov et al. [10–12], the trained model can capture syntactic and semantic information of words in a language.

4.4   Other Improvements

Besides the introduction of language models and word embedding to replace some functionality of the FuzzyED distance metric, we have also made other minor improvements. The previous 2ED algorithm does not separate the period from the last word in a sentence during its tokenisation phrase. Since many approximately matched pairs are exact matches if we strip the period (dot) from the last token in the substring, we make this operation an optional feature in the implemented post-processing algorithm.

5   Implementation

The improved methods described in Sect. 4 is implemented in a pipeline. All improvements are applied as post-processing steps to filter, examine and (possibly) re-score matched pairs selected by previous 2ED algorithm. We will walk through the pipeline step by step in the rest of this section.

5.1   Obtain Candidate Pairs

The first step is finding matched pairs with character-level edit-distance as candidates for future re-scoring work. We apply the previous 2ED algorithm to our corpus against a dictionary with token-level similarity threshold $\delta = 0.8$ and character-level similarity threshold $\tau = 0.8$. was chosen according to the parameter optimization work in [16]; was chosen for error tolerance with the previous algorithm. After obtaining the list of matched pairs, we filter out exact matches (i.e. 2ED score = 1) because they are not the part of the result we are trying to improve. For the rest of the matched pairs, we apply the following steps for each pair.

5.2   Rescore Candiadte Pairs

Filter Out Pairs with Tokenisation Problems: An approximately matched pairs with tokenisation problems as described in Sect. 4.2 is not processed into the next step. Rather, we simply strip the ending period from the substring and assume it an exact match. The stripping step is operational and improvement from this operation is separately analysed as in Sect. 6.

Generate n-gram to Check Validity: With an approximately matched pair, we compare each token pair in the corresponding position of the substring and the entity to identify whether there is (only) a character-level edit-distance between this pair. In this process, we have also obtained the position of the ts and te as per notation in Sect. 4.1 if the token pair does exist. We then generate (token-level) n-gram pairs surrounding ts and te in the substring and the entity term respectively. We first generate 3-grams. If the substring is too short that it contains less than 3 tokens. We use the substring and the entity as a whole, i.e. 2-grams or 1-gram, for a pair. The next step is to check the validity of these n-grams in a language model to help us distinguish a typo from an intended word according to the conditions described in Sect. 4.1. We use a tolerant criteria for this validity check, where the unmatched token in the substring ts is considered an intended word as long as any n-gram pair from ts and te are both valid or both invalid in the language model. For each (token-level) n-gram, we use two thresholds accounting for the log-probability and raw count in the language model respectively to help check its validity. The thresholds are set according to empirical observations. The threshold for log-probability is -10.8 and the threshold for raw count is 0.

Apply Cosine Similarity to Rescore: When an unmatched token is identified as an intended word in the last step, we use the trained word2vec embedding to calculate the similarity between the token pair ts and te. For the examples in Sect. 4.1, the cosine similarity are shown in the table below. As we can see, these scores represents the distance between the token pairs in English: the similarity between "honor" and "honour" is significantly higher than that between "premise" and "promise" since the former consists of variations of the same word while the latter consists of two distinct words (Table 4).

Table 4. Cosine similarity for examples in Table 3

#	Substring	Entity	Cosine similarity
1	About the premise	About the promise	0.245628
2	Code of honor	Code of honour	0.637478

The cosine similarity between ts and te is normalised using the following formula. This formula is chosen according to empirical observation of the distribution of the cosine similarity (denoted by cos in the formula). It guarantees the following features: (i) normalised edit-distance is 0 when cos is 1, i.e. the edit-distance is 0 for two identical words; (ii) normalised edit-distance is 1 when cos is 0 (although cos is within range $[-1,1]$, we observe that most empirical results sits in $[0, 1]$); (iii) normalised edit-distance punishes low cos scores using an exponential formula; (iv) base is a tunable parameter affecting the curve of the normalization function: $ED_{norm} = \frac{base^{1-cos}-1}{base-1}$. A final score is applied to the post-processed pair of substring and entity using the following formula. We take the length of the entity as a normalizing parameter. This approach is similar to the normalization in FuzzyED when we assign a uniform weight to the tokens in the entity: $Rescore = 1 - \frac{ED_{norm}}{length(entity)}$.

6   Experimental Studies

Evaluation Setup: The validation was performed on the NeCTAR research cloud [3] using a 12-core computing instance with 48 GB of RAM. The test data set was obtained from a public corpus of Amazon reviews [9]. The corpus consists of (i) millions of reviews on the Amazon website, further divided into subsets by product category; (ii) metadata of the products available on the Amazon website. From the review data set, we selected the books subset which contains more than 8 million reviews and sampled 1000 reviews as the text for the task. From the metadata which contains information about 9.4 billion product items, we extracted only the titles of these items and use the result as the dictionary for the task. Due to missing fields in the metadata, the dictionary consists of 7.99 million product titles.

The corpus for training word2vec embeddings is obtained from various resources on the web using the script provided in the toolset on [1]. The resulting training set consists of 6.1 billion tokens. After two runs of the word2phrase pre-processing [1], we train the word2vec embedding with the Continuous Bag of Word (CBOW) method and a vector size of 300 dimensions on the data set. Another training method skipgram was also attempted but achieved lower precision using the provided validation tool in [1]; and it was not used in future steps. The training process takes less than a day to finish on the cloud instance.

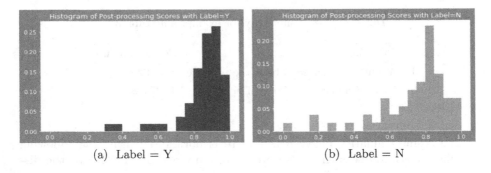

(a) Label = Y   (b) Label = N

Fig. 1. Histogram of post-processing scores

We use (i) the distribution of the scores of re-visited pairs for positive pairs and negative pairs respectively, and (ii) the Receiver Operating Characteristic (ROC) curve to validate the effectiveness of the post-processing. We manually labelled 113 pairs from the re-scored set, which comprises over 10% of its size and use that labelled data to evaluate the result.

Effectiveness: Figure 1 shows the distribution of the re-visited scores separated by their labels, where label Y means the matched pair is valid (according to human evaluation) and label N means the pair is not. As we can see, by applying the post-processing, the two groups have their scores distributed in two clusters in distinct centroids.

The two ROC curves below compare the performance of using 2ED score and post-processed score to predict validity of extracted substrings. As we can see, the post-processed score achieves a higher true positive rate without sacrificing

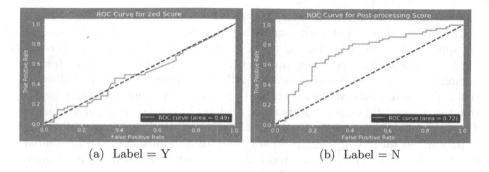

(a) Label = Y   (b) Label = N

Fig. 2. ROC curves for 2ED score and post-processing score

the false positive rate, while 2ED score performs like random guess in evaluation of extracted substrings. Overall the post-processed score achieved an area under curve (AUC) of 0.72, and outperforms 2ED score by 47%.

Efficiency: The efficiency of the algorithm is not the major concern in this paper. We evaluate the performance of the post-processing algorithm by the time taken to complete the task on the data set described earlier in this section. The task typically finishes within 10 min, depending on the status of the cloud instance. Majority of the time taken is on loading trained models into memory, so the performance should also depend on the physical RAM available on the evaluation instance. After loading the models, the application finishes processing over 2000 items in less than 5 s. Therefore, this algorithm should be suitable as a post-processing step for the previous 2ED algorithm in terms of its performance.

7   Conclusion and Future Work

In this paper, we proposed several improvements to our previous entity extraction algorithm called "2ED". Our proposed improvements include language models for typo detection, word embedding to measure word distances to capture semantic features, and more advanced tokenization. We have implemented the proposed techniques as a post-processing step on top of 2ED. Our proposed techniques bring significant improvement to 2ED. The improvement mainly lies in the introduction of web-scale corpora used for training relatively comprehensive and versatile models. This finding shows that more information from the web-scale corpora can facilitate entity extraction.

Some improvements and extensions to this work can be made to further generalise its applicability, boost its performance and make better use of the web-scale corpus. First, it is possible to combine evidence from postags. The new version of Google Books Ngram Corpus features part-of-speech tag (i.e., postag) information. Such labels can be further utilised for measuring the distance between a token pair in addition to the n-gram used in the current implementation. Furthermore, beyond the post-processing approach, postags can facilitate the candidate substring generation process in 2ED. Second, it is promising to tokenise text with punctuations. 2ED uses a tokenisation method which does not separate the period of a sentence with its ending word. One major concern of stripping periods from the ending words in the previous implementation is it is hard to distinguish a "true" punctuation which ends a sentence or clause from an ending dot of an abbreviation lexically. With the language models introduced in this paper, potentially we are able to find effective ways to improve the tokenisation using linguistic evidence from these models. Third, learning parameters for 2ED is also helpful for users. The current implementation uses empirical settings of parameters for judging n-gram validity and for normalising the cosine similarity of a token pair. These parameters can be learned from labelled data. Finally, our approach extracts entities in English, and our approach can be extended to other languages.

References

1. Bengio, Y., Ducharme, R., Vincent, P., Jauvin, C.: A neural probabilistic language model. J. Mach. Learn. Res. **3**(Feb), 1137–1155 (2003)
2. Chiu, J.P., Nichols, E.: Named entity recognition with bidirectional LSTM-CNNs. Trans. Assoc. Comput. Linguist. **4**, 357–370 (2016)
3. Corbet, S.A., Delfosse, E.S.: Honeybees and the nectar of echium plantagineum l. in Southeastern Australia. Aust. J. Ecol. **9**(2), 125–139 (1984)
4. Harper, F.M., Konstan, J.A.: The movielens datasets: history and context. ACM Trans. Interact. Intell. Syst. (TIIS) **5**(4), 19 (2016)
5. Heafield, K.: KenLM: faster and smaller language model queries. In: Workshop on Statistical Machine Translation, pp. 187–197. ACL (2011)
6. Jagadish, H.V., Ooi, B.C., Tan, K.-L., Yu, C., Zhang, R.: iDistance: an adaptive B+-tree based indexing method for nearest neighbor search. Trans. Database Syst. **30**(2), 364–397 (2005)
7. Lin, Y., Michel, J.-B., Aiden, E.L., Orwant, J., Brockman, W., Petrov, S.: Syntactic annotations for the google books ngram corpus. In: ACL, pp. 169–174 (2012)
8. Maas, A.L., Daly, R.E., Pham, P.T., Huang, D., Ng, A.Y., Potts, C.: Learning word vectors for sentiment analysis. In: Proceedings of the 49th Annual Meeting of the Association for Computational Linguistics: Human Language Technologies, vol. 1, pp. 142–150. Association for Computational Linguistics (2011)
9. McAuley, J., Leskovec, J.: Hidden factors and hidden topics: understanding rating dimensions with review text. In: Proceedings of the 7th ACM Conference on Recommender Systems, pp. 165–172. ACM (2013)
10. Mikolov, T., Chen, K., Corrado, G., Dean, J.: Efficient estimation of word representations in vector space. arXiv preprint arXiv:1301.3781 (2013)
11. Mikolov, T., Sutskever, I., Chen, K., Corrado, G.S., Dean, J.: Distributed representations of words and phrases and their compositionality. In: Advances in Neural Information Processing Systems, pp. 3111–3119 (2013)
12. Mikolov, T., Yih, W.-T., Zweig, G.: Linguistic regularities in continuous space word representations. In: Proceedings of the 2013 Conference of the North American Chapter of the Association for Computational Linguistics: Human Language Technologies, pp. 746–751 (2013)
13. Pauls, A., Klein, D.: Faster and smaller n-gram language models. In: ACL, pp. 258–267. ACL (2011)

14. Tseytlin, E., Mitchell, K., Legowski, E., Corrigan, J., Chavan, G., Jacobson, R.S.: Noble-flexible concept recognition for large-scale biomedical natural language processing. BMC Bioinf. **17**(1), 32 (2016)
15. Wei, Q., Chen, T., Xu, R., He, Y., Gui, L.: Disease named entity recognition by combining conditional random fields and bidirectional recurrent neural networks. Database **2016** (2016)
16. Wen, Z., Deng, D., Zhang, R., Kotagiri, R.: An efficient entity extraction algorithm using two-level edit-distance. In: ICDE, pp. 998–1009. IEEE (2019)
17. Wen, Z., Zhang, R., Ramamohanarao, K., Qi, J., Taylor, K.: MASCOT: fast and highly scalable SVM cross-validation using GPUs and SSDs. In: ICDM, pp. 580–589. IEEE (2014)
18. Whitelaw, C., Hutchinson, B., Chung, G.Y., Ellis, G.: Using the web for language independent spellchecking and autocorrection. In: EMNLP, pp. 890–899. ACL (2009)

Short Papers

Graph-Based Relation-Aware Representation Learning for Clothing Matching

Yang Li[✉], Yadan Luo, and Zi Huang

The University of Queensland, Brisbane, Australia
yang.li@uq.edu.au, lyadanluol@gmail.com, huang@itee.uq.edu.au

Abstract. Learning mix-and-match relationships between fashion items is a promising yet challenging task for modern fashion recommender systems, which requires to infer complex fashion compatibility patterns from a large number of fashion items. Previous work mainly utilises metric learning techniques to model the compatibility relationships, such that compatible items are closer to each other than incompatible ones in the latent space. However, they ignore the contextual information of the fashion items for compatibility prediction. In this paper, we propose a Graph-based Type-Relational Neural Network (GTR-NN) framework, which first generates item representations through multi-layer ChebNet considering k-hop neighbour information, and then outputs compatibility score by predicting the binary label of an edge between two nodes under a specific type relation. Extensive experiments for two fashion-related tasks demonstrate the effectiveness and superior performance of our model.

Keywords: Fashion compatibility · Graph Neural Network

1 Introduction

The increasing demands of fashion recommender systems have boosted the development of fashion-related researches, such as visual recognition [8–10,14], fashion retrieval [1], fashion recommendation [11] and fashion compatibility learning [5,13]. Different from fashion retrieval and conventional fashion recommendation that mainly focus on recommending visually similar items to users, fashion compatibility learning aims at suggesting complementary items to users, which finally forms an aesthetically pleasing outfit.

The mainstream of modelling pair-wise fashion compatibility mainly relies on embedding learning and metric learning strategies, which maps item features into a fashion style latent space where compatible items are closer to each other than incompatible ones based on the Euclidean distance function or learnt metric function. However, this kind of approaches suffers from two issues. Firstly, they measure compatibility between two items in a single-relational space, such

© Springer Nature Switzerland AG 2020
R. Borovica-Gajic et al. (Eds.): ADC 2020, LNCS 12008, pp. 189–197, 2020.
https://doi.org/10.1007/978-3-030-39469-1_15

that the distance function is fixed for compatibility estimation, e.g., Euclidean distance or inner product. Such type-unaware latent space is likely to force incompatible items to be close when inappropriate triangle situation occurs. More concretely, if a t-shirt A matches pants B and a pair of shoes C match B, then A is forced to be compatible with C in the same style latent space, which is under-than-desirable. Secondly, due to the pair-wise training strategy, these approaches model each compatibility relationship in an item-independent manner, which does not consider the item's other associated compatible items for prediction. As a result, the distance between two items under the context-unaware space is fixed, which may lead to sub-optimal performance.

To solve the above-mentioned limitations, in this paper, we propose an end-to-end graph-based framework that explores compatibility relationships through graph data structure as well as captures type-to-type relations by exploiting edge features, namely Type-Relational Graph Neural Network (GTR-NN). The overall architecture of our model is illustrated in Fig. 1, which has two main components: graph-based item representation generator and Type-relation-aware Compatibility Estimator. Specifically, we first construct an item graph where the nodes represent different items and edges link compatible fashion items. Then, we use graph convolutional network to generate items' representation by aggregating their neighbours' information. Finally, the prediction of compatibility score between two items are output through a multilayer perceptron where the type relations are taken into consideration. To increase the robustness of our model, we also introduce edge-wise dropout regularisation which significantly helps our model converge faster and achieve better performance. Our main contributions can be summarised as below:

- We incorporate type-to-type relational information in Graph Neural Network for fashion compatibility modelling by exploring edge relation labels.
- We design type-aware pair-wise projections for item-to-item compatibility comparison.
- We introduce edge-wise regularisation training strategy that can be helpful to increase the performance and robustness of our model.
- Extensive experiments have been conducted for fill-in-the-blank, compatibility score estimation and compatible fashion item retrieval tasks, which shows that our model outperforms other baseline methods.

2   Related Work

2.1   Fashion Compatibility Learning

The main approaches of modelling fashion compatibility among fashion items are to project the item features into a shared style latent space, such that compatible items are made to be closer than incompatible ones. McAuley et al. [11] propose to learn an underlying compatibility space by Low-rank Mahalanobis Transformation to minimise the distance between compatible pairs as well as

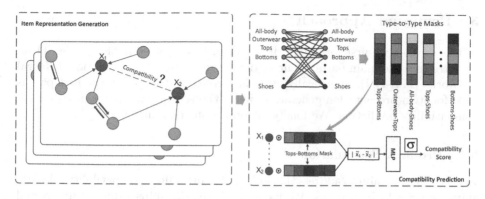

Fig. 1. The overview of our proposed Type-Relational Graph Neural Network (GTR-NN) framework. It mainly contains two parts: a graph-based item representation generator and a type-aware compatibility estimator.

maximise those of incompatible ones. Veit et al. propose to learn a metric function that is trained with Siamese CNNs in an end-to-end manner. Following that work, they introduce Conditional Similarity Network (CSN), which claims that the compatibility measurement should be assessed from multiple aspects, i.e., colours, shapes, patterns, etc. Vasileva et al [13] develop a type-aware embedding learning framework, which points that type label information would have a positive impact on compatibility measurement, and thus items with different type labels should be compared in different type-specific spaces.

2.2 Graph Neural Networks

Recently, Graph Neural Networks (GNNs) are proven to be an efficient and effective framework for representation learning on graph-structured data, which leads to breakthroughs in various areas. Technically, GNNs follow transformation and aggregation schemes to merge neighbour information into each node, such that each node's representation is able to capture more contextual information from its neighbours. The concept of Graph Neural Network is first introduced by Scarselli et al. [12], which utilises a feed-forward network for information propagation. After this work, an extensive number of GNN-based approaches have been proposed. Generally, GNN-related methods can be categorised into two groups according to the propagation types: spectral-based and spatial-based. Spectral methods generalise convolution operations into graph domain. Defferrard et al. [4] introduced to use a truncated expansion of Chebyshev polynomials to recursively aggregate information from K orders. Kipf et al. [6] proposed Graph Convolutional Network, which restricts the depth of convolution to 1, such that it only considers 1th order aggregation operation on each GCN layer.

3   Proposed Approach

In this section, we first formulate the problem to be solved in this paper. Then, we introduce the main parts of our model, Graph-based Type-Relational Neural Network (GTR-NN). Specifically, it mainly contains two parts, the first part is used for item presentation generation, while the second part is for item-to-item compatibility prediction. We finally introduce our training strategy.

3.1   Problem Formulation

In this paper, we aim to address the problem for modelling compatibility relationships between fashion items. We model such relationships using an undirected graph. We have a set of type labels denoted as τ, a collection of fashion items denoted as $S = x_1, x_2, x_3, \ldots, x_n$. Each item x_i is associated with visual features and type label t_i from τ. Denote $\mathcal{G} = (\mathcal{V}, \mathcal{E})$ be an undirected graph where node i represents item x_i, and edge $e = (I, j) \in \mathcal{E}$ connects two items x_i and x_j which are observed to be compatible with each other and linked with a type-relational label r^{t_i, t_j}.

3.2   Part 1: Item Representation Generation

The initial features of items are visual features extracted from pre-trained ResNet, which contain multiple attributes, such as clothing colours, shapes and patterns. We think that when measuring the compatibility score between two items x_i and x_j, using other items that x_i and x_j are compatible with as references would help the model to better capture the important characteristics for compatibility prediction. In this paper, we use graph convolutional network proposed by [4] to incorporate contextual information (i.e., information from neighbour compatible items) into each node's representation. Specifically, the graph-based representation generator can be considered as a non-linear transition function that changes item i's representation $h_i \in \mathbb{R}^d$ into $\tilde{h}_i \in \mathbb{R}^{d'}$. More concretely, it applies an efficient convolution-like operation on graph domain using a Laplacian operator. We denote a normalised normalised Laplacian graph as L, which is calculated as follows:

$$L = I - D^{\frac{1}{2}} A D^{\frac{1}{2}} \tag{1}$$

Here, I is an identity matrix, A is an adjacency matrix and D is a diagonal degree matrix, where $D_{ii} = \sum_{k=0}^{j} A_{ik}$. The node representations are updated following the formulas below:

$$\tilde{H} = \sum_{k=1}^{K} Z^{(k)} \cdot \Theta^{(k)} \tag{2}$$

where $\Theta^{(k)}$ denotes the trainable parameters at k hop that transforms item features $\mathbb{R}^d$ into $\mathbb{R}^{d'}$. $Z^{(k)}$ represents the calculated $k - hop$ features. It is computed recursively by the following equations:

$$Z^{(1)} = H \tag{3}$$

$$Z^{(2)} = \hat{L} \cdot H \tag{4}$$

$$Z^{(k)} = 2 \cdot \hat{L} \cdot Z^{(k-1)} - Z^{(k-2)} \tag{5}$$

where $\hat{L}$ is the scaled and normalised Laplacian computed by $\frac{2L}{\lambda_{max} - I_n}$, which limits the scaled eigenvalues ranged between -1 and 1.

3.3 Part 2: Type-Aware Compatibility Prediction

The compatibility score prediction between item pairs can be considered as a link prediction problem on the graph. Therefore, the goal of the compatibility estimator in our framework is to give a score ranging between 0 and 1 based on two given node features. The common way for achieving this is to learn a metric function $f()$ that can represent a distance between two $n - D$ vectors. Inspired by the metric learning-related work [2,7], we choose to compute the compatibility probability using the following formula:

$$compatibility = \sigma(W^{\top} |H_i - H_j| + b) \tag{6}$$

where H_i and H_j are the features of two nodes i and j output from graph-based representation generator. W is a weight matrix and b is R. $\sigma()$ is a sigmoid function that limits the output value to be a valid probability score, i.e., $p \in (0,1)$. We use absolute function to guarantee the symmetry of pair-wise measurement, i.e., the value of $f(H_i, H_j)$ is the same as $f(H_j, H_i)$. Moreover, we think that items associated with different type labels should be treated differently when measuring their distance. This idea is based on the fact that when people compare whether two clothes are matching, they may focus on different aspects for different type pairs. For example, we usually focus on the size and shape when we measure the compatibility between a pair of pants and a t-shirt, while we may pay attention to colour and pattern when we are about to find a hat to match our tops. Therefore, we propose to construct type-relation-aware subspaces to model such observation. Specifically, assume there are τ types in the dataset, then there will be $\frac{\tau^2 - \tau}{2}$ type-relations (we also consider pairs of same types). Therefore, as illustrated in Fig. 1 we design type-relation-specific masks that project item features into their associated type-relational subspaces. Thus, the compatibility score p of item i and j is computed as:

$$p = \sigma(W^{\top} \left| H_i \odot m^{r^{t_i, t_j}} - H_j \odot m^{r^{t_i, t_j}} \right| + b) \tag{7}$$

where t_i and t_j are the type labels of item i and j, while H_i and H_j are the features of item i and j respectively. $\odot$ represents dot product operation.

3.4   Training Strategy

We treat the compatibility measurement task as graph completion task on a large graph. More concretely, to train our model, we first randomly discard a set of edges $e_{ij} \in \mathcal{E}^{positive}$ from the training adjacency matrix where $A_{ij} = 1$, which are labelled as 1. We then randomly sample the same sized set of negative edges $e_{ij} \in \mathcal{E}^{negative}$ labelled as 0 from the A, i.e., $A_{ij} = 0$. The adjacency matrix A now becomes an incomplete adjacency matrix $\hat{A}$ with a training edge set $\mathcal{E}_{train} = \mathcal{E}^{positive} + \mathcal{E}^{negative}$. Finally, we use binary cross entropy objective function to train the model to predict 1 for positive edges (i.e., items that are compatible) and 0 for negative edges (i.e., incompatible pairs). The objective function is defined as follows:

$$\mathcal{L} = -((a+b)log(p) + (1-a)log(1-p) + (1-b)log(1-p)),$$
$$a = 1, b = 0, p \in (0,1) \tag{8}$$

where p represents the compatibility score calculated by Eq. (7).

To increase the robustness of our approach, we introduce edge-wise regularisation strategy. Specifically, we randomly remove some edges from $\hat{A}$ where $A_{ij} = 1$. In this way, the structure of the constructed item graph is continuously changed over the training phase, and the model will be trained to be more robust when less contextual information is given for representation learning.

4   Experiments

4.1   Dataset

Our experiments are conducted on the public fashion outfit dataset collected from a fashion-focused online community, Polyvore, by Han et al. [5]. It contains 21,889 outfits with rich information including title, item description, image, number of likes and type label. We split the dataset into three subsets, i.e., training set (17,316 outfits), validation set (1,497 outfits) and test set (3,076 outfits).

Table 1. Comparison on PolyvoreMaryland dataset based on two fashion-related tasks: fill-in-the-blank (Accuracy) and compatibility estimation (AUC).

Method	Maryland Polyvore			
	FITB Accuracy	FITB (Hard) Accuracy	Compat. AUC	Compat. (Hard) AUC
Siamese Net	54.2	54.4	0.85	0.85
Bi-LSTM	68.6	64.9	0.90	0.94
TA-CSN	86.1	65.0	0.98	0.93
CA-GAE	95.9	90.9	0.98	0.98
GTR-NN	**97.3**	**92.1**	**0.99**	**0.98**

4.2   Baselines

The brief descriptions of state-of-the-art methods are provided below.

Siamese Net: A metric learning method that minimises the distance of compatible image features and maximises the distance between incompatible images through contrastive loss.

Bi-LSTM: The method uses a bidirectional LSTM to capture the underlying compatibility relationships trained under cross-entropy optimisation criterion.

TA-CSN: The method constructs type-pair subspaces where items with different type labels are compared in different subspaces trained via triplet loss.

CA-GAE: The state-of-the-art method employs Graph AutoEncoder architecture, which has an encoder for item representation generation and a decoder for pair-wise compatibility prediction. It receives the state-of-the-art result in both fill-in-the-blank and compatibility prediction tasks.

4.3   Implementation Details

We implement GTR-NN using Tensorflow deep learning framework. The visual features of each fashion item are extracted using ResNet with 2048 dimensions. We stack three ChebNet layers with 350 hidden units in the item representation generator and apply 0.5 and 0.3 to dropout layer in representation generator and compatibility estimator respectively. We set the edge-wise dropout rate to be 0.1. The whole item graph is fed into the model without a mini-batch training strategy. The optimiser we use is SGD with Adam updating strategy. The learning rate is set to be 0.001 and a momentum of 0.9.

4.4   Task Description

To evaluate our model, we conduct experiments for two widely-applied fashion-related tasks: fill-in-the-blank and outfit compatibility estimation on Polyvore dataset. The details and analysis of these two tasks are described below.

Fill in the Blank. This task is to select the most suitable item from four candidates to form a compatible outfit. In particular, we form four outfits with the given four candidate items respectively. The candidate with the highest score is selected as the answer. We also design a hard version of this task where all four candidates are from the same category. The metric we use for evaluation in this task is accuracy, which is widely used in recommendation evaluation [3,5].

Compatibility Prediction. This task requires the model to output an overall compatibility score $s, s \in (0, 1)$ for the given outfit. The test set contains 10,000 compatible outfits and 10,000 incompatible outfits. The negative outfits are generated by randomly replacing items in outfits with other fashion items. We use AUC as our evaluation metric, whose value represents the probability that a randomly chosen positive example is ranked higher than a randomly chosen negative example, in this task.

4.5   Performance Comparison

The results of the fill-in-the-blank task and compatibility prediction is represented in Table 1. It can be observed that GTR-NN achieves the best performance in most cases. SiameseNet and Bi-LSTM methods perform poorly mainly because they do not consider type information. The graph-based methods, CA-GAE and our approach both receive better performance than BiLSTM. This proves that modelling outfit data in graph structure can better capture second-order relationships than in sequence structure. TA-CSN achieves 86.1% accuracy in FITB task but receives similar performance result in the hard version of FITB task, which proves that pair-wise learning strategy could not distinguish the intra-type items in the type-specific space well. CA-GAE reaches nearly 96% and 91% in FITB&FITB(hard) task and 0.99 in compatibility prediction task, however, their performance is lower than ours especially in terms of FITB tasks. This mainly because our model measures compatibility relationships under type-specific relations, which helps the model identify subtle patterns from different types.

5   Conclusion

In this paper, we introduce a graph-based type-aware framework that not only models item-to-item relationships via graph convolutional network but also incorporate type relational information into final compatibility estimation. The experiments conducted on Polyvore dataset have shown that our model can achieve state-of-the-art performance on both fill-in-the-blank and compatibility estimation tasks. As for future work, we would like to study type-relation information by directly exploring edge features during aggregation procedure in graph convolutional network.

References

1. Bell, S., Bala, K.: Learning visual similarity for product design with convolutional neural networks. ACM Trans. Graph. **34**(4), 98:1–98:10 (2015)
2. Cucurull, G., Taslakian, P., Vazquez, D.: Context-aware visual compatibility prediction. In: Proceedings of the IEEE Conference on Computer Vision and Pattern Recognition, pp. 12617–12626 (2019)
3. Cui, Z., Li, Z., Wu, S., Zhang, X., Wang, L.: Dressing as a whole: outfit compatibility learning based on node-wise graph neural networks. In: The World Wide Web Conference, WWW 2019, pp. 307–317 (2019)
4. Defferrard, M., Bresson, X., Vandergheynst, P.: Convolutional neural networks on graphs with fast localized spectral filtering. In: Advances in Neural Information Processing Systems 29: Annual Conference on Neural Information Processing Systems 2016, pp. 3837–3845 (2016)
5. Han, X., Wu, Z., Jiang, Y., Davis, L.S.: Learning fashion compatibility with bidirectional LSTMs. In: Proceedings of the 2017 ACM on Multimedia Conference, MM 2017, pp. 1078–1086 (2017)

6. Kipf, T.N., Welling, M.: Semi-supervised classification with graph convolutional networks. In: 5th International Conference on Learning Representations, ICLR 2017 (2017)
7. Koch, G., Zemel, R., Salakhutdinov, R.: Siamese neural networks for one-shot image recognition. In: ICML Deep Learning Workshop, vol. 2 (2015)
8. Luo, Y., Huang, Z., Zhang, Z., Wang, Z., Li, J., Yang, Y.: Curiosity-driven reinforcement learning for diverse visual paragraph generation. In: Proceedings of the 27th ACM International Conference on Multimedia, MM 2019, pp. 2341–2350 (2019)
9. Luo, Y., Wang, Z., Huang, Z., Yang, Y., Zhao, C.: Coarse-to-fine annotation enrichment for semantic segmentation learning. In: Proceedings of the 27th ACM International Conference on Information and Knowledge Management, CIKM 2018, pp. 237–246 (2018)
10. Luo, Y., Yang, Y., Shen, F., Huang, Z., Zhou, P., Shen, H.T.: Robust discrete code modeling for supervised hashing. Pattern Recogn. **75**, 128–135 (2018)
11. McAuley, J.J., Targett, C., Shi, Q., van den Hengel, A.: Image-based recommendations on styles and substitutes. In: Proceedings of the 38th International ACM SIGIR Conference on Research and Development in Information Retrieval, Santiago, Chile, 9–13 August 2015, pp. 43–52 (2015)
12. Scarselli, F., Gori, M., Tsoi, A.C., Hagenbuchner, M., Monfardini, G.: The graph neural network model. IEEE Trans. Neural Networks **20**(1), 61–80 (2009)
13. Vasileva, M.I., Plummer, B.A., Dusad, K., Rajpal, S., Kumar, R., Forsyth, D.: Learning type-aware embeddings for fashion compatibility. In: Ferrari, V., Hebert, M., Sminchisescu, C., Weiss, Y. (eds.) ECCV 2018. LNCS, vol. 11220, pp. 405–421. Springer, Cham (2018). https://doi.org/10.1007/978-3-030-01270-0_24
14. Wang, Z., Luo, Y., Li, Y., Huang, Z., Yin, H.: Look deeper see richer: depth-aware image paragraph captioning. In: 2018 ACM Multimedia Conference on Multimedia Conference, MM 2018, Seoul, Republic of Korea, 22–26 October 2018, pp. 672–680 (2018)

Evaluating Random Walk-Based Network Embeddings for Web Service Applications

Olayinka Adeleye[1]([✉]), Jian Yu[1], Ji Ruan[1], and Quan Z. Sheng[2]

[1] Department of Computer Science, Auckland University of Technology,
Auckland 1010, New Zealand
{olayinka.adeleye,jian.yu,ji.ruan}@aut.ac.nz
[2] Department of Computing, Macquarie University, Sydney, NSW, Australia
quan.sheng@macq.ac.au

Abstract. Network embedding models automatically learn low-dimensional and neighborhood graph representation in vector space. Even-though these models have shown improved performances in various applications such as *link prediction* and *classification* compare to traditional graph mining approaches, they are still difficult to interpret. Most works rely on visualization for the interpretation. Moreover, it is challenging to quantify how well these models can preserve the topological properties of real networks such as *clustering*, *degree centrality* and *betweenness*. In this paper, we study the performance of recent unsupervised network embedding models in Web service application. Specifically, we investigate and analyze the performance of recent random walk-based embedding approaches including *node2vec*, *DeepWalk*, *LINE* and *HARP* in capturing the properties of Web service networks and compare the performances of the models for basic web service prediction tasks. We based the study on the Web service networks constructed in our previous works. We evaluate the models with respect to the precision with which they unpack specific topological properties of the networks. We investigate the influence of each topological property on the accuracy of the prediction task. We conduct our experiment using the popular ProgrammableWeb dataset. The results present in this work are expected to provide insight into application of network embedding in service computing domain especially for applications that aim at exploiting machine learning models.

Keywords: Embedding · Web service network · Link prediction

1 Introduction

Network (also known as Graph) models are important for encoding information, and data in network format exist in various fields in real-world including social, World Wide Web [3] and academics [7]. There has been significant progress over the last decades in mining network data and unveiling global properties of these networks. Various empirical observations emphasizing the universal nature of certain topological features like the high clustering coefficient, heavy

R. Borovica-Gajic et al. (Eds.): ADC 2020, LNCS 12008, pp. 198–205, 2020.
https://doi.org/10.1007/978-3-030-39469-1_16

tail node degree distribution [3] and community formation in many real-world networks [12] have been observed. In web service domain, there have been a number of studies based on network analysis investigating topological features and evolutionary properties of Web service ecosystem [1]. Some existing works have demonstrated the potentials of mining Web service network features especially in common tasks such as service recommendation, network prediction [10] and service discovery [2]. These applications usually exploit certain node or edge features, which are predictive of their properties. The most straightforward network representation used in the applications includes Mashups-APIs *bipartite network* which could in turn be compressed by applying *one-mode projection* to form an *API-API* network. The networks can be presented inform of sparse adjacency matrix where edges between nodes are presented as an entry into a square matrix [10]. This sort of data representation requires further transformation in low-dimensional vector space before they can be used as input for machine learning related tasks. Recently, network embedding techniques which aim to automatically learn low-dimensional, neighborhood and community-aware graph representation in vector space has drawn increasing attention. These techniques have been exploited in diverse domains and have shown promising performances in various downstream tasks such as *link-prediction* and *classification* [6,8].

In this paper, we investigate the performance of the state-of-the-art, random walk-based network embedding approaches including *node2vec* [9], *Deep-Walk* [11], *LINE* [14] and *HARP* [5] in transforming Web service networks into low-dimensional vector representation of the network elements. The resulting representations can then be used as input to various machine learning models. We consider our analysis in three key phases: First, we present three different Web service complex networks and their global characteristics. Then, we evaluate how well a particular embedding model can unpack the topological features encoded in the networks. We achieved this by quantifying the accuracy with which each embedding model can replicate the topological properties like node degree, betweeness, clustering coefficient and so on. Second, we consider the best performing embedding model for Web service prediction task with respect to a given service network. This is done by building a node property prediction classifier that is capable of predicting node-specific feature value given the node embedding. We conjecture that achieving a high node-feature prediction accuracy (score) by the classifier signifies effective encoding of the feature in the embedding space. Hence, we score each embedding model by its ability to train the classifier such that high performance in prediction task can be achieved given the embedding. This idea is motivated by recent literature [6,8,13] that attempted to interpret sentence and node representations in vector space. For this work, we uniquely map various representations learning with the Web service networks constructed in our previous works [1,2]. We aim to provide insights into *why an embedding algorithm performs better for a particular downstream task in Web service domain?*, and unearth the principal topological features responsible for optimum performance of a given node embedding approach in service discovery/prediction task. The main contribution of this paper includes:

1. We investigate and evaluate the performances of random walk-based network embedding models in preserving global topological characteristics of Web service ecosystem, which could be exploited in various machine-learning based Web service applications.
2. From network perspective, we examine how well node-specific properties encoded by the embedding models can be used to facilitate an elementary web service recommendation application defined as a link-prediction task.

The rest of this paper is organized as follows. Section 2 presents overview of various Web service networks. Section 3 presents the detail of our experimental procedure, analysis and results; Finally, we draw our conclusion and discuss future work in Sect. 4.

2   Web Service Networks and Their Properties

In this section, we present the overview of various Web service networks considered in this study. We focus on the networks that have been used in previous Web service applications. We visualize these networks and discuss their topological properties.

2.1   Composition - Service Network

A simple and most common way to build a social network for service ecosystems such as ProgrammableWeb is to model Composition-Service (or Mashup-API) invocation relationship in the service ecosystem as a *affiliation network*. This network can then be compressed to form a *Service-Service* (or *API-API*) network by applying *One-mode projection* to the service side of the *affiliation network*. This approach have been employed in several service related application [1,10] to model Web service network. Technically, this network is a bipartite graph, where the edges indicate which Web services are invoked by which composition. We define this network as *affiliation Network* $G = (M \uplus A, E)$ where M is the set of service compositions (Mashups) and A is the set of Web services (Web-APIs), and for any edge $(m, a) \in E, m \in M$ and $a \in A$ [1]. The overview of the affiliation network visualized using the *Force-Atlas* layout in Gephi[1] is shown in Fig. 1a. The *hubs* are clearly visible in the figure as disks with *Google-Maps* API being the largest one sitting at the bottom on of the network. Popular social media Web-APIs such as *Twitter*, *Youtube*, *Flickr*, and *Facebook* also appear 667, 557, 484, and 382 times respectively in the network.

2.2   Popularity and Fitness-Based Service Evolving Networks

The affiliation network described in Sect. 2.1 is solely based on *composition-service* usage record. However, the network show an apparent limitation in that

---

[1] https://gephi.org/.

only Web services used in Compositions (suppose every composition contains at least two Web service) will appear on the projected network. For example, the ProgrammableWeb affiliation network contains only 1,525 Web-APIs, which is less than 10% of the total 17,138 Web-APIs acquired from the repository. Therefore, to generate a network that connects all the Web services in the ecosystem, one way is to use generative network models that are capable of capturing/preserving specific node attributes and structural properties of the service ecosystem. Various mechanisms including *Node fitness, Preferential Attachment-PA* and *homophily* have been advanced for this purpose. Among these mechanisms, Preferential Attachment (PA) and node fitness have been more prominent because of their simplicity and capability to explain certain universal topological properties that emerge in real-world networks [12]. Topological properties not found in most classic models of sparse random networks such as − *scale-independence* (characterized with heavy-tailed degree distribution), *self similarity* and *hierarchy* − all appear in most real-word networks like WWW, citation network and internet [3]. We have shown details in our previous work [1] how to built a preferential attachment-based (or Popularity-based) Web service network using the well-established Barabási-Albert (BA) generative model [3] where attachment probabilities are proportional to target API node degree or API popularity. Figure 1b shows the visual overview of the BA *popularity-based* Web service network with the popular nodes labelled.

Another synthetic web service network considered in this work is the *Preferential Attachment with Fitness based* network which is an extension of *BA* model proposed by *Bianconi-Barabási* (called BB or fitness model) [4]. Fitness generative model captures certain intrinsic qualities other than popularity (or node

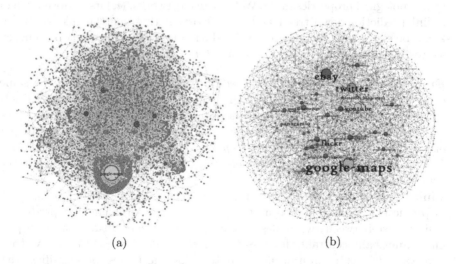

(a)   (b)

Fig. 1. Visualization of Web service networks. 1a shows the overview of the *Mashup-API bipartite Network* and 1b shows the overview of *Popularity-based service* network [1].

degree) posses by nodes in a network that influence the rate at which the nodes can acquire new link. *BA* set-up makes it difficult for a node which enters late into an open network to compete with the already established hubs of the network. However, this is not always true in real-world scenario, *latecomers* like *Google* service or nodes with minimal degree can actually acquire links relatively quickly and others who arrived earlier like *Alta Vista* and *Inktomi* services may not make it. The fitness model captures this behaviour by having on top of *growth* and *PA* another concept called the *fitness*, which capture the intrinsic quality of vertices. Fitness here is a quantitative measure of a node's ability to stay in front of the competition [3]. The higher the fitness, the higher the probability of attracting new edges. For detail construction of the fitness-based service network − see [2].

We analyse the topological properties of Web services networks from *node-level*. Since the Web service networks considered in this work are mainly driven by node's specific attributes (i.e. node's popularity and fitness), we consider key centrality indicators that characterized important nodes within the networks. We measure node's *degree centrality*[2], *betweenness centrality*[3], *clustering coefficient* and *eigenvector centrality*[4].

3   Analysis and Results

In this section, we describe the experimental procedure, analysis and the results for both prediction tasks: links and network properties predictions. Given the Web service networks described in Sect. 2, we aim to evaluate the performance of each of the *random-walk-based* embedding model based on (*i*) its ability to encode certain topological properties in the Web service networks. (*ii*) its performance in basic link prediction downstream tasks. It is worth noting that the link prediction task can be extended as service recommendation task [10]. We use two accuracy measures including *precision* and variants of *F-1 score*.

– **Embedding Models:** All the embedding models used here have the same objective, which is to learn a low-dimensional representation of a given network in a vector space, such that the representation can preserve the topological features of the network. We get the embeddings of each network per embedding model (*node2vec* [9], *DeepWalk* [11], *LINE* [14] and *HARP* [5]). For details of the embedding models, we encourage readers to consult the original publications.
– **Link Prediction Task:** For the link prediction task, we formulate the task of predicting missing links as a *binary classification* problem that predicts if a link exist between two nodes or not. We use *Schur product* of node pair embeddings and centrality features to construct *edge* representation. We then give the *edge* representation as input to a logistic regression classifier with

---

[2]   https://en.wikipedia.org/wiki/CentralityDegree-centrality.
[3]   https://en.wikipedia.org/wiki/CentralityBetweenness-centrality.
[4]   https://en.wikipedia.org/wiki/CentralityEigenvector-centrality.

$L2$ regularization from the $Scikit - learn - api$ and compute the precision of the prediction. Since we are working with numerical data, we tried various classifiers - starting from basic decision trees, SVM, logistic regression, Random forest, Multi-Layer Perception (MLP). We finally based our evaluation on $RandomForest$ due to its superior accuracy in learning the embeddings and predicting missing links. We evaluate how well the embedding models node interaction by predicting unobserved connections.

First, we give the embeddings generated for each Web service network by an embedding model to the link prediction model, and measure the accuracy using precision and recall metrics for each network. For each network dataset, we split into 2:8, with the 80% of the edges as the training set used to learn the embeddings. The remaining 20% were used as test set to predict the edges which are not observed in the training data using the learned embedding.

Figure 2 shows the prediction accuracy of each embedding models for all the service networks. Eventhough the datasets used to construct the Web service affiliation network is smaller compare to the other two synthetic networks (BA and BB), the network produced better prediction results across the three networks for all the models with the HARP model producing superior accuracy 71.5% at top-50 service follow by $node2vec$ and $DeepWalk$ − with 58.0% and 56.2% precisions respectively. We believe this could be attributed to direct projection of service interactions ProgrammableWeb Ecosystem, which is expected include lesser noise compare to the other two models. For BA and BB models both $node2vec$ and $HARP$ provides better results. We believe the low accuracy score in BA and BB model is due to the amount of noise introduced to the networks during construction.

– **Network Properties Prediction:** For network property prediction task, we build a *feed-forward* neural network (NN) model with *Keras and Scikit-Learn API*[5] for mapping the non-linear relationship between a node embedding as input of the NN model to the node's different centrality measures as single output variable [13]. The architecture of our NN model comprises of the *input layer, two hidden layers, rectifier* and *Optimizer* and *output layer* and. The input layer takes the node representation from each of the embedding models. The dimension of this layer is based on the embedding dimension. The two hidden dense layers use rectifier activation functions $ReLU$ activation unit. For the output layer, a *Softmax function* is defined to get the prediction as discrete probability distribution. We use a logarithmic loss-function − *categorical-cross entropy*. We perform *grid search* over different combinations of possible hyper-parameter values to get the best combination. We evaluate how well the embedding models capture specific node centrality measures by predicting unobserved node features. Given a node embedding, we try to predict the node attributes. We present the *F1-score* in Fig. 3 across the 3 networks for each embedding model with higher score signifying superior performance. The results show that $HARP$, $node2vec$ and $DeepWalk$ perform well in preserving specific topological features in the embedding space, espe-

---

[5]   https://keras.io/scikit-learn-api/.

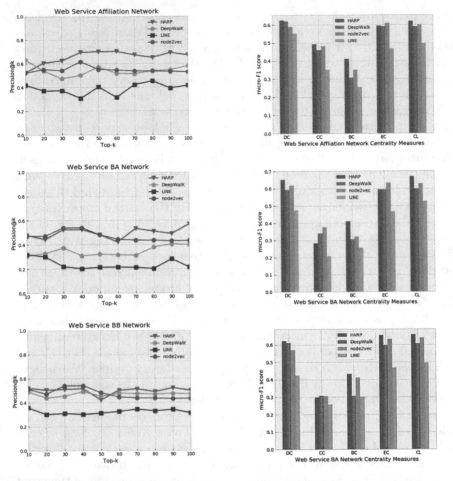

Fig. 2. Precision@K of Link Prediction for service Web service networks

Fig. 3. F1-Score of centrality measures prediction for service Web service networks

cially *node degree*, *eigenvector* and *closeness* information, with *HARP* and *node2vec* providing above 0.45 *F1-score* on average. These results validate our hypothesis that embedding models can map the approximate network topological features of Web service ecosystem to the vector space.

4   Conclusion and Future Work

In this paper, we studied the performance of recent unsupervised network embedding models in Web service domain. We evaluate the models with respect to the precision with which they unpack specific topological properties of the networks. We investigate the influence of each topological property on the accuracy of the prediction task. We conduct our experiment using the popular ProgrammableWeb dataset. Our results show that *HARP*, *node2vec* and *DeepWalk* perform well in preserving specific topological features in the embedding space, especially *node degree*, *eigenvector* and *closeness* information, with *HARP* and *node2vec* providing superior results. In future work, we plan to incorporate these features into Web service application like Web service recommendation application and study their individual influence on the performance of the application.

Acknowledgement. This work is partially supported by the National Key Research and Development Program of China (No. 2018YFB1402500) and National Natural Science Foundation of China (No. 61832004 and No. 61672042).

References

1. Adeleye, O., Yu, J., Yongchareon, S., Han, Y.: Constructing and evaluating an evolving web-API network for service discovery. In: Pahl, C., Vukovic, M., Yin, J., Yu, Q. (eds.) ICSOC 2018. LNCS, vol. 11236, pp. 603–617. Springer, Cham (2018). https://doi.org/10.1007/978-3-030-03596-9_44
2. Adeleye, O., Yu, J., Yongchareon, S., Sheng, Q.Z., Yang, L.H.: A fitness-based evolving network for web-APIs discovery. In: Proceedings of the Australasian Computer Science Week Multiconference, p. 49. ACM (2019)
3. Barabási, A.-L.: Network Science. Cambridge University Press, Cambridge (2016)
4. Bianconi, G., Barabási, A.-L.: Bose-Einstein condensation in complex networks. Phys. Rev. Lett. **86**(24), 5632 (2001)
5. Chen, H., Perozzi, B., Hu, Y., Skiena, S.: HARP: hierarchical representation learning for networks. In: AAAI Conference, 3rd ed. (2018)
6. Dalmia, A., Gupta, M., et al.: Towards interpretation of node embeddings. In: Companion Proceedings of the The Web Conference 2018, pp. 945–952. International World Wide Web Conferences Steering Committee (2018)
7. Dawson, S., Gašević, D., Siemens, G., Joksimovic, S.: Current state and future trends: a citation network analysis of the learning analytics field. In: Proceedings of the Fourth International Conference on Learning Analytics and Knowledge, pp. 231–240. ACM (2014)
8. Goyal, P., Ferrara, E.: Graph embedding techniques, applications, and performance: a survey. Knowl. Based Syst. **151**, 78–94 (2018)
9. Grover, A., Leskovec, J.: node2vec: scalable feature learning for networks. In: Proceedings of the 22nd ACM SIGKDD International Conference on Knowledge Discovery and Data Mining, pp. 855–864. ACM (2016)
10. Huang, K., Fan, Y., Tan, W.: Recommendation in an evolving service ecosystem based on network prediction. IEEE Trans. Autom. Sci. Eng. **11**(3), 906–920 (2014)
11. Perozzi, B., Al-Rfou, R., Skiena, S.: DeepWalk: online learning of social representations. In: Proceedings of the 20th ACM SIGKDD International Conference on Knowledge Discovery and Data Mining, pp. 701–710. ACM (2014)
12. Pham, T., Sheridan, P., Shimodaira, H.: Joint estimation of preferential attachment and node fitness in growing complex networks. Sci. Rep. **6**, 32558 (2016)
13. Rizi, F.S., Granitzer, M.: Properties of vector embeddings in social networks. Algorithms **10**(4), 109 (2017)
14. Tang, J., Qu, M., Wang, M., Zhang, M., Yan, J., Mei, Q.: LINE: large-scale information network embedding. In: Proceedings of the 24th International Conference on World Wide Web, pp. 1067–1077 (2015)

Query-Oriented Temporal Active Intimate Community Search

Md Musfique Anwar[(⊠)]

Jahangirnagar University, Dhaka, Bangladesh
manwar@juniv.edu

Abstract. Most of the existing research works on finding local community mainly focus on the network structure or the attributes of the social users. Some recent works considered users' topical activeness in detecting communities. However, not enough attention is paid to the degree of temporal topical interactions among the members in the retrieved communities. We propose a method to search temporal active intimate community in which community members are densely-connected as well as actively participate and have active temporal interactions among them with respect to the given query consisting of a set of query nodes (users) and a set of attributes. Experiments on real datasets demonstrate the effectiveness of our proposed approach.

Keywords: Active intimate community · Topical activeness · Query cohesiveness

1   Introduction

Discovering communities in Online Social Networks (OSNs) is classified into two categories: (i) community detection and community search [1]. Earlier approaches mainly concentrate on the network topology of OSNs ignoring the rich attributes of the nodes. Some works taking into account the properties of the users' to find meaningful communities [4, 10]. However, the above methods tried to scan all the nodes of a graph to discover the desired communities which is computationally very expensive, especially for larger graph. Again, they are not customized for a query request (e.g., a user-specified query node).

Recently, some works try to find query oriented community also known as community search [1, 7] which aims to find densely connected communities containing query node(s) and query attributes. However, these methods ignore the topical interactions among the community members resulting less interactive community. To avoid this inactivity problem, authors in [12] have proposed an approach where they considered the frequency and pattern of users' interactions.

We observe that users' have different degree of intimacy among them for different attributes. In this research work, we propose a method to find topic oriented *highly interactive* temporal communities in OSNs, where the community members should have certain degree of topical activeness as well as interactions

© Springer Nature Switzerland AG 2020
R. Borovica-Gajic et al. (Eds.): ADC 2020, LNCS 12008, pp. 206–215, 2020.
https://doi.org/10.1007/978-3-030-39469-1_17

with others related to a given query. We also emphasize that the members in the retrieved communities should actively interact with at least k other members within the community. Below, we summarize our contributions:

- We investigate the users' temporal activeness and degree of interactions related to the given query to search active intimate community;
- We use a modified version of CL-tree index mechanism to efficiency search the desired community and then further improve the result by introducing an improved greedy algorithm.
- We conduct extensive experiments using real datasets to show the effectiveness of our approach.

2   Related Work

Earlier methods for community detection are based on structural information of the social graph such as modularity [3], edge betweenness [2] etc. Some approaches like Topic-Link LDA model [10] and probabilistic generative model named as CESNA [4] consider both the linkage structure and content similarities of the edges to detect communities.

More recent approaches have focused on the interaction strengths between the users to discover active communities. Kim et al. [12] proposed Highly Interactive Community Detection (HICD) method which generates a weighted network using the frequency of direct interactions between users. Correa et al. [5] proposed *iTop* algorithm which greedily maximizes the local modularity in a weighted graph based on user interactions and a set of seed users. Yang et al. [1] recently proposed an approach based on k-core for community search. However, all these methods ignored topic-wise users' temporal interactions.

3   Preliminary and Problem Definition

k-CORE: Given an integer $k(k \geq 0)$, the k-core of a graph G, denoted by C^k, is the largest subgraph of G, such that $\forall u \in C^k, deg_{C^k}(u) \geq k$, where $deg_{C^k}(u)$ refers to the degree of node u in C^k. The core number of a node u in G is the maximum k for which u belongs in the k-core of G.

Query: An input query $Q = \{U_q, \mathcal{T}_q\}$ consisting of a set of query nodes U_q and a set of query topics $\mathcal{T}_q$.

Activity: An activity tuple $\langle u_i, \psi_{u_i}, t_n \rangle$ represents an action where ψ_{u_i} indicates the set of topics covered by the action performed by user u_i at time t_n. Again, $\langle u_i, u_j \psi_{u_i u_j}, t_n \rangle$ is used to indicate an action where $\psi_{u_i u_j}$ shows the set of topics covered during the interaction between u_i and u_j at time t_n.

Active User: An active user u performed at least $\gamma(\geq 1)$ activities related to $\mathcal{T}_q$ i.e., $|\{\langle u, \psi_u, t_j \rangle\}| \geq \gamma$, where $\psi \in \mathcal{T}_q\}$. The set of active users denoted as U^A are h hops away from the query nodes U_q. The number of edges between the users in U^A is denoted as E^A.

Recency Score: We apply exponential time-decay function in Eqs. 1 and 2 to emphasize greater importance to user's most recent activities by a measure called *recency score*, denoted by $\mu \in [0,1]$. The parameter a is used to control the decaying speed and $age_{\langle u_i, \psi, t_n \rangle}$ indicates the amount of time passed since the activity occurred [9].

$$\mu_{\langle u_i, \psi_{u_i}, t_n \rangle} = exp(-a \times age_{\langle u_i, \psi, t_n \rangle}) \tag{1}$$

$$\mu_{\langle u_i, u_j, \psi_{u_i u_j}, t_n \rangle} = exp(-a \times age\langle u_i, u_j, \psi, t_n \rangle) \tag{2}$$

Topical Activeness and Intimacy Score: For each user $u_i \in U^A$, we compute individual activeness score (σ_{u_i}) as well as pairwise (u,v) activeness score ($\sigma_{u_i u_j}$) to measure the involvement of u_i towards query topics $\mathcal{T}_q$, using Eqs. 5, where $t_j \in I_m$, and $\psi_{(u_i, T_x, I_m)}$ is the user's degree of activeness compared to the total number of activities performed by all the active users.

$$\Omega_{u_i} = \frac{\sum \mu_{\langle u_i, \psi_{u_i}, t_n \rangle} \times |\{\langle u_i, \psi_{u_i}, t_n \rangle\}|}{\sum_{u_z \in U^A} |\{\langle u_z, \psi_{u_z}, t_n \rangle\}|} \tag{3}$$

$$\Omega_{u_i u_j} = \frac{\sum \mu_{\langle u_i, u_j \psi_{u_i u_j}, t_n \rangle} \times |\{\langle u_i, u_j \psi_{u_i, u_j}, t_n \rangle\}|}{\sum_{u_x, u_y \in U^A} |\{\langle u_x, u_y, \psi_{u_x u_y}, t_n \rangle\}|} \tag{4}$$

$$\sigma_{u_i} = \frac{\Omega_{u_i}}{max_{u_z \in U^A}\{\Omega_{u_z}\}} \quad , \quad \sigma_{u_i u_j} = \frac{\Omega_{u_i u_j}}{max_{u_x, u_y \in U^A}\{\Omega_{u_i u_j}\}} \tag{5}$$

Then the overall interaction strength between users u_i and u_j is,

$$w_{u_i u_j} = \alpha \times (\sigma_{u_i} \times \sigma_{u_j}) + (1 - \alpha) \times \sigma_{u_i u_j} \tag{6}$$

Definition 1 (Active Intimate Community (AIC)). *Given an input query* Q, *two integers* k *and* h *(hop numbers), we generate an weighted sub-graph* $G_h^Q(U^A, E^A, W^A)$ *from* G, *where* W^A *is the set of weights* ($w_{uv} \in [0,1]$) *indicates the interaction strength of the edge* $e_{uv} \in E^A$. *Then an active intimate community* H_j^k *is an induced subgraph that meets the following constraints:*
(i) Connectivity. $H_j^k \subset G_h^Q$ *is connected; (ii) Structure cohesiveness.* $\forall u \in H_j^k$ *has interaction degree of at least* k; *and (iii) Active intimacy.* $\forall e_{uv} \in H_j^k$, $w_{uv} \geq \theta$ *and* $\theta \in [0,1]$ *is a threshold.*

We define an intimacy score function denoted as $f(H_j^k, Q)$ for the detected communities that establishes a balance of attribute homogeneity, coverage and the structure cohesiveness.

$$f(H_k^j, Q) = \frac{\eta}{|Q|} \times \frac{|E(H_k^j)|}{|U(H_k^j)|}, \quad \text{and} \quad \eta = \sum_{T_i \in Q} \frac{|E_{T_i} \cap E(H_k^j)|}{|E(H_k^j)|} \tag{7}$$

where $E_{T_i} \in E(H_k^j)$ is an edge that overs query topic $T_i \in \mathcal{T}_q$. In Eq. 7, η captures the popularity of each query topic T_i inside the community H_j^k by calculating the fraction of edges of H_j^k that cover T_i. Finally, the factor $\frac{|E(H_j^k)|}{|U(H_j^k)|}$ is used to reward the communities that are structurally more cohesive.

Problem Definition. Given an attributed graph G, an input query Q, and parameters k, h, the problem is to search an AIC with highest intimacy score.

Figure 1(a) shows a graph G with the core number for each node. Figure 1(b) shows the active interaction edges for a given query $Q = \{U_q = (B,C), T_q = (T_1, T_2, T_3)\}$. Suppose, we want to find the active intimate communities for $k = 2$ and $\theta = 0.4$. There are few

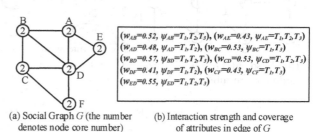

(a) Social Graph G (the number denotes node core number)

(b) Interaction strength and coverage of attributes in edge of G

Fig. 1. A graph G with interactive edges

subgraphs that satisfy the criteria, for example, we get the candidate AICs $H_1^k = \{A, B, C, D, E\}$, $H_2^k = \{A, C, D, E, F\}$, $H_3^k = \{A, B, C, D, E, F\}$ etc. We see that the query topic T_1 is covered by all the edges in all the candidate AICs. Topics T_2 and T_3 are covered by 6 edges in H_1^k, hence the intimacy score of H_1^k is $f(H_1^k, Q) = \frac{(1+0.86+0.86)}{3} \times \frac{7}{5} = 1.27$. In H_2^k, T_2 and T_3 are covered by 6 and 5 edges respectively. So the intimacy score of H_2^k is $f(H_2^k, Q) = \frac{(1+0.86+0.71)}{3} \times \frac{7}{5} = 1.2$. Similarly, $f(H_3^k, Q) = \frac{(1+0.78+0.78)}{3} \times \frac{9}{6} = 1.28$. Although the coverage of the query topics in H_3^k is lower than that of H_1^k, but H_3^k is structurally more cohesive than H_1^k, hence H_3^k has slightly better intimacy score.

4   AIC Detection Algorithm

We adjusted an indexing mechanism called `CL-tree` (Core Label tree) [1] to efficiently discover AIC. The CL-tree index is built based on the observations that cores are nested, i.e., a $(k+1)$ core must be contained in a k-core. Therefore after computing the k-core of G, we assign each connected components induced by k-core as a child node of a tree. Each node in the tree contains four elements: (i) *coreNum:* the core number of the k-core, (ii) *nodeSet:* set of graph nodes, (iii) *invertedList:* a list of $<key, value>$ pairs, where the *key* is an attribute contained by the nodes in *nodeSet* and the *value* is the list of nodes in *nodeSet* containing *key*. In our proposed work, for each node, we add the number of activities related to *key*, and (iv) *childList:* a list of child nodes.

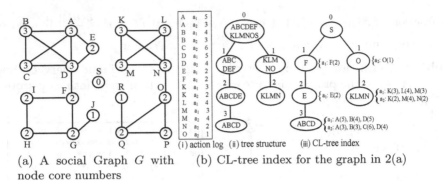

(a) A social Graph G with   (b) CL-tree index for the graph in 2(a)
node core numbers

Fig. 2. Example of CL-tree index

4.1 Baseline Solution

In AIC-Basic (shown in Algorithm 1), we first compute the induced subgraph G_h^Q from the set of active nodes U^A in G who are h hops away from any query nodes of U_q (line 1–3). Then, We remove the inactive edges (whose $w_{uv} < \theta$) from each connected k-core component H_j^k and compute $f(H_j^k, Q)$ if exists (line 5–8). Removal of an edge e_{uv} decreases the degree of the end points (u and v) of e_{uv} by 1 which may result into violation of the cohesiveness constraint by either u or v or both. Finally, it outputs the desired H_j^k (line 9).

Algorithm 1. AIC-Basic

Input: $G = (U, E, \mathcal{T}), Q, k, h, \alpha, \beta, \gamma, \theta$
Output: An AIC H_j^k with the maximum $f(H_j^k, Q)$
1: Find the set of active users U^A who are h hops away from any of query nodes U_q
2: compute the induced graph G_h^Q on U^A
3: Maintain G_h^Q as a k-core
4: **for** each connected k-core component H_j^k from G_h^Q **do**
5:     remove edge e_{uv} that has smallest weight w_{uv}
6:     Maintain H_j^k as a k-core
7:     **if** H_j^k exists **then**
8:         Compute the intimacy score $f(H_1^k, Q)$
9: Output the H_j^k with the maximum $f(H_j^k, Q)$ from G_h^Q

4.2 Improved Greedy Algorithm

The basic algorithm has a limitation that they ignore the impact of the removal of an inactive edge which may trigger the deletion of other nodes due to the violation of k-core constraints. If these nodes have many query attributes, it can severely limit the effectiveness of the algorithm. Thus, we need to look ahead the effect of each removal node, and then decide which ones are better to be deleted.

Definition 2 *(Node Marginal Gain). Given a graph H_j^k, query topics $\mathcal{T}_q$ and a node $u \in U(H_j^k)$, the marginal gain of u is defined as $gain_{H_j^k}(u, H_j^k) = f(H_j^k + L_{H_j^k}(u), Q) - f(H_j^k, Q))$, where $L_{H_j^k}(u) \subset H_j^k$ is the set of nodes together with u that violate k-core after the removal of u from H_j^k.*

For example, consider the graph G in Fig. 1 with $Q = \{U_q = (B, C), \mathcal{T}_q = (T_1, T_2, T_3)\}$, $\theta = 0.45$ and $k=2$, we get $H_1^2 = \{A, B, C, D\}$ due to the removal of the edges e_{AE}, e_{CF} and e_{DF} which also delete nodes E and F resulting $f(H_1^2, Q) = 1.08$. Now, $L_{H_1^2}(F) = \{F\}$ and we get $H_1^2 + L_{H_1^2}(F) = \{A, B, C, D, E\}$ with $f(H_1^2 + L_{H_1^2}(F), Q) = 1.13$. So the marginal gain of node F ($gain_{H_1^2}(F, H_1^2) = f(H_1^2 + L_{H_1^2}(F), Q) - f(H_1^2, Q)) = (1.13 - 1.08) = 0.05$) doesn't contribute much to the intimacy score $f(H_1^2, Q)$. Again, $L_{H_1^2}(E) = \{E\}$ and we get $H_1^2 + L_{H_1^2}(E) = \{A, B, C, D, E\}$ with $f(H_1^2 + L_{H_1^2}(E), Q) = 1.27$. We can see that node E has significant marginal gain ($gain_{H_1^2}(F, H_1^2) = f(H_1^2 + L_{H_1^2}(F), Q) - f(H_1^2, Q)) = (1.27 - 1.08) = 0.19$) in this case and should be included in H_1^2. So, we can get better community using marginal gain as it estimates more accurately the effectiveness of node deletion.

We propose an improved Algorithm 2 (`AIC-Greedy`) based on node marginal gain that finds the set of nodes S (due to the removal of inactive edge w_{uv}) and compute their marginal gain $gain_{H_j^k}(S, H_j^k)$ for each H_j^k (line 5–6). If $gain_{H_j^k}(S, H_j^k) < \epsilon$ (($< \epsilon$ where $\epsilon > 0$)), then it removes S and with their incident edges (line 7–8).

5   Experiment and Result

All experiments are performed on an Intel(R) Core(TM) i7-4500U 2.4 GHz Windows 7 PC with 16 GB RAM. We choose two Twitter datasets: CRAWL [11] and SNAP[1] and apply Twitter-LDA [8] topic modeling to identify different topics as node attributes. We set the input query topics as {*politics, entertainment, online social network service, food and health*} in both CRAWL and SNAP datasets. A user in Twitter interacts with others in the form of replies, mentions and retweets. We use an academic coauthor (DBLP) dataset [6] and apply latent dirichlet allocation (LDA) topic modeling [13] method on the abstracts of the research papers to find the research topics. We set the input query topics as {*social network analysis, semantic web, machine learning, text mining*}. Table 1 shows the statistics of our experimental data.

We compare `AIC-Basic` and `AIC-Greedy` algorithms with two other methods. We select `HICD` method [12] based on users' interaction frequencies with their following links of celebrities of particular interest category. We also consider `iTop` [5] that detects topical communities by first selecting a set of seed users who are identified based on a textual search of their Twitter user profile biography. In all cases, we set $\theta = 0.5, \alpha = 0.5, \gamma = 5$.

---

[1] http://snap.stanford.edu/data/twitter7.html

Algorithm 2. AIC-Greedy

Input: $G = (U, E, T), Q, k, h, \alpha, \beta, \gamma, \theta, \epsilon$
Output: An AIC H_j^k with the maximum $f(H_j^k, Q)$
1: Find the set of active users U^A who are h hops away from any of query nodes U_q
2: compute the induced graph G_o on U^A
3: Maintain G_h^Q as a k-core
4: **for** each connected k-core component H_j^k from G_h^Q **do**
5:     **if** $(w_{uv} \in E(H_j^k)) < \theta$ **then**
6:         Find a set of nodes S and compute gain $gain_{H_j^k}(S, H_j^k)$
7:         **if** $gain_{H_j^k}(S, H_j^k) < \epsilon$ **then**
8:             Remove S and their incident edges
9:             Maintain H_j^k as a k-core
10:     **if** H_j^k exists **then**
11:         Compute the intimacy score of $f(H_j^k, Q)$
12: Output the H_j^k with the maximum $f(H_j^k, Q)$

Table 1. Datasets

Dataset	# of Nodes	# of Edges	# of Acivities
CRAWL	9,355	1,372,978	5,913,331
SNAP	100,000	3,916,456	847,536
Coauthor	16,614	49,758	192,721

5.1 Efficiency

Figure 3 shows the running time at different values of k. Observe that iTop requires more time compare with other methods as it needs to recursively perform several steps in order to maximize local modularity. HICD also takes more time as it requires to perform the Clique Percolation Method (CPM) on the network generated by the set of celebrities and their followers. A lower k renders more subgraphs, due to which it takes more computation time for all the

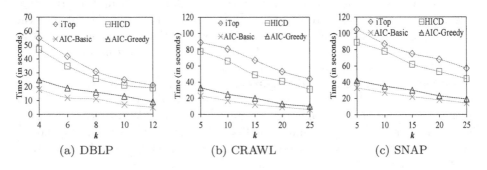

    (a) DBLP   (b) CRAWL   (c) SNAP

Fig. 3. Run-time for different values of k

methods. Both `AIC-Basic` and `AIC-Greedy` outperforms the other methods. `AIC-Greedy` takes more time than `AIC-Basic` as it requires to check the node marginal gains.

5.2 Community Quality Evaluation

We vary the length of query topics $|\mathcal{T}_q|$ of Q to $2, 3, 4$ and use two measures of modularity and entropy to evaluate the quality of the generated candidate communities generated. The definition of modularity and entropy are as follows:

$$modularity(\{\mathcal{G}_j\}_{j=1}^n) = \frac{1}{2m} \sum_{ij} [A_{ij} - \frac{d_i d_j}{2m}] \delta(s_i, s_j) \tag{8}$$

Here, m denotes the number of edges corresponding to an adjacency matrix A of G, d_i denotes the degree corresponding to node n_i, s_i denotes the community membership of node n_i and $\delta(s_i, s_j) = 1$ if $s_i = s_j$.

$$entropy(\{H_j^k\}_{j=1}^r) = \sum_j^r \frac{|U(H_j^k)|}{|U|} entropy(H_j^k) \quad , \text{where} \quad entropy(H_j^k) = -\sum_{i=1}^n p_{ij} log_2 p_{ij}$$

and p_{ij} is the percentage of nodes in community H_j^k that are active on query topic T_i. $entropy(\{H_j^k\}_{j=1}^r)$ measures the weighted entropy considering all the query topics over top-r communities. Entropy indicates the randomness of topics in communities. A good community should have high modularity and low entropy.

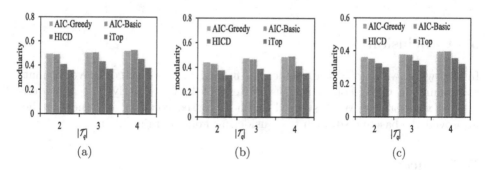

(a)   (b)   (c)

Fig. 4. Modularity comparison on datasets: (a) DBLP, (b) CRAWL, (c) SNAP

Figure 4 shows the modularity comparison between the four methods. We set $k = 4$ for DBLP as it has many small-sized research groups. In CRAWL, we set $k = 10$ as it has very densely connected network. We set $k = 7$ in SNAP as it is very sparse in structure. Both `AIC-Basic` and `AIC-Greedy` perform better than `iTop` and `HICD` due to the consideration of users' degree of intimacies and topical activeness. The increase rate of modularity value by `iTop` method is not as good as `AIC-Basic` and `AIC-Greedy` because it does not focus on the interactions between the non-seed users. Similarly, HICD achieves poor modularity values because it requires connection between normal users to the high profile users.

Figure 5 shows the entropy comparison between the four methods. Both AIC-Basic and AIC-Greedy achieve better performance as they take into account the relevance (topical activeness) of the users w.r.t. the query topics while forming a community. As AIC-Greedy considers the node marginal gain, so it has better percentage of users related to the query topics resulting better entropy value than AIC-Basic. On the other hand, HICD achieves higher entropy value because many connected normal users do not have interest in all the common topics. iTop also achieves higher entropy value because it does not focus on topic wise interactions between the seed users and their followers.

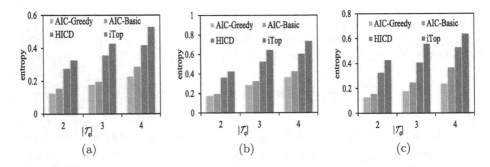

Fig. 5. Entropy comparison on datasets: (a) DBLP, (b) CRAWL, (c) SNAP

6   Conclusion

In this work, we studied the problem of finding query-oriented active intimate community in OSNs considering users' temporal topical activeness and interactions with others. We first used an index based solution and then further improved the baseline solution by considering node marginal gain.

References

1. Fang, Y., Cheng, R., Luo, S., Hu, J.: Effective community search for large attributed graphs. In: VLDB, pp. 1233–1244 (2016)
2. Newman, M.E.J., Park, J.: Why social networks are different from other types of networks. Phys. Rev. E **68**, 036122 (2003)
3. Clauset, A., Newman, M.E.J., Moore, C.: Finding community structure in very large networks. Phys. Rev. E **70**, 066111 (2004)
4. Yang, J., McAuley, J., Leskovec, J.: Community detection in networks with node attributes. In: ICDM, pp. 1151–1156 (2013)
5. Correa, D., Sureka, A., Pundir, M.: iTop - interaction based topic centric community discovery on Twitter. In: PIKM, pp. 51–58 (2012)

6. Tang, J., Zhang, J., Yao, L., Li, J., Zhang, L., Su, Z.: ArnetMiner: extraction and mining of academic social networks. In: KDD, pp. 990–998 (2008)
7. Huang, X., Lakshmanan, L.V.S.: Attribute-driven community search. In: VLDB, pp. 949–960 (2017)
8. Zhao, W.X., et al.: Comparing twitter and traditional media using topic models. In: ECIR, pp. 338–349 (2011)
9. Anwar, M., Liu, C., Li, J., Anwar, T.: Discovering and tracking active online social groups. In: WISE, pp. 59–74 (2017)
10. Liu, Y., Niculescu-Mizil, A., Gryc, W.: Topic-link LDA: joint models of topic and author community. In: ICML, pp. 665–672 (2009)
11. Bogdanov, P., Busch, M., Moehli, J., Singh, A.K., Szymanski, B.K.: The social media genome: modeling individual topic-specific behavior in social media. In: ASONAM, pp. 236–242 (2013)
12. Lim, K.H., Datta, A.: An interaction-based approach to detecting highly interactive Twitter communities using tweeting links. In: Web Intelligence, pp. 1–15 (2016)
13. Blei, D.M., Ng, A.Y., Jordan, M.I.: Latent Dirichlet allocation. J. Mach. Learn. Res. **3**, 993–1022 (2003)

A Contextual Semantic-Based Approach for Domain-Centric Lexicon Expansion

Muhammad Abulaish[1], Mohd Fazil[1], and Tarique Anwar[2,3(✉)]

[1] South Asian University, New Delhi, India
abulaish@sau.ac.in, mohdfazil.jmi@gmail.com
[2] Macquarie University, Sydney, Australia
tarique.anwar@mq.edu.au
[3] CSIRO Data61, Sydney, Australia

Abstract. This paper presents a contextual semantic-based approach for expansion of an initial lexicon containing domain-centric seed words. Starting with a small lexicon containing some domain-centric seed words, the proposed approach models text corpus as a weighted word-graph, where the initial weight of a node (word) represents the contextual semantic-based association between the node and the target domain, and the weight of an edge represents the co-occurrence frequency of the respective nodes. The semantic-based association between a node and the target domain is calculated as a function of three contextual semantic-based association metrics. Thereafter, a random walk-based modified `PageRank` algorithm is applied on the weighted graph to rank and select the most relevant terms for domain-centric lexicon expansion. The proposed approach is evaluated over five datasets, and found to perform significantly better than three baselines and three state-of-the-art approaches.

Keywords: Text mining · Keyword extraction · Lexicon expansion · Contextual similarity

1 Introduction

Extraction of keywords or keyphrases from large text corpora is an important task in many text information processing applications, in which important and relevant words are extracted from the corpora. Such words are generally related to all the different domains of interest. Research on this problem in the past few decades has resulted into a rich literature [4]. While keywords are relevant to multiple domains of interest, they are not much effective in highlighting some specific domains. Lexicons, on the other hand, are able to effectively conceptualize one particular domain with relevant words from the text corpus. Lexicon-based approaches are highly effective in many applications, such as spam email classification, abusive language detection, sentiment analysis, and emotion mining. Although there exists many works on lexicon generation in the literature, they

© Springer Nature Switzerland AG 2020
R. Borovica-Gajic et al. (Eds.): ADC 2020, LNCS 12008, pp. 216–224, 2020.
https://doi.org/10.1007/978-3-030-39469-1_18

predominantly ignore the contextual semantics. It makes them ineffective over online social networks (OSN) data. Moreover, most of the existing lexicons are generally curated through crowd-annotation [7,10], which is a time-consuming and tedious task. There exists some well-established benchmark lexicons such as Hatebase[1], SocialSent[2]. But still there is a lack of sufficient lexicons to cover every domain of interest. For example, there is no such lexicon of radical words used by different extremist groups in the South Asian region. Through human efforts, one can possibly identify only a limited number of radical words such as *kashmirfreedom, gazwaehind, khalistan*. It is not feasible to manually identify all other contextual words that are used by such extremist groups. Therefore, automated lexicon expansion from a given initial lexicon of few seed words, is an important research problem.

There exists some works in the direction of domain-centric lexicon expansion from a text corpus, most of which use the concepts of contrasting corpora and graph-based approaches [3,8,9]. Sarna et al. [9] utilized an initial lexicon of seed words using a statistical significance analysis-based approach for its expansion. However, it ignores the contextual semantic of corpus words with the seed words. Overall, the existing works suffer from three major limitations. Firstly, most of the existing approaches are based on simple statistical measures like frequency count and co-occurrence count ignoring the contextual semantics between the terms. Secondly, to the best of our knowledge, all existing approaches except [9] are for lexicon generation rather than expansion. Finally, no approach exists that utilizes the strengths of both the contrasting-corpora and graph-based approaches incorporating contextual semantics towards initial lexicon expansion over the OSN data. To this end, this paper utilizes the advantages of both the statistics of contrasting-domain corpora and contextual semantics of latest word vector representation for domain-centric lexicon expansion. Further, proposed approach exploits an initial lexicon of few seed terms to bias the initial contextual semantic-based scores of corpus-words towards the target domain.

2 Proposed Approach

2.1 Candidate Words Extraction

The selection of content-bearing candidate words from the corpus is an important step of the lexicon expansion process. OSNs are a conversation platform where users generally use an informal and noisy language. Therefore, firstly, uninformative symbols and special characters like "@", "#", "RT" are filtered out from tweets, which are further converted to lower case to avoid ambiguity between words. The filtered tweets are further passed to a part-of-speech tagger to find *noun* and *adjective* phrases [5], which are generally important words in user-generated contents conceptualizing the text corpus. Finally, identified *noun* and *adjective* phrases are lemmatized to construct the set of potential candidate words for graph modeling.

---

[1] https://hatebase.org/.

[2] https://nlp.stanford.edu/projects/socialsent/.

2.2 Contextual Semantic-Based Graph Construction

The candidate words are modeled as a word co-occurrence graph $G = \langle W, E \rangle$, where W is the set of nodes representing the candidate words and E is the set of links connecting the nodes (words). Further, we compute the initial vertex score of each word representing the contextual semantic-based association between the word and target domain, and edge weight is assigned to show the co-occurrence frequency between every pair of words. An edge between a pair of words is created only when they have co-occurred in at least one document of the corpus (in our case, it is a tweet).

Vertex Relevance Score. The initial weight assigned to a node (word) $w \in W$ is based on three association measures – (i) contextual semantic-based similarity of w with S, (ii) domain relevance of w with respect to a set of contrasting corpora, and finally (iii) occurrence-probability of w with seed words.

Embedding-Based Semantic Similarity. The semantic similarity of w with the seed words of S is based on numeric vector representation of words. In the existing literature, several neural network-based methods have been presented to train the low dimensional numeric vector representation of words. In such an approach, Mikolov et al. [6] presented a computationally efficient and widely accepted approach to learn the word representation from unlabeled corpus using two models – (i) a continuous bag of words (CBOW) representation model and (ii) skip-gram model. In the proposed approach, we use the $CBOW$ model to train a word embedding model that maps each word of the corpus into a low-dimensional vector in a vector space of latent concepts. Thereafter, semantic similarity between the lexicon of seed words and each word in the graph is computed based on the trained word-embedding vectors. The contextual semantic-based similarity of each word of G is the average of cosine similarity of the word with each seed word of S as given in Eq. 1, where e_w and e_s represent the embedding vectors of w and $s \in S$ respectively.

$$\mathcal{S}(w) = \frac{\sum\limits_{s \in S} Cos(e_w, e_s)}{|S|} \tag{1}$$

Domain Relevance. In the proposed approach, domain relevance of a word w is defined as the ratio of the occurrence probability of w in domain-specific corpus to the average of its occurrence probability in the contrasting corpora. If the domain-specific corpus is D and contrasting corpora C, then domain relevance $\mathcal{D}(w)$ of a word w is defined as given in Eq. 2, where P_w^D represents the occurrence probability of w in D and P_w^C represents the average of the occurrence probability of w in C.

$$\mathcal{D}(w) = \frac{P_w^D}{P_w^C} = \frac{tf_w^D/N^D}{\sum_{c \in C} \frac{tf_w^c}{N^c}/|C|} \tag{2}$$

Co-occurrence-Based Contextual Proximity. The frequent occurrence of a word with seed words reflects its contextual proximity with seed words. Therefore, we define a metric called co-occurrence-based contextual proximity, $\mathcal{P}$, to capture the co-occurrence of a word with seed words. For a word w, it is the average of conditional probability of w with each $s \in S$ as defined using Eq. 3, where $p(s/w)$ represents the conditional probability of s given that w has already occurred.

$$\mathcal{P}(w) = \left(\sum_{s \in S} p(s/w) \right) / |S| \tag{3}$$

Finally, vertex score $\mathcal{V}(w)$ of w is defined as given in Eq. 4

$$\mathcal{V}(w) = (\mathcal{S}(w) + \mathcal{D}(w) + \mathcal{P}(w)) / 3 \tag{4}$$

Edge Score. This section captures the contextual semantic-aware association between every pair of words $(w_i, w_j) \in G$ to create edges between them. We define the edge weight between a pair of words (w_i, w_j) of G as the number of tweets in which they co-occur regardless of any window size to incorporate tweet-level context. It is defined using Eq. 5, where $I_t(w_i, w_j)$ is the identify function which is one when both the words occur in a tweet t otherwise zero as given using Eq. 6.

$$\mathcal{E}(w_i, w_j) = \sum_{t \in D} I_t(w_i, w_j) \tag{5}$$

$$I_t(w_i, w_j) = \begin{cases} 1 & if \ w_i \in t \ and \ w_j \in t \\ 0 & otherwise \end{cases} \tag{6}$$

Finally, we normalize the edges weight using Eq. 7, where $\mathcal{E}_{max}$ represents the weight of the edge with the highest value.

$$\mathcal{E}(w_i, w_j) = \frac{\mathcal{E}(w_i, w_j)}{\mathcal{E}_{max}} \tag{7}$$

$$\mathcal{V}'(w_i) = \frac{1 - d}{N} + \sum_{w_i' \in Adj(w_i)} C * \frac{\mathcal{E}(w_i', w_i) * \mathcal{V}(w_i')}{|Adj(w_i')|} \tag{8}$$

2.3   Words Ranking and Lexicon Expansion

In `PageRank`, initial weight of nodes follows uniform distribution with an equal weight of 1. Thus, every node has equal probability of random jump to other nodes of the graph. On contrast, in the proposed approach, weights on nodes follow a non-uniform distribution such that the nodes having higher contextual semantic with seed words are assigned higher weights emulating the personalized `PageRank`. The non-uniform distribution of weights biases the computation towards certain nodes in the recursive procedure. It allows the nodes of the graph to spread their importance to other nodes depending on their weights. This spread of a node score is also affected by the weights of adjacent edges such that the flow of weight will be higher between two strongly connected nodes. Therefore, the final weight of a node is not only based on its contextual semantic with the seed words but also depends on the strength of co-occurrence. Finally, a modified `PageRank` [2] is applied on G to identify the most relevant words for expansion of the initial lexicon of seed words. In the modified `PageRank` algorithm, importance score of a word is updated using Eq. 8, where $\mathcal{V}'(w)$ represents the updated score of $w \in W$, d is a damping constant (0.85), C is a scaling constant (0.95), and N is the number of words (nodes) in the graph. The iterative procedure of score updation of each word is repeated until a stationary distribution of words score is reached. Thereafter, words are sorted based on their final scores and high ranked words are selected for lexicon expansion.

3   Experimental Setup and Results

This section presents a detailed description of datasets and embedding learning, evaluation results, and comparative analysis.

3.1   Dataset and Embedding Learning

The proposed approach is evaluated on five different domains of datasets prepared using two main datasets – D_1 and D_2. The dataset D_1 is a benchmark dataset of 80000 tweets related to three categories of offensive languages – *hateful*, *spam*, and *abusive* [1] including *normal* tweets. We crawled 64963 tweets (remaining were suspended) and their related metadata information from the provided tweet-ids to construct D_1 and learn the 100-d word-embeddings using `Word2Vec` model. Thereafter, a random set of 1000 tweets, called D_h, D_s, and D_a respectively, each from *hateful*, *spam*, and *abusive* categories are selected to evaluate the proposed approach. Further, three sets of 286, 343 and 264 keywords are extracted from D_h, D_s and D_a, respectively using the `Natural Language Understanding` tool. Thereafter, three annotators are asked to rate the extracted keywords on a 11-point scale from 0 to 10, where 0 is assigned when annotator is 100% confident that keyword does not belong to a particular category and it is assigned 10 when annotator is 100% confident that keyword belongs to a particular category. Finally, average of the three rating scores is compared with 5 to create an annotated set of 76 hate words (A_h), 130 spam words (A_s), and 105 abusive words (A_a).

To further evaluate the proposed approach, another dataset D_2 is crawled during August 5, 2019 to August 28, 2019 using `Twitter` based on 14 radical keyphrases related to *Khalistan* and *Kashmir* movements. Thereafter, same procedure is repeated on D_2 as on D_1 to learn embedding vectors and generate the set of ground-truth keywords. As a result, we have annotated sets of 48 and 90 keywords for *Khalistan* and *Kashmir* related tweets represented as A_{kh} and

Table 1. A brief statistic of five datasets

Category	Benchmark dataset D_1					Crawled dataset D_2		
	Abusive	Hateful	Spam	Normal	Total	Khalistan	Kashmir	Total
Total tweets	12878	2740	9048	40297	64963	3888	560	4448
Evaluation tweets	1000	1000	1000	1000	4000	1000	560	1560

A_{ka}, respectively. A brief statistic about the five evaluation datasets is given in Table 1.

Table 2. Performance evaluation results using an initial lexicon of 3 seed words

	Datasets with 1000 tweets					Datasets with 500 tweets				
	D_h	D_s	D_a	D_{kh}	D_{ka}	D_h	D_s	D_a	D_{kh}	D_{ka}
P@80	0.350	**0.738**	0.500	0.463	0.600	0.338	0.588	0.437	0.337	**0.537**
R@80	0.368	0.454	0.381	**0.771**	0.533	0.355	0.362	0.333	**0.562**	0.477
F@80	0.359	0.562	0.432	**0.578**	0.565	0.346	0.447	0.378	0.421	**0.506**

3.2 Evaluation Results

The proposed approach is evaluated using three standard evaluation metrics – *precision*, *recall*, and *f-score* at K. The domain relevance $\mathcal{D}(w)$ for each word w of G is computed using a single contrasting corpus D_c of 1000 normal tweets from D_1. Table 2 presents the evaluation results of the proposed approach at $K = 80$ over the five datasets using S containing 3 seed words. This table shows that in terms of $P@80$, proposed approach exhibits lower performance over D_h because the ground-truth set A_h has a number of words like *nazi*, *muslim*, *crazy* which are contextually used in hateful tweets but they were labeled by the annotators as *non-hatred* words. Moreover, many words like *terrorism*, *russia*, *gay*, which are used as hatred words in certain contexts were not extracted by the NLU. Accordingly, they are missing from the annotated set of words. In terms of $P@80$, proposed approach performs best on D_s as shown in bold typeface in the third row of Table 2, whereas, in terms of $R@80$, it performs best over D_{kh} dataset as shown in the fourth row of Table 2. It is because that D_{kh} has the least number of manually annotated keywords, thereby, increases the recall. Similarly, performance evaluation results over the five datasets of 500 tweets in each is shown in the last five columns of Table 2. On analysis of evaluation results over 1000 and 500 tweets from Table 2, it can be observed that the performance of the proposed approach goes down as we decrease the number of tweets in

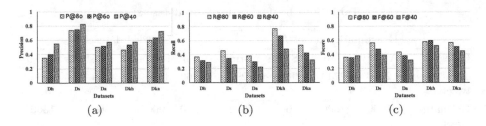

Fig. 1. Performance evaluation results at different k values (80, 60 and 40)

Table 3. Comparative performance evaluation results

Approach	Datasets														
	D_h			D_s			D_a			D_{kh}			D_{ka}		
	P@80	R@80	F@80	P@80	R@80	F@80	P@80	R@80	F@80	P@80	R@80	F@80	P@80	R@80	F@80
Proposed approach	**0.350**	**0.368**	**0.359**	**0.738**	**0.454**	**0.562**	**0.500**	**0.381**	**0.432**	**0.463**	**0.771**	**0.578**	**0.600**	**0.533**	**0.565**
Sarna and Bhatia [9]	0.244	0.128	0.168	0.318	0.121	0.175	0.209	0.086	0.122	0.250	0.102	0.144	0.286	0.106	0.155
Park et al. [8]	0.175	0.184	0.179	0.149	0.085	0.108	0.175	0.133	0.151	0.075	0.083	0.079	0.100	0.067	0.080
Kit and Liu [3]	0.163	0.171	0.167	0.350	0.215	0.267	0.025	0.019	0.022	0.075	0.125	0.094	0.125	0.111	0.118
tf	0.175	0.184	0.179	0.150	0.092	0.114	0.175	0.133	0.151	0.262	0.437	0.328	0.263	0.233	0.247
tf-idf	0.063	0.066	0.064	0.238	0.146	0.181	0.138	0.105	0.119	0.025	0.041	0.031	0.038	0.033	0.035
Embedding-based similarity	0.075	0.079	0.077	0.113	0.069	0.086	0.325	0.248	0.281	0.262	0.438	0.328	0.388	0.344	0.364

the evaluation datasets to 500. A comparative evaluation of performance of the purposed approach over different values of k over the five evaluation datasets of 1000 words is shown in Fig. 1. It can be observed from this figure that as we select less number of top ranked keywords for lexicon expansion, precision increases sharply whereas recall shows downgrading pattern as expected.

3.3   Comparative Analysis

The proposed approach is compared with three baselines and three state-of-the-art approaches [3,8,9]. In the first baseline, we ranked and extracted the words based on their frequency count in text-corpus, whereas, second baseline extracts the top-ranked words based on their *tf-idf* value. Finally, in the third baseline, the embedding-based similarity of words with the lexicon of seed words is computed to extract the top ranked contextually semantic terms. Table 3 presents the performance evaluation results of the proposed approach in terms of all the three evaluation metrics for $K = 80$ in comparison to six approaches. It can be observed from this table that the proposed approach performs significantly better than all the comparison approaches. Among the three standard state-of-the-art approaches, [9] performs best though it shows poor performance in comparison to the proposed approach. Among the three baseline methods, words extracted using embedding-based similarity performs best over D_a, D_{kh}, and D_{ka} datasets whereas *tf-idf* based relevant word extraction performs worst. The *tf*-based relevant words extraction also shows good performance but not comparable to the proposed approach. The better results by embedding-based similarity also confirm the strength of the proposed approach, which uses contextual semantics based on the distributional representation of words as a measure of association between the corpus words and initial lexicon of seed words.

4 Conclusion

In this paper, we presented a contextual semantic-based approach utilizing the strengths of both the distributional word representation and contrasting-domain corpus for domain-specific lexicon expansion from text-corpus. We validated the performance of our approach by conducting experiments on five different Twitter datasets. Our approach performs significantly better in comparison to three baselines and three state-of-the-art approaches. The proposed approach is very useful for the domains in which the text corpus is not fixed, rather keeps incrementing with time.

Acknowledgment. The authors would like to thank the South Asian University, Delhi, for the financial support under the start-up research grant provided to the first author.

References

1. Founta, A.M., et al.: Large scale crowdsourcing and characterization of Twitter abusive behavior. In: Proceedings of the 12th International Conference on Web and Social Media, pp. 491–500. AAAI, Palo Alto, June 2018
2. Hassan, S., Mihalcea, R., Banea, C.: Random-walk term weighting for improved text classification. In: Proceedings of the International Conference on Semantic Computing, California, USA, pp. 242–249, September 2007
3. Kit, C., Liu, X.: Measuring mono-word termhood by rank difference via corpus comparison. Terminology. Int. J. Theor. Appl. Issues in Specialized Commun. **14**(2), 204–229 (2008)
4. Matsuo, Y., Ishizuka, M.: Keyword extraction from a single documentusing word co-occurrence statistical information. In: Proceedings of the 16th Int'l Florida Artificial Intelligence Research Society Conference, pp. 392–396. AAAI, Florida, May 2003
5. Mihalcea, R., Tarau, P.: Textrank: bringing order into text. In: Proceedings of the International Conferences Empirical Methods in Natural Language Processing, pp. 404–411. ACL, Barcelona, July 2004
6. Mikolov, T., Chen, K., Corrado, G., Dean, J.: Efficient estimation of word representations invector space. arXiv:1301.3781 (2013)
7. Mohammad, S., Turney, P.: Crowdsourcing a word-emotion association lexicon. Comput. Intell. **29**(3), 436–465 (2013)

8. Park, Y., Patwardhan, S., Visweswariah, K., Gates, S.C.: An empirical analysis of word error rate and keyword error rate. In: Proceedings of the 9th Annual Conference of the International Speech Communication Association, Brisbane, Australia, pp. 270–273, September 2008
9. Sarna, G., Bhatia, M.: A probalistic approach to automatically extract new words from social media. In: Proceedings of the International Conference on Advances in Social Networks Analysis and Mining, San Francisco, USA, pp. 719–725, August 2016
10. Staiano, J., Guerini, R.M.: Depechemood: a lexicon for emotion analysis from crowd-annotated news. In: Proceedings of the 52nd Annual Meeting of the ACL, Maryland, USA, pp. 427–433, June 2014

Data-Driven Hierarchical Neural Network Modeling for High-Pressure Feedwater Heater Group

Jiao Yin[1,2], Mingshan You[3], Jinli Cao[1(✉)], Hua Wang[4], MingJian Tang[5], and Yong-Feng Ge[1]

[1] Department of Computer Science and Information Technology,
La Trobe University, Melbourne, VIC 3083, Australia
{j.yin,j.cao,g.ge}@latrobe.edu.au
[2] School of Artificial Intelligence, Chongqing University of Arts and Sciences,
Chongqing 402160, China
[3] Shenhua Tianming Power Generation Company, Sichuan 621700, China
youmingshan2019@gmail.com
[4] Institute for Sustainable Industries & Liveable Cities, Victoria University,
Melbourne, VIC 3083, Australia
Hua.Wang@vu.edu.au
[5] Huawei Technologies Co., Ltd., Shenzhen 518129, China
tang.ming.jian@huawei.com

Abstract. This paper proposes a data-driven hierarchical neural network modeling method for a high-pressure feedwater heater group (HPFHG) in power generation industry. An HPFHG is usually made up of several cascaded high-pressure feedwater heaters (HPFH). The challenge of modeling an HPFHG is to formulate not only the HPFHG as a whole but also its components at the same time. Physical modeling techniques based on dynamic thermal calculation can hardly be applied in practice because of lacking necessary parameters. Based on big operating data, modeling by neural networks is feasible. However, traditional artificial neural networks are black boxes, which are difficult to describe the subsystems or inner components of a system. The proposed modeling approach is inspired by the physical cascade structure of the HPFHG to tackle this problem. Experimental results show that our modeling approach is effective for the entire HPFHG as well as its every single component.

Keywords: High-pressure feedwater heater group · Hierarchical neural networks · Modeling techniques

1 Introduction

A feedwater heater is a power plant component used to preheat feedwater delivered to a steam-generating boiler [2]. To fully make use of the regenerative extraction steam, most fossil fuel-fired power plants contain a low-pressure feedwater

© Springer Nature Switzerland AG 2020
R. Borovica-Gajic et al. (Eds.): ADC 2020, LNCS 12008, pp. 225–233, 2020.
https://doi.org/10.1007/978-3-030-39469-1_19

heater group (LPFHG) and a high-pressure feedwater heater group (HPFHG). Both LPFHG and HPFHG play a vital role in improving the thermal efficiency of a power plant and reducing certain emissions, such as carbonic oxide [4].

Simulating and modeling an HPFHG is important for finding out its optimal operating conditions in a dynamic industrial environment, improving operational efficiency and detecting faults [5,7]. Traditional physical modeling techniques based on accurate mathematical expressions are ideal for theoretically understanding of how an HPFHG works. However, in practice, it is very difficult to determine the heat transfer coefficient, because it changes dynamically according to operating status [9,12]. Furthermore, some key coefficients have no sensor to measure in industrial fields, such as the extraction steam flow and the drain water flow of the superior heater in the same heater group [1].

Leveraging big operational data, data-driven and machine-learning-based methods are widely used in thermal power plant component modeling, including the feedwater heater group [3,8]. Artificial neural network (ANN) is a nonlinear statistical data modeling tool by imitating the structure and function of human brain. According to the universal approximation theorem, a feedforward network with a single layer is sufficient to represent any function [6]. However, the mechanics of the ANN models are mysterious. They are regarded as black boxes and their internal relationships are uninterpreted. For many applications, especially for those industry applications with physical prototypes, it is desirable to model a system as a whole as well as to model its subsystems at the same time. Thus, the traditional "black-box" neural networks need to be improved. Hierarchical Neural Networks [10,11] allow designing the model architecture based on some pre-set rules, which can be used for industry system modeling, including HPFHGs.

An HPFHG could be treated as a system consisted of several subsystems—HPFHs. Considering the physical cascade structure of an HPFHG, we proposed a data-driven hierarchical regression model. It models the relationship between the feedwater outlet temperature and other related variables recorded by the sensors in the industrial field. Compared with the "black-box" neural network model, the proposed model can formulate not only the working state of the entire HPFHG but also every single HPFH of the group in detail.

The remaining sections are organized as follows. Section 2 introduces the industrial background. Section 3 presents the architecture and training method of the proposed data-driven hierarchical neural network model. Experimental setting and results are reported in Sect. 4. At last, a brief summary is made in Sect. 5.

2   Industrial Background

2.1   Thermal Power Plant Regenerative System

The high-pressure feedwater heater group is important equipment in the regenerative system of a thermal power plant. In this part, we introduce the basic principle of a typical thermal power plant regenerative system. As shown in

Fig. 1, feedwater is heated by a boiler to generate steam, which pushes the turbine to rotate, causing the turbo generator to generate electricity. After working through the turbine, one part of the discharging steam condenses into condensated water and then enters into the LPFHG; while another part is working as regenerative extraction steam to heat the feedwater in the LPFHG and HPFHG. Being heated, feedwater re-enters the boiler and produces steam for the turbine. Such a regenerative system is beneficial for the thermal power plant to improve thermal efficiency, save fuel and reduce pollution.

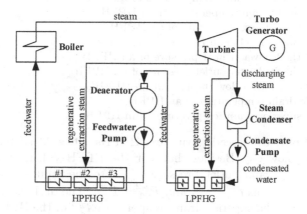

Fig. 1. A thermal power plant regenerative system

2.2   High-Pressure Feedwater Heater Group

The HPFHG is a complex system, which usually consists of three high-pressure feed-water heaters, numbered by #3, #2, #1 respectively, as shown in Fig. 2. Feedwater flows into the HPFH #3 first to be heated and then flows into #2 and lastly #1 for getting a higher temperature. Among them, #1 is the most superior HPFH connected with the boiler, and #3 is the most inferior HPFH.

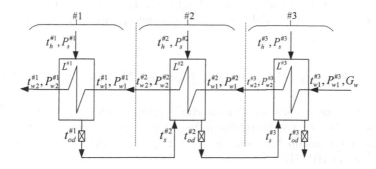

Fig. 2. The input/output relationship of a high-pressure feedwater heater group

Based on thermodynamics, the higher the feedwater outlet temperature of an HPFHG is, the less fuel will be consumed by the boiler to heat the feedwater and the thermal power plant regenerative system would be more efficient. Therefore, modeling the HPFHG is to find out the relationship between the feedwater outlet temperature and other variables. Based on the data could be collected in the industrial field and the domain knowledge, we define the notations below to represent the related variables of an HPFH.

t_{w2} (°C)—the feedwater outlet temperature of an HPFH
t_{w1} (°C)—the feedwater inlet temperature of an HPFH
t_h (°C)—the inlet steam temperature of an HPFH
P_s (MPa)—the inlet steam pressure of an HPFH
L (mm)—the water level in an HPFH
P_{w1} (MPa)—the feedwater inlet pressure of an HPFH
P_{w2} (MPa)—the feedwater outlet pressure of an HPFH
G_w (t/s)—the feedwater flow throughout an HPFHG
t_{od} (°C)—the drain temperature of an HPFH
t_s (°C)—the superior drain temperature of an HPFH

Because of the physical cascade structure, HPFHs #1, #2, #3 share the same input feedwater flow G_w. Besides that, for the HPFH #3, its feedwater outlet temperature $t_{w2}^{\#3}$ and outlet pressure $P_{w2}^{\#3}$ are the input variables for the HPFH #2, which means $t_{w1}^{\#2} = t_{w2}^{\#3}$ and $P_{w1}^{\#2} = P_{w2}^{\#3}$. The drain temperature $t_{od}^{\#2}$ of the HPFH #2 is the superior drain temperature $t_s^{\#3}$ of the HPFH #3, which means $t_{od}^{\#2} = t_s^{\#3}$, as demonstrated in Fig. 2. Similarly, $t_{w1}^{\#1} = t_{w2}^{\#2}$, $P_{w1}^{\#1} = P_{w2}^{\#2}$ and $t_{od}^{\#1} = t_s^{\#2}$.

From the perspective of modeling, the output of the HPFH #3 is $t_{w2}^{\#3}$, and the input is $x^{\#3} = [G_w, t_{w1}^{\#3}, t_h^{\#3}, P_s^{\#3}, L^{\#3}, P_{w1}^{\#3}, P_{w2}^{\#3}, t_{od}^{\#3}, t_s^{\#3}]$. Similarly, for the HPFH #2, the output is $t_{w2}^{\#2}$, and the input is $x^{\#2} = [G_w, t_{w1}^{\#2}, t_h^{\#2}, P_s^{\#2}, L^{\#2}, P_{w1}^{\#2}, P_{w2}^{\#2}, t_{od}^{\#2}, t_s^{\#2}]$; for the HPFH #1, the output is $t_{w2}^{\#1}$, and the input is $x^{\#1} = [G_w, t_{w1}^{\#1}, t_h^{\#1}, P_s^{\#1}, L^{\#1}, P_{w1}^{\#1}, P_{w2}^{\#1}, t_{od}^{\#1}]$. Obviously, to model the HPFHG composed by HPFHs #3, #2, #1, the output is $y = t_{w2}^{\#1}$ and the input is $X = x^{\#3} \cup x^{\#2} \cup x^{\#1}$. Based on the big operational history data, it is easy to establish a regression model to fit the functional relationship $y = f(X)$ for a HPFHG using a fully connected neural network. However, the challenge is how we can get the accurate models for the three single HPFH #3, #2, #1 based on the model $y = f(X)$.

3   Data-Driven Hierarchical Neural Network Modeling

To provide one possible solution for the challenging problem mentioned in Sect. 2, we propose a data-driven hierarchical neural network modeling method to formulate the relationship between the output $y = t_{w2}^{\#1}$ and the input $X = x^{\#3} \cup x^{\#2} \cup x^{\#1}$ of an HPFHG.

3.1   Architecture of the Proposed Model

The proposed data-driven hierarchical neural network model is designed based on traditional "black-box" neural networks. Figure 3 presents a 3-layer full connection neural network. The first layer is the input layer, which stands for all variables related to the output, denoted as $x = [x_1, x_2, \ldots, x_n]$, where n is the dimension of inputs. The middle layer is a hidden layer, denoted as $a^{(2)} = [a_1^{(2)}, a_2^{(2)}, \ldots, a_{n_h}^{(2)}]$, where n_h stands for the number of hidden nodes and the superscript (2) indicates this is the second layer of the network. The last layer is the output layer, which can be denoted as $y = a_1^{(3)} = h_\Theta(x)$, where h stands for the hypothesis of the model and Θ stands for all parameters of the networks.

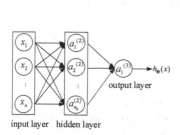

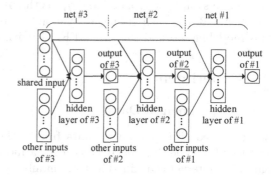

Fig. 3. A traditional 3-layer neural networks

Fig. 4. The architecture of the proposed data-driven hierarchical neural network mode

The proposed model consists of three full connection networks with hierarchical relationships, namely, net #3, net #2 and net #1, as demonstrated in Fig. 4. This hierarchical structure is enlightened by the psychical cascaded structure of the HPFHG illustrated in Fig. 2.

Net #3 is the most inferior 3-layer fully connection neural network. The input layer of net #3 includes a shared input G_w and other inputs of the HPFH #3, namely, $t_{w1}^{\#3}$, $t_h^{\#3}$, $P_s^{\#3}$, $L^{\#3}$, $P_{w1}^{\#3}$, $P_{w2}^{\#3}$, $t_{od}^{\#3}$ and $t_s^{\#3}$. The output of net #3 is $t_{w2}^{\#3}$.

Similarly, net #2 is the middle 3-layer fully connected neural network. The input layer of net #2 includes three parts, namely, the shared input G_w, the output of net #3 $t_{w2}^{\#3}$ and other inputs of the HPFH #2, namely, $t_h^{\#2}$, $P_s^{\#2}$, $L^{\#2}$, $P_{w1}^{\#2}$, $P_{w2}^{\#2}$, $t_{od}^{\#2}$ and $t_s^{\#2}$. The output of net #2 is $t_{w2}^{\#2}$.

Net #1 is the most superior 3-layer fully connection neural network. The input layer of net #1 includes the shared input G_w, the output of net #2 $t_{w2}^{\#2}$ and other inputs of the HPFH #1, namely, $t_h^{\#1}$, $P_s^{\#1}$, $L^{\#1}$, $P_{w1}^{\#1}$, $P_{w2}^{\#1}$ and $t_{od}^{\#1}$. The output of #1 is $t_{w2}^{\#1}$, which is also the output of the whole hierarchical neural network model.

3.2   Model Training Process

To formulate not only a HPFHG but also every single HPFH, we jointly train net #3, #2 and #1 at the same time. More generally, for a hierarchical network model with N subnets, the loss function to be minimized is a weighted sum of Mean Squared Error (MSE) of all subnets, expressed in (1),

$$L = \sum_{j=1}^{N} \left(W_j \sum_{i=1}^{m} \left(y_j^{(i)} - \hat{y}_j^{(i)} \right)^2 \right) \tag{1}$$

where N is the number of subnets in the hierarchical network model; W_j is the weight of subnet j; m is the number of training samples; $y_j^{(i)}$ is the true output of the i-th sample of subnet j and $\hat{y}_j^{(i)}$ is the predicted output of subnet j. In our cases, $N = 3$ and each subnet corresponding to an HPFH. It is easy to extend this modeling method to other HPFHGs with different number of HPFHs.

4   Experiments

4.1   Experimental Data

We collected all experimental data from a thermal power unit whose capacity is 1000 MW. The data is collected over a month without interruption, and the sampling interval is 5 min. The total number of samples $m = 10081$. All data are valid without abnormal values. Three datasets corresponding to HPFHs #3, #2, #1 are collected: $(t_{w2}^{\#3}, x^{\#3})$, $(t_{w2}^{\#2}, x^{\#2})$ and $(t_{w2}^{\#1}, x^{\#1})$.

4.2   Performance Evaluation Criteria

The HPFHG modeling problem is a nonlinear regression problem, so we choose four widely used criteria to evaluate the proposed modeling method, namely, mean average error (MAE), root mean square error (RMSE), mean absolute percentage error (MAPE) and root mean squared percentage error (RMSPE). We denote the true output values as y, and the predicted values as $\hat{y}$, then, $MAE = \frac{1}{m} \sum_{i=1}^{m} |y^{(i)} - \hat{y}^{(i)}|$; $RMSE = \sqrt[2]{\frac{1}{m} \sum_{i=1}^{m} (y^{(i)} - \hat{y}^{(i)})^2}$; $MAPE = \left(\frac{1}{m} \sum_{i=1}^{m} |(y^{(i)} - \hat{y}^{(i)})/y^{(i)}| \right) \times 100\%$ and $RMSPE = \left(\sqrt[2]{\frac{1}{m} \sum_{i=1}^{m} ((y^{(i)} - \hat{y}^{(i)})/y^{(i)})^2} \right) \times 100\%$.

4.3   Experimental Setting and Results

All datasets are in chronological order and divided into a training set and a test set by a 70%:30% ratio. The layer "DenseNN" and the functional API "Model" in Keras are used to implement the hierarchical model. Hidden nodes for all three subnets are set to 10. Other parameters are set as defaults. We set $W_3 : W_2 : W_1 = 1 : 1 : 1$ in (1) to make the three subnets equally important.

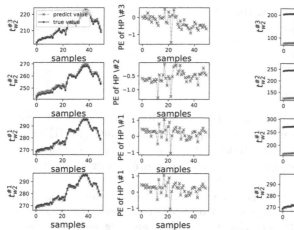

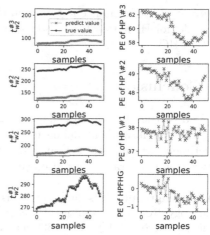

Fig. 5. Results on the proposed hierarchical neural network

Fig. 6. Results on a black-box neural network

Figure 5 shows the regression results of the first 50 samples on the test set. The left four subplots are the regression results for HPFHs #3, #2, #1 and the whole PHFHG, in which the blue lines with dot markers are the true values while the red lines with "x" markers are the predicted values. The right four subplots are the percentage error (PE) of each model, where $PE = \dfrac{y^{(i)} - \hat{y}^{(i)}}{y^{(i)}} \times 100\%$.

To compare our method with a "black-box" neural network, we built a full connection neural network with three hidden layers and each hidden layer has 10 nodes. When training the model, the output is $y = t_{w2}^{\#1}$ and the input set is $X = x^{\#3} \cup x^{\#2} \cup x^{\#1}$. The regression results of this black-box neural network are shown in Fig. 6. As shown in Fig. 6, although the black-box neural network modeling method can model the HPFHG with a comparative performance, it failed to model every single HPFH.

Table 1 lists four regression modeling evaluation criteria to compare the performance of the proposed method and the black-box neural network modeling method on the whole test set. It also shows that the proposed model can

Table 1. Performance comparison

Methods	The proposed method				The 'black-box' method			
Criteria	MAE (°C)	RMSE (°C)	MAPE (%)	RMSPE (%)	MAE (°C)	RMSE (°C)	MAPE (%)	RMSPE (%)
HPFH#3	0.936	1.073	0.458	0.525	125.14	125.17	61.19	61.22
HPFH#2	1.764	1.980	0.731	0.832	120.70	120.78	49.03	49.03
HPFH#1	0.691	0.894	0.253	0.326	102.89	103.01	37.75	37.75
HPFHG	0.691	0.894	0.453	0.326	1.1254	1.3643	0.409	0.494

achieve good performance not only on the HPFHG model but also on every single model for HPFHs #3, #2, #1, while the 'black-box' method can only model the HPFHG.

5   Conclusion

Inspired by the physical cascade structure of the HPFHG, a data-driven hierarchical neural network modeling method is proposed to formulate the HPFHG. Experimental results show that it can model not only the entire high-pressure heater group accurately but also every single high-pressure heater in the group.

Acknowledgment. This first author is partially supported by the Science and Technology Research Program of Chongqing Municipal Education Commission of China (Grant No. KJQN201901306 and KJQN201801325) and the Industrial Technology Development Project of Chongqing Development and Reform Commission of China(Grant No.2018148208).

References

1. Almedilla, J., Pabilona, L., Villanueva, E.: Performance evaluation and off design analysis of the HP and LP feed water heaters on a 3× 135 MW coal fired power plant. J. Appl. Mech. Eng. **7**(3), 14 (2018)
2. Blair, T.H.: Energy Production Systems Engineering. 1st edn. Wiley-IEEE Press (2016)
3. De, S., Kaiadi, M., Fast, M., Assadi, M.: Development of an artificial neural network model for the steam process of a coal biomass cofired combined heat and power (CHP) plant in Sweden. Energy **32**(11), 2099–2109 (2007)
4. Devandiran, E., Shaisundaram, V., Ganesh, P.S., Vivek, S.: Influence of feed water heaters on the performance of coal fired power plants. Int. J. Latest Technol. Eng. Manag. Appl. Sci, **5**, 115–119 (2016)
5. Gong, M., Peng, M., Zhu, H.: Research of multiple refined degree simulating and modeling for high pressure feed water heat exchanger in nuclear power plant. Appl. Therm. Eng. **140**, 190–207 (2018)
6. Hornik, K., Stinchcombe, M., White, H.: Multilayer feedforward networks are universal approximators. Neural Netw. **2**(5), 359–366 (1989)
7. Hossienalipour, S., Karbalaee, S., Fathiannasab, H.: Development of a model to evaluate the water level impact on drain cooling in horizontal high pressure feedwater heaters. Appl. Therm. Eng. **110**, 590–600 (2017)
8. Kang, Y.K., Kim, H., Heo, G., Song, S.Y.: Diagnosis of feedwater heater performance degradation using fuzzy inference system. Expert Syst. Appl. **69**, 239–246 (2017)
9. Kumar, A.A., Buckshumiyanm, A.: Performance analysis of regenerative feedwater heaters in 210 MW thermal power plant. Int. J. Mech. Eng. Technol. **8**(8), 1490–1495 (2017)
10. Serban, I.V., Sordoni, A., Bengio, Y., Courville, A., Pineau, J.: Hierarchical neural network generative models for movie dialogues. arXiv preprint arXiv:1507.04808. **7**(8) (2015)

11. Serban, I.V., Sordoni, A., Bengio, Y., Courville, A., Pineau, J.: Building end-to-end dialogue systems using generative hierarchical neural network models. In: Thirtieth AAAI Conference on Artificial Intelligence. AAAI Press (2016)
12. Weber, G., Worek, W.: Development of a method to evaluate the design performance of a feedwater heater with a short drain cooler. J. Eng. Gas Turbines Power **116**(2), 434–441 (1994)

Early Detection of Diabetic Eye Disease from Fundus Images with Deep Learning

Rubina Sarki[✉], Khandakar Ahmed, Hua Wang, Sandra Michalska, and Yanchun Zhang

Institute for Sustainable Industries and Liveable Cities, Victoria University, Ballarat Road, Melbourne 3011, Australia rubina.sarki@live.vu.edu.au

Abstract. Diabetes is a life-threatening disease that affects various human body organs, including eye retina. Advanced Diabetic Eye disease (DED) leads to permanent vision loss, thus an early detection of DED symptoms is essential to prevent disease escalation and timely treatment. Up till now, research challenges in early DED detection can be summarised as follows: *Firstly*, changes in the eye anatomy during its early stage are frequently untraceable by human eye due to subtle nature of the features, and *Secondly*, large volume of fundus images puts a significant strain on limited specialist resources, rendering manual analysis practically infeasible. Thus, Deep Learning-based methods have been practiced to facilitate early DED detection and address the issues currently faced. Despite promising, highly accurate detection of early anatomical changes in the eye using Deep Learning remains a challenge in wide scale practical application. Consequently, in this research we aim to address the main three research gaps and propose the framework for early automated DED detection system on fundus images through Deep Learning.

Keywords: Diabetic disease · Diabetic Retinopathy · Deep Learning · Glaucoma · Image processing · Macular Edema · Transfer Learning

1 Introduction

The World Health Organization (WHO) has been publishing general guidelines for DED detection and classification for more than 50 years. According to the indication of the International Diabetes Federation (IDF) in 2013, around 385 million people worldwide were diagnosed with Diabetes. What is more, the number of sufferers is predicted to rise to 592 million by 2035. Medical, social and economical expenses of Diabetes already constitute an overwhelming burden in public health governance.

Effects of Diabetes can be observed in various part of the body including eye retina. Eye diseases caused by Diabetes, i.e. Diabetic Retinopathy (DR), Diabetic Macular Edema (DME), and Glaucoma (GL), eventually lead towards the vision loss and permanent blindness. These conditions mainly occur due to a high blood

© Springer Nature Switzerland AG 2020
R. Borovica-Gajic et al. (Eds.): ADC 2020, LNCS 12008, pp. 234–241, 2020.
https://doi.org/10.1007/978-3-030-39469-1_20

sugar level in the body causing uneven growth of blood vessels, damage of optic nerve due to intraocular pressure, and formation of hard exudates area near macula region. Detection of the anatomical changes in the eye using fundus photography has brought up the number of challenges. *Firstly*, the continuously increasing scale of information on patient's health, such as medical images poses a significant strain in terms of diagnosis, treatment and check-up using limited specialist resources. Manual identification of features from high volume of retinal images as well as beneficial knowledge extraction cause unnecessary time delays between detection and treatment. The time taken for diagnosis further depends on the years of practice and professional experience. *Secondly*, manual retinal image analysis and grading of DED performed by the ophthalmologist does not always produce accurate results as the very minute changes in the eye anatomy are not always detectable by the human eye. Moreover, the human evaluation tends to suffer from subjectivity leading to potentially inconsistent diagnoses across practices. At this point, early automated detection proves essential to provide early treatment and minimise the risk of future vision loss. *Finally*, automatic retinal image analysis already plays an important role in screening for early DED detection. Since the last few decades, many efforts have been made to establish a reliable computer-based DED analysis systems. With the help of image processing techniques and Deep Learning methods, the workload associated with manual detection can be avoided to eventually reduce the time and cost associated with DED diagnosis. Currently, the most common binary classification of DED and non-DED using Deep Learning has already achieved high validation accuracy. At the same time, early DED classification and multi-stage classification from colour fundus images are still an open problem [1].

Thus, we focus our research on the main three research gaps in the development of Deep Learning-based early (normal and mild) DED classification systems, and propose a conceptual framework to achieve this goal. In our literature study, it is observed that none of the previous work addresses the early detection of Diabetic Eye Disease, i.e Diabetic Retinopathy, Glaucoma, Diabetic Macular Edema and Cataract jointly in one system. Detection of DED in one system is considered to be a crucial factor for treatment in terms of specific areas of lesions. Identification of lesions in those specific areas can provide specialist treatment to the target region of the eye, which is mostly affected.

2   Literature Review

Diabetic Eye Disease leads to blindness and its prevalence is predicted to rise continuously. A group of DED damages eye retina at its various parts. Severe DED is the main cause of blindness among adults between 20–70 years of age. Glaucoma is the main leading cause in the group of DED, which causes irreversible blindness. Diabetic Retinopathy (DR) can be classified as Non-Proliferative DR (NPDR) and Proliferative DR (PDR). Specific DR features can define the different stages of condition advancement. The following are the three subclasses of NPDR as well as PDR, namely Mild NPDR, Moderate NPDR, Severe NPDR, and PDR [17].

Gulshan et al. [10] proposed a DL algorithm for detection of DR. They yielded a result in two validation sets of 1748 and 9963 images. The algorithm achieved the Sensitivity of 90.3% and 87.0%, and 98.1% and Specificity of 98.5% for each data set respectively. Vahadane et al. [11] proposed a system to detect DME in optical coherence tomography scans using deep Convolutional Neural Network (CNN). Their method achieved Precision of 96.43%, Recall of 89.45%, and F1-score of 0.9281. Prentasic et al. [12] presented a fusion approach based on CNN and landmark detection for identification of exudates. They obtained 0.78 in F_1 measure. Otalora et al. [13] introduced a CNN model that used gradient length. Automated segmentation of exudates and other features using 10 layers of CNN was employed by Tan et al. [14]. Their system used 149 images for training and another 149 images for testing which yielded 0.8758 and 0.7158 in terms of Sensitivity for exudates and dark lesions, respectively. In their work, Chai et al. [15] used DL model with retinal images for automatic diagnosis of Glaucoma. They used Multi-Branch Neural Network (MB-NN) model to obtain the features. The Accuracy achieved was 0.9151, with Sensitivity of 0.9233, and Specificity of 0.9090. Li et al. [16] developed a DL method for automatic detection of Non-Glaucoma and Glaucoma based on visual fields (VFs). Their CNN-based algorithm achieved 0.876 of Accuracy, 0.826 of Specificity, and 0.932 of Sensitivity. Raghavendra et al. [17] proposed the 18 layers CNN framework for Glaucoma diagnosis. They evaluated their model with 589 Normal and 837 Glaucoma images, for which they obtained the Accuracy of 98.13%, Sensitivity of 98%, and Specificity of 98.3%.

3   Research Challenges

Deep Neural Network model use advance mathematical operations to process pixel value in the image [2], where the training is conducted by introducing the network with diversified examples, as opposed to solid rule-based programming underlying the conventional methodologies [3]. Deep Learning have been used extensively for knowledge finding and Predictive Analysis for example [18,19]. In Deep Learning, Convolutional Neural Network (CNN) has been extensively explored in the domain of DED [4–6], surpassing previous methodologies such as image recognition. In literature, numerous challenges have been identified in automatic DED detection. Neural Networks strive to learn deep, and often nuanced, features to detect the sophisticated aspect of mild DED [6]. Regardless, the research on DED detection using Deep Learning persistently reports the high performance on severe cases, while mild DED detection remains still an open challenge. In order to address the current challenges in automatic DED detection using Deep Learning, our research questions can be formulated as follows:

1. How the nature of the images affect the accuracy of Deep Learning techniques in terms of (i) image quality (ii) image volume, and (iii) an object in the image?

2. How the concept of the Transfer Learning can be effective to detect the features of mild DED and enhance the accuracy?
3. How to design more robust Deep Learning models that will produce promising results in the field of DED?

4   Contribution to Knowledge

In this sub-section, we present different research gaps that academic researchers were not fully able to address in the previous studies on Diabetic Eye Disease detection. Thorough research, it is still required to enhance the performance of Deep Learning techniques for *early* Diabetic Eye Disease detection. The image pre-processing for feature extractions is considered crucial for classification performance enhancement. It is often observed that publicly available images consist of low fidelity data, and the images were taken with various fundus cameras that leads to large variation in image quality. The identified issues along with the proposed solutions are detailed below:

1. **Image Enhancement:** Retinal image pre-processing is considered a crucial step due to its capability to enhance the visual aspect of an image for improved classification performance. Following is a brief description of the pre-processing techniques, which we aim to adopt in our research. Green Channel Extraction is employed to extract the green band from an RGB of an image. Green channel of an image provides more insight into the relevant information from an image. Many researchers have used this method to pre-process fundus images in their experiments. Contrast enhancement based on CLAHE (Contrast Limited Adaptive Histogram Equalization) is used in our research to enhance the contrast of the images. An example before and after CLAHE application to fundus images is presented in Fig. 1. After contrast enhancement, illumination correction is applied to increase the brightness and luminance of the images. Finally, the noise is removed to smooth out an image using Gaussian filtering.

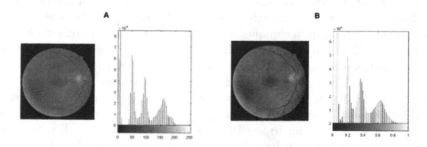

Fig. 1. Contrast Limited Adaptive Histogram Equalization enhances contrast in an image: A. Before and B. After CLAHE application. (Color figure online)

2. **Image Augmentation:** Another issue that needs to be addressed is the annotated data limitation. In order to train a Deep Learning architecture, a large set of data is required. If training sample size is insufficient, the model can easily overfit the data resulting in poor classification performance on unseen fundus images. This problem can be solved by applying data augmentation methods such as cropping, rotating, and mirroring of the images. Lastly, the same labelled data from different sources can be combined to increase the volume and improve accuracy. For example, the number of normal-labelled Kaggle image set K_0 images can be combined with the number of normal-labelled Messidor image set M_0 (Eq. 1). Similarly, the number of mild-labelled Kaggle image set K_1 can be combined with the number of mild-labelled Messidor image set M_1 (Eq. 2).

$$K_0 \bigcup M_0 = x : \forall x \in K_0 \quad or \quad \forall x \in M_0 \tag{1}$$

$$K_1 \bigcup M_1 = x : \forall x \in K_1 \quad or \quad \forall x \in M_1 \tag{2}$$

Hence, we can input $K_0 \bigcup M_0$ and $K_1 \bigcup M_1$ number of images into the model training to increase the volume of dataset.

3. **Region of Interest:** Colour fundus images are used as an input to build an early DED detection system. RGB fundus images for DR, Gl and DME are used as an input. To detect DR, the most important region of interest is a blood vessel. Similarly, to detect Gl and DME, the most significant regions of interest are optic disk and macular region, respectively. Hence, instead of training the entire retinal image, the region of interest can be extracted for training the system.

4.1   Analysis of Diabetic Eye Disease Using Deep Learning

This section discusses Deep Learning (DL) based approaches for DED detection. Deep learning is the extension of Machine Learning, where the multiple-layered network is designed to extract the most salient features from images using the examples provided. Here, the term *"deep"* signifies the depth of the network in Deep Learning architecture. Firstly, training and testing data sets are collected. Then, the pre-processing techniques are applied to images in order to increase their clarity, and improve subsequent features extraction. For feature extraction and classification the previously pre-processed images are forwarded to the DL model. In DL training process, output of the previous layer is passed onto the next layer as an input. Lastly, the top, or the last, layer produces the result. Various studies employed Deep Learning methods for detection of DR, Gl and DME. In our study, we aim to use Deep Learning-based approach with Transfer Learning, as well as own built Deep Learning architecture for classification performance comparison.

1. **Transfer Knowledge application:** For object identification several pre-trained Convolutional Neural Network (CNN) architectures are available in

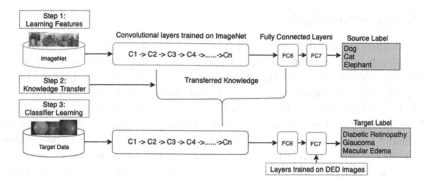

Fig. 2. Learning features and knowledge transferred using Convolutional Neural Network for detection of Diabetic Eye Disease.

the field of Deep Learning namely: *VGG16, VGG19, ResNet50, Inception V3, InceptionResNet V2, Xception, MobileNET, MobileNET V2, DenseNet 121, DenseNet 169, DenseNet 201, NASNetMobile,* and *NASNetLarge.* The top layers of these architectures can be retrained with the target task (normal/mild Diabetic Eye Disease) for feature extraction and classification. The concept of knowledge transfer from source task to target task can be useful in the case of limited training data. However, these pre-trained architectures are not suitable for medical images in terms of classification performance enhancement as they were initially developed for generic images identification, such as animals, foods, cars, etc. Therefore, Deep Learning models have to be re-adapted for Diabetic Eye Disease detection task shown in Fig. 2, usually by removal and re-train of the final layers in the network. The comparison of various architectures implementing Transfer Learning has to be conducted to demonstrate their applicability in niche domains such as mild DED detection.

2. **CNN architecture development:** Another option is to develop and train the CNN model entirely from scratch, without reliance on the pre-trained architectures adopted from Transfer Learning. This approach necessitates large number of annotated data, which can also be generated through appropriate augmentation techniques, e.g. mirroring, rotating. CNN has already produced promising results in the classification of normal/severe DED, but normal/mild is still an open challenge. To increase the performance of the classifier one can increase the computational power by increasing the size of the network. Another solution could be object-oriented identification, i.e. blood vessels, optic disc, macular region. Object-oriented detection is more beneficial than the use of an entire image-based. Still an extensive evaluation has to be conducted in order to provide empirical validation for their practical usage due to an increased computational resources required for new CNN network development.

4.2   Statement of Significance

Like academic contribution, our work on early DED detection has a strong practical significance. Prior research has already investigated the automatic detection of various stages of Diabetic Retinopathy (normal, Non Proliferative Diabetic Retinopathy and Proliferative Diabetic Retinopathy) using Deep Learning techniques [4–6]. Similarly, other researchers have managed to detect various stages of Glaucoma (normal to severe) [7], Diabetic Macular Edema [8] and Cataract [9], all using Deep Learning models. In our research, we aim to analyse, classify and detect *all* types of DED in the end-to-end fashion. Moreover, we aim to develop a system which will detect the *early* stage of all potential forms of DED.

5   Conclusions

This paper presents a Deep Learning-based conceptual framework, while addressing the three main research challenges in the domain of *early* Diabetic Eye Disease detection, as identified from the most recent literature. We have discussed the limitations of publicly available data sets (low fidelity, lack of publicly available dataset for specific conditions such as Cataract, etc.), and how they can be corrected by appropriate image pre-processing approaches application. Techniques such as Green Channel Extraction and contrast enhancement using CLAHE has improved subtle features visibility.

References

1. Carson Lam, D.Y., Guo, M., Lindsey, T.: Automated detection of diabetic retinopathy using deep learning. AMIA Summits Transl. Sci. Proc. **2018**, 147 (2018)
2. Poplin, R., et al.: Prediction of cardiovascular risk factors from retinal fundus photographs via deep learning. Nat. Biomed. Eng. **2**(3), 158 (2018)
3. Gardner, G.G., Keating, D., Williamson, T.H., Elliott, A.T.: Automatic detection of diabetic retinopathy using an artificial neural network: a screening tool. Br. J. Ophthalmol. **80**(11), 940–944 (1996)
4. Mateen, M., Wen, J., Song, S., Huang, Z.: Fundus image classification using VGG-19 architecture with PCA and SVD. Symmetry **11**(1), 1 (2019)
5. Sankar, M., Batri, K., Parvathi, R.: Earliest diabetic retinopathy classification using deep convolution neural networks. pdf. Int. J. Adv. Eng. Technol. (2016)
6. Pratt, H., Coenen, F., Broadbent, D.M., Harding, S.P., Zheng, Y.: Convolutional neural networks for diabetic retinopathy. Procedia Comput. Sci. **90**, 200–205 (2016)
7. Orlando, J.I., Prokofyeva, E., del Fresno, M., Blaschko, M.B.: Convolutional neural network transfer for automated glaucoma identification. In: 12th International Symposium on Medical Information Processing and Analysis, January 26, vol. 10160, p. 101600U). International Society for Optics and Photonics (2017)
8. Gelman, R.: Evaluation of transfer learning for classification of: (1) diabetic retinopathy by digital fundus photography and (2) diabetic macular edema, choroidal neovascularization and drusen by optical coherence tomography. arXiv: 1902.04151. 26 January 2019

9. Pratap, T., Kokil, P.: Computer-aided diagnosis of cataract using deep transfer learning. Biomed. Signal Process. Control. **53**, 101533 (2019)
10. Gulshan, V., et al.: Development and validation of a deep learning algorithm for detection of diabetic retinopathy in retinal fundus photographs. Jama **316**(22), 2402–2410 (2016)
11. Vahadane, A., Joshi, A., Madan, K., Dastidar, T.R.: Detection of diabetic macular edema in optical coherence tomography scans using patch based deep learning. In: 2018 IEEE 15th International Symposium on Biomedical Imaging (ISBI 2018), April 4, pp. 1427–1430. IEEE (2018)
12. Prentašić, P., Lončarić, S.: Detection of exudates in fundus photographs using deep neural networks and anatomical landmark detection fusion. Comput. Methods Programs Biomed. **137**, 281–292 (2016)
13. Otálora, S., Perdomo, O., González, F., Müller, H.: Training deep convolutional neural networks with active learning for exudate classification in eye fundus images. In: Cardoso, M.J., et al. (eds.) LABELS/CVII/STENT -2017. LNCS, vol. 10552, pp. 146–154. Springer, Cham (2017). https://doi.org/10.1007/978-3-319-67534-3_16
14. Tan, J.H., et al.: Automated segmentation of exudates, haemorrhages, microaneurysms using single convolutional neural network. Inf. Sci. **420**, 66–76 (2017)
15. Chai, Y., Liu, H., Xu, J.: Glaucoma diagnosis based on both hidden features and domain knowledge through deep learning models. Knowl.-Based Syst. **161**, 147–156 (2018)
16. Li, F., Wang, Z., Qu, G., Qiao, Y., Zhang, X.: Visual field based automatic diagnosis of glaucoma using deep convolutional neural network. In: Stoyanov, D., et al. (eds.) OMIA/COMPAY -2018. LNCS, vol. 11039, pp. 285–293. Springer, Cham (2018). https://doi.org/10.1007/978-3-030-00949-6_34
17. Raghavendra, U., Fujita, H., Bhandary, S.V., Gudigar, A., Tan, J.H., Acharya, U.R.: Deep convolution neural network for accurate diagnosis of glaucoma using digital fundus images. Inf. Sci. **441**, 41–49 (2018)
18. Subramani, S., Michalska, S., Wang, H., Du, J., Zhang, Y., Shakeel, H.: Deep learning for multi-class identification from domestic violence online posts. IEEE Access **7**, 46210–46224 (2019)
19. Peng, M., et al.: Neural sparse topical coding. In: Proceedings of the 56th Annual Meeting of the Association for Computational Linguistics, vol. 1, Long Papers, pp. 2332–2340 (July 2018)

Author Index

Printed in the United States
By Bookmasters